Janmichelsand
March 1971

THE MIND OF CHESTERTON

The Mind of
CHESTERTON

CHRISTOPHER HOLLIS

UNIVERSITY OF MIAMI PRESS
Coral Gables, Florida

ACKNOWLEDGMENTS

The Author gratefully acknowledges the permission of Miss D. Collins and of the following publishers to quote from the works of G. K. Chesterton: from *Autobiography*, Hutchinson & Co Ltd.; from *Collected Poems*, Methuen and Co. Ltd. and Dodd, Mead Inc.; from *The Common Man*, Sheed & Ward Inc.; from *The Defendant* and *The Wild Knight*, J. M. Dent Ltd. and Dodd, Mead Inc.; from *The Everlasting Man* and *St. Thomas Aquinas*, Hodder & Stoughton Ltd. and Sheed & Ward Inc.; from *Orthodoxy*, The Bodley Head Ltd. and Dodd, Mead Inc.; from *A Short History of England*, Chatto & Windus Ltd.; from *The Thing*, Sheed & Ward Ltd., and Sheed & Ward Inc.

The Author also gratefully acknowledges permission to quote from the following publications: from Hilaire Belloc's works, by courtesy of Mrs Raymond Asquith; from Thomas Hardy's verse, by courtesy of Macmillan & Co. Ltd. and Macmillan Inc.; from Rudyard Kipling, *The Years Between* and *Puck of Pook's Hill*, by courtesy of Mrs George Bambridge; from Monsignor Ronald Knox's verse, by courtesy of the Earl of Oxford and Asquith; and from Walter de la Mare's verse, by courtesy of the Literary Trustees of Walter de la Mare and The Society of Authors as their representatives.

Manufactured in Great Britain

CONTENTS

1

Chesterton and the World
of Today

Until a few years ago general opinion took it for granted that the Catholic Church differed from other bodies in that it was more uncompromising in its claim to rule by authority. Others were content to suggest. The Church did not hesitate to command. Tom Kettle's *mot* that the Catholics take their religion *table d'hôte* and the Protestants *à la carte* was quoted and it was generally accepted that it described the truth. The Church's critics complained that the Church allowed no sufficient room for freedom. Its loyal members contrasted its discipline and unity with the alleged 'puerilities and the despairs' which—to quote a phrase used by Belloc in his open letter to Dean Inge—were found outside its discipline. No serious critic denied or doubted that within the boundaries of the Church was to be found an abundance of charity and self-sacrifice, but, it was thought, the last word was with authority. The Church, allowing and encouraging its children's personal exercises of dedication, nevertheless set the bounds within which such exercises were to be confined. It said to them without apology 'Thus far and no farther.' And over it all as the final master of authority was the Pope—always in all modern times a holy and good man, as all but the utterly bigoted unhesitatingly admitted, but nevertheless by the nature of his office a detached man, who had of necessity to live a life that was remote from the general run of the world. It was into such a world that there erupted the astonishing figure of John XXIII. John did not on analysis have any spiritual discoveries to proclaim that had never previously been enunciated. He made no such claim. But his was an achievement greater than that of originality. He succeeded in breaking a sound barrier. He had had doubtless great predecessors who were aflame with the love of souls. But he had no predecessors who were, like him, able to break through all inhibitions —to make manifest to all the world his love for them—and to win, as he did, the love of men and women of every race and colour in every corner of the globe.

Nothing would have astonished and shocked Chesterton more than to hear his name coupled with that of the great Pope, had he lived to see his day, and indeed of course Chesterton in no way filled a place on the world's stage at all comparable to that of Pope John. Trite and silly jokes about their size inevitably suggest themselves. One remembers the story of the American travelling down Fleet Street with Chesterton and saying 'Everybody seems to know you, Mr Chesterton,' to elicit the answer 'Yes, and if they don't they ask.' But to be a familiar figure in Fleet Street and in the passing newspapers is something very different from being the Pope of Rome. Yet there was a certain similarity of personality between them. There was a tang of Chestertonism in the soubriquet of John the Jolly which came to be attached to Pope John.

In much the same way on the smaller scale nineteenth-century Catholicism—indeed nineteenth-century religion in general—was a serious and indeed a solemn business. The Victorians did not joke about it and thought it in the worst of taste if others joked about it. It was left to those who rejected religion to make their jokes, and 'scoffer' and 'atheist' came to be almost interchangeable terms. It was Chesterton's first achievement that he turned the joke against the sceptic. Just as General Booth refused to let the devil have all the best tunes, so Chesterton refused to let him have all the best jokes, and claimed that those who had the faith should also be allowed to have the fun. His first triumph was when his agnostic opponent Joseph McCabe was reduced, almost with tears in his eyes, to beg Chesterton to be serious on the high moral issue of McCabe's atheism.

Chesterton of course made excellent jokes which were widely quoted. But his achievement was not merely that of making jokes. Belloc made jokes which were as excellent as those of Chesterton.

But Belloc's jokes were all too often bitter and satiric. Their aim was to make the object of them ridiculous. He struck to wound. There was, as Chesterton himself said of him to Douglas Woodruff, a sundering quality in his controversies. Chesterton's jokes were warm jokes—the jokes of a kindly man. Those from whom he differed most deeply were nevertheless devoted to him. H. G. Wells wrote of him, 'It is exactly like him. From first to last he and I were very close friends. I never knew anyone so steadily true to form as G.K.C.' Shaw, his most constant antagonist, was also his most constant friend. Walter de la Mare summed up the affectionate respect in which his contemporaries held him in the lines

> Knight of the Holy Ghost, he goes his way
> Wisdom his motley, Truth his loving jest;
> The mills of Satan keep his lance in play,
> Pity and innocence his heart at rest.

It would, I think, be widely accepted that to the Catholic of today John XXIII appears as the *beau idéal* of the Catholic. We have accepted him as our champion. Avoiding the extravagances of the extreme progressives, he has called on the Church to address the modern world in language which it can understand. He has brought to the tasks of the spirit humility, reverence and cheerfulness. To those of us who are English and who are now old Chesterton spoke on his smaller scale in something of the same spirit when we were young. He made of course no sort of claim to enunciate what were purely personal opinions as authoritative, and there were plenty who disagreed with him on various points and they were fully entitled to their disagreements. Yet wide circles of us among the Catholic young of those days took Chesterton for our champion and, attracted alike by the gentility of his character and the high spirits of his literary style, accepted as esoteric Catholicism the whole gamut of his opinions. Even when he spoke of matters that were admittedly in no sort of way of faith we tended to proclaim ourselves Chestertonians and perhaps sometimes to think, beyond question a little absurdly and arrogantly, that those who did not fully share our beliefs were not inheritors of the ultimate secrets of Catholicism. It is therefore of interest now to look back and to see which of the Chestertonian positions are now no longer in fashion. For the moment my concern is merely to enumerate rather than to pass judgement. If it be true, as Johnson said, that most men's opinions are no more than the consequence of fashion, that is not a truth that is all to men's credit. It is not necessarily a condemnation of a man of the past to say that his opinions are out of date. There are some dates which it is very good to be out of, and it is most possible that the present is of that type. Still it is well in the beginning of our study to set out the list of the points on which opinion seems to have moved. There would seem to be in the main six of them.

In the first place certainly, were Chesterton to return to earth today, he would be surprised—and at first discovery dismayed— by the decline of the predominance of Latin in the liturgy of the Church. It was until recently a commonplace of Catholic apologetic for the Catholic to contrast the universality of his worship with the local parochialism of the denominations. The Church of England, he claimed, was a Church mainly of Englishmen.

> To foreign lands no sound of her is come,
> Humbly content to be despised at home,

he quoted from Dryden. In contrast the Catholic prayed in the majestic language that had 'fought and conquered the centuries.' He prayed as Saint Ambrose had prayed. His priests offered the Sacrifice as Saint Augustine had offered it. As he travelled abroad he could go into a church in any part of the world and see Mass being celebrated exactly as it was celebrated in his own land. It is not to my purpose to inquire into the qualifications that might have been urged against these generalised claims. Latin, it was said, was not the language of the Last Supper or of Our Lord. The Church did not even grow up with Latin as its language. When it turned from Aramaic it turned not to Latin but to Greek. Latin, when it was adopted, far from being adopted because it was a universal language was adopted precisely because it was then a vernacular language, and indeed the language of the Mass is in some ways very vernacular indeed with strange phrases like *Dic Verbo* and *Habemus Ad Dominum*, so unlike any phrases that would have been admitted into Ciceronian prose. Latin, it was said again, was not the universal language of the Church. The other rites had been preserved throughout the Church's history. When Latin was a general language of educated people throughout the Western world it was perhaps reasonable to preserve it as the language of the liturgy. When, with the decline of classical education, Latin was no longer the predominant language of education it was only reasonable to follow the custom of the Orientals and to allow the vernacular language a place in our worship. Bishop Christopher Butler tells us that we should speak to God in the language in which we make love. The integralists with a strong tradition behind them argue that on the contrary the demands of reverence require that we should use to God a special language more secret than that of ordinary speech. Doubtless the truth lies in a middle line. It is not for this work to settle exactly where it should be drawn. 'In writing,' says a character in one of Conrad's novels, 'you should always pitch the language a little higher than that of ordinary life.' 'Yes,' comes the reply, 'but you shouldn't let the reader catch you at it.' But of course Chesterton was of a generation, as indeed were we who were his juniors, when Latin, for good reason or bad, had still the prestige behind it that it was the normal vehicle of education. The day when school learning was exclusively Latin and Greek had passed, but, though other subjects were offered, specialisation in them was thought to be an inferior option. The Classics offered the best prizes for scholarships. The classical scholars had the first prestige among scholars. To offer to God any language less than the Latin would have seemed an irreverence. Chesterton, though not of the first rank as a classical scholar, was himself brought up in that tradition. He accepted the Latin liturgy of the Church as a part of the Catholic tradition and doubtless hardly thought, any more than did the rest of us, for many years afterwards, that there was any alternative to it. Vernacularists in those days were thought of as cranks like vegetarians.

But what is curious is that though a neglect to consider even the possibility of a vernacular liturgy may be one of the great marks of difference between Chesterton and the modern Johannine Catholic, it is not so much a difference between Chesterton and John himself. For though a largely vernacular liturgy turned out to be the first practical reform that emerged out of John's Council, it was not in itself a reform that John especially favoured. Indeed John in his *Veterum Sapientiae* had very outspokenly championed the cause of Latin; and even among those who most welcome the vernacular now that it has come, and have learnt from experience of the great value of a language at the altar that is understood by simple members of a congregation, many would, unless they are very intransigent, admit it as an irreparable loss—as keenly as Chesterton would have felt it—if the knowledge and memory of Latin should be entirely banished from all the services of the Church.

The decline of the classics in secular education has been one of the important factors, making desirable liturgical reforms which would perhaps have been undesirable fifty or more years ago. But it is only one factor. The twentieth century has seen a more important development, the second great change from the Catholicism which Chesterton knew. The Christian religion was not born in Europe. The Incarnation did not take place in Europe. In the Church's early centuries its Asian and African provinces were at least as vigorous as its European province. The first Councils and the debates out of which the creeds were formed did not take place in Europe. Greek, not Latin, was the Church's first language. If the Church was forced back into being a predominantly European body that was not because the Christian message was in any sort of way a message addressed especially to Europeans but simply because by the Mahomedan invasion of the fifth century the African and Asian provinces of Europe were virtually destroyed, and Christendom forced back into Europe as into a city under siege. So it was as a matter not of divine promises but of mere secular history that Christendom became an almost exclusively European thing for fifteen hundred years. That condition lasted up till the early years of this century—till the years when Chesterton was a young man and was breaking upon the world. A few years later, at the time of the First World War, his friend Belloc wrote in *Europe and the Faith* 'The Faith is Europe and Europe is the Faith.' When the century began the government of the Church was still entirely in European hands. There were only two Cardinals who were not residents of Europe—Gibbons in America and Moran in Australia —and they were of course both European by origin. Today, half a century later, with Cardinals of every race and from every continent, the Church presents a very different picture. The Church almost everywhere in a minority, is nevertheless for the first time in its history a Catholic Church in reality as well as in profession —in the sense that it is a world-wide Church.

Chesterton lived and wrote in this earlier world and he is not to be blamed that he did not foresee the conditions of the new world. Who did foresee them? He was no imperialist and no racialist. He advocated no policies of suppression. Yet he did in his youth, as did almost everyone else at that time, take it for granted that the world was about Europeans. He condemned in retrospect the savageries of some of the acts of suppression of the Indian Mutiny, but when he argued about the rights and wrongs of the Boer War the whole issue to his mind was whether South Africa should be ruled by the British or the Dutch. He was suspicious from the first of the Japanese and the Japanese alliance, and he was even— less pardonably—quite absurdly offensive about men of white blood who lived outside geographical Europe within the British Empire—about in particular the Australians. Now this expansion of the boundaries of Christendom has obviously changed the whole balance of the argument about a Latin Liturgy. It was one thing to impose a Latin liturgy on a Christian community whose members were substantially inhabitants of countries that had all been provinces of the Roman Empire and who all spoke languages of their own that derived from Latin. To such a body Latin might well be a reminder of a lost unity that had once been possessed and then disastrously shattered and which it was a pious hope to see one day recreated. But to ask Japanese and Africans, Indians and Malaysians—the inheritors of languages and cultures that had no trace of Latin in them—to accept a purely Latin liturgy was a very different proposition. To them, to bid them pray in Latin was to remind them of a claim to hegemony which Europeans had advanced but which Asians and Africans thought of as an usurpation to which they had no right. Chesterton saw up to a point that the Church, if its claims were true at all, must of its nature be something much more than a European imperialism—that its message was of its nature for all men. In an essay he records how he had said that he would not at all mind one day seeing a black Cardinal but he would not care himself to see a black Pope. Then, as he recounts it, he checked himself and apologised and said that it was not for him to set bounds to what might be the purpose of God. It is valueless to speculate on what he might have come to think had he lived on into different times. It is valueless alike to say that he would have supported such developments or that he would have opposed them. All that we can record is the fact that he never came to envisage them as possible.

The third great point of difference between Chesterton's teaching and that of Pope John is on the distribution of property. Chesterton of course made himself the champion of what came—perhaps not very happily—to be called distributism. Opposed alike to the capitalists who thought that effective property should be concentrated in the hands of a few rich men, and to the Socialists who thought that it should all be vested in the state, he advocated that property should be as widely distributed as possible so that as nearly as possible every head of a family should have his little parcel of it.

Leo XIII in his *Rerum Novarum* in 1891 advocated such a wide distribution of property and Pius XI forty years later in *Quadragesimo Anno* repeated the demand. But John XXIII's *Mater et Magistra* broke entirely new ground. Paying verbal tribute, as is the custom of the Vatican, to his predecessors, he sketched a wholly new programme. *Rerum Novarum* and *Quadragesimo Anno* had been essentially nationalist documents. They laid down the principle by which property and power should be distributed within the national state. How far it was right that there should be wide differences of standards between nation and nation and continent and continent and, if wrong, how that evil was to be remedied, they did not discuss. It would have been hardly possible within the climate of their times for them to have done so. By Pope John's time the problems of the gap between the have's and the have-not's, between the developed and the underdeveloped, the allegation that the gap is ever widening, the certainty that, if means are not found to narrow it, it will lead ultimately to war have become the main problems of the day; and it was these problems that John XXIII in *Mater et Magistra*, and after him Paul VI in *Progressio Populorum*, had, above all others, in mind when they wrote their encyclicals.

To that extent Chesterton's writings are now dated. But of course it is ridiculous to judge Chesterton by the details of his plans for social reform. It might be reasonable to judge Belloc or even Chesterton's brother by such tests, for they professed to speak on such matters as authorities. But Chesterton made no claims to understand such details. When he spoke on such matters he spoke only as an obedient disciple, repeating what Belloc told him to repeat, nor would anyone have ever dreamed of thinking otherwise had it not been for the accident which caused him out of loyalty to take on his brother's paper after his brother's death and as a consequence of the paper's poverty to write so large a proportion of it himself, since the paper could not afford to pay anyone else to write it. It is as a result of this that so large a proportion of his writing in mere quantity was on such topics, and that the public came to speak of him as a distributist almost at times as if such writings was the sole task to which he devoted himself. Not only was this not the truth but it obscured the truth. For Chesterton was no master of the constructive details of a plan, but he was a prophet. In so far as he sketched out practical policies he wrote only of things that were at the best true for the moment but, when the moment was past, out of date. But in so far as he saw that it was of the essence of a Christian system that it must respect every individual as the creature of God, and that there was much in modern materialistic civilisation, as indeed in different ways there had been in all the various previous civilisations, which failed to pay this respect to many of its members, he was abundantly right; whatever the details upon which they differed, he of course on that point joined hands with Pope John. He did not know all the answers, any more indeed than did anyone else, but in every age it is necessary to ask the question and the age is only lost when it ceases to ask the question. Chesterton did not know the answers, which are ephemeral, but he knew the questions which are eternal.

Chesterton's beliefs about international affairs are dated in a similar way. The problem of war is for a Christian an exceedingly difficult one. The general mind of the Church throughout the ages has rejected unconditional pacifism. Though Our Lord might condemn violence and aggression, the problem, it has been generally held, cannot be solved by a mere assertion of a duty of unconditional non-resistance. The purpose must be to preserve peace, but there are times when a modicum of violence now is the only means to prevent injustice and larger violence in the long run. So the Church, laying down indeed very strict conditions which must be satisfied before a war can be called a just war, nevertheless does not preach unconditional pacifism. That being so, it was not surprising that Chesterton should reject pacifism. Yet, even if absolute pacifism cannot be accepted, the Christian can surely hardly fail to respect that creed when held, as so often it is, not out of mere cowardice but from high motives. He must believe that those who draw the sword do usually perish by the sword, that violence has, to use the modern word, a fatal tendency to escalate, that man has a better nature which can often be more effectively tamed by mildness than by violence and that therefore, even if total pacifism cannot be accepted, men should use violence only as a last resort. What was odd about Chesterton was not that he was not a pacifist; it was the passion, peculiar for a man of so kindly a nature, with which he constantly assailed pacifism and the strange readiness with which in so many of his stories he allowed his characters to use weapons of violence. He spoke with bitterness of pacifists such as Cadbury, the owner of *The Daily News*, whom he accused without qualification of responsibility for the war of 1914 because in the years before the war Cadbury had opposed the increase of armaments and the assumption of a firm British commitment to come to the support of France, if she should be attacked by Germany. Such a commitment would, he thought, have prevented a German attack and thus have prevented a war. He thought of the war as an unqualified aggression by Germany against her neighbours. It is true that the Germany of 1914 was a power with imperialistic ambitions; but, in so far as the world was at that time parcelled out between rival imperialisms Germany, through being a late comer, had a far smaller share of the markets than that to which she was entitled by her industrial potential; and Britain, through being the first in the field, had the lion's share. A man who had spent so much energy in the vigorous denunciation of imperialistic greed should surely have reflected that it was the very system of imperialism which was to some degree the cause of the war and should have felt that it was an oversimplification to see it as a mere conflict between black and white.

Chesterton had no deep knowledge of continental ways. He had no more than a schoolboy's knowledge of French and I have not come across any evidence of his ever staying in any foreigner's house. From schooldays onwards he made from time to time visits to the Continent but they were no more than the visits of a cultured tourist. He was in no real way interested in the detailed private life—as opposed to the general historical story—of any country but his own. It may be true, as Shaw said, that he had a Gallic wit. It is not very certain what phrases of that sort mean. But he was essentially an Englishman of the English and the details of his opinions on international affairs were certainly adopted as an almost unquestioning disciple of Belloc. The two had come across one another for the first time over the Boer War, to which they were united in their opposition. From that comradeship Chesterton came to accept Belloc as his master on all matters of foreign affairs.

Belloc's standpoint on such matters was essentially that of a Frenchman. Chesterton, on the other hand, was by nature a lover of small places and a hater of vast dehumanised agglomerations. It was in many ways an attractive faith and it caused him to rebuke the folly of those Englishmen who nattered in woolly generalisation of the Anglo-Saxon race or the English Speaking Union and took it for granted that Britain could always count on American support for all her policies. He was in no way anti-American. He found much to admire in American habits—thought that on the whole there was a truer democracy in America than in Britain. But he was concerned to insist that the two countries were totally different from one another and as a condition of friendship must recognise one another's differences. Here he was certainly right and the passage of time—the increasing absurdity of pretending that there was a 'special relationship' between the two countries—has proved him a wise prophet.

But his love of small units caused him to be suspicious of cosmopolitan projects for the League of Nations with which Woodrow Wilson filled the post-war world. The hostility of the masonic government of Italy, where at that time the quarrel with the Vatican had of course not as yet been composed, prevented the Pope from playing an active part in the League, but in these years after the Second World War the Popes by their strong support of the League's successor, the United Nations, have shown themselves the champions of the creation of the international authority. Perhaps the invention of the more horrible and utterly destructive weapons have impressed men—Popes and others—with a greater urgency than was felt fifty years ago. Perhaps the truth is rather that fifty years ago no one imagined that, whatever they did, there was any possibility that there would be another world war in their lifetimes and therefore did not think it of any special importance that they should behave responsibly. Whatever the truth, it is certain that Chesterton, unlike the modern Popes, was quite without sympathy for plans of international organisation. He may well have been right in insisting on the importance, if we were to preserve a colourful world, of preserving national peculiarities, and the day might come when the supranational authority was so strong that it was necessary to take special measures to preserve these local peculiarities against its overweening power. But in a real world men take their precautions against the real dangers and leave the precautions against the reaction to those dangers to a time when the reactions themselves have become dangerous. A day might come when nationalism was too weak a force in the world. In the proliferation of new nations which the formula of self-determination brought to birth the danger in modern times was manifestly not that there should be too little but that there should be too much nationalism. It was Chesterton's argument that the League of Nations was a façade behind which the bankers were seeking to put Germany again on her feet and to build her up until she should be again a danger to Europe.

Chesterton's opinions then—at least these secondary opinions on political or economic matters which he had so largely adopted from Belloc—were, as are all men's opinions, to a large extent the products of his own particular age and necessarily appear dated in the different conditions of today. Belloc was an aggressive Catholic whose controversies had always about them 'a sundering quality.' It is easy to condemn such aggressiveness. But it is necessary to remember how different a place was nineteenth-century England from twentieth-century England. Attitudes towards Catholics had softened a little during the nineteenth century—but only a very little. Catholic Emancipation had in the end been granted. The attempt to prevent the Catholics by law from organising themselves into dioceses had in the end been abandoned and indeed had been generally conceded to be ridiculous. First the University authorities and then the Catholic authorities had agreed to allow Catholics to go to Oxford and Cambridge. Newman had in the end won a place in English respect that had not been previously attained by any Catholic ecclesiastic. Yet the gulf was still wide. Many Catholics in England still lived in a ghetto community, almost without contact with their Protestant fellow citizens. Most Protestants in fact hardly ever met a Catholic. Englishmen took for granted a version of history which depicted Protestantism as the unvarying champion of liberty and Catholicism as its unvarying enemy. Catholicism was thought to be the religion of the Irish and the Latins, both of whom on account of their religion were inferior people. The Irish claim to Home Rule exacerbated anti-Catholic feeling among the English.

It was into such an atmosphere that Belloc erupted. It was his deliberate conclusion that in its defence courtesy would be a weapon of no avail. Complacency could only be broken down if it was treated with contempt. That Belloc was somewhat too violent in his methods and too sweeping in his generalisations, that his history was often inaccurate in detail, was certainly true. But whether or not we entirely approve his methods it is necessary to understand the purpose of them. The purpose of them was to break down by battering a brick wall of prejudice. And, if today history is taught in the English universities fairly and without bias, in a vastly different fashion from that in which it was taught in the last century, we must remember that a large part of the credit is due to Belloc; and that if the well-mannered moderate-minded Catholic of our day can receive courteous treatment and fair-minded criticism, to a large extent he is able without encumbrance to walk through the gap in the wall largely because Belloc opened the gap for him. Chesterton rendered a similar, perhaps a more important, service in a slightly different field. He showed the English public that the Catholic could laugh—and not only laugh but laugh in so good-humoured a fashion that even his antagonist could not bear malice. Indeed he, like Pope John after him, showed that the Catholic could be both full of love and lovable.

Yet of course once he became a Catholic Chesterton was absolutely uncompromising in his Catholicism. The voice of the Church was to him the voice of God and he would admit no qualification of any of the truths which it taught. If anything he tended to exaggerate the authority of the Church and to claim as essential Catholicism some accidental quirks which Catholics at the moment might happen to hold but which were in no way of the essence of the faith. 'All jolly Catholics wear size tens', wrote Guedalla in a good-humoured parody of Belloc. This manner again throws Chesterton into very strong contrast with the modern Catholicism where every claim is so constantly thrown into controversy—sometimes properly and sometimes improperly— where Catholic writers fall over one another in their anxiety to repudiate triumphalism. But, again, we must understand that the contrast is not merely a personal contrast between Chesterton and some modern writer. It is a contrast between two ages of the Church. Chesterton's mind on these matters was formed, even though he was indeed then still an Anglican, in the first decade of the twentieth century—in years when Pius X was Pope and when the Church's life was dominated by the campaign against the modernists. He was on Pius's side because he had himself come out of and still largely moved in a world where people were content to collect into their minds an assortment of uncoordinated opinions and hold them as their faith. In opposition to such moods he believed that if Christianity was true then the teachings of Christ must be accepted. They were not matters for mere debates and therefore it was of the essence of Christianity that it spoke with a single vioce. His general opposition to the principle of modernism was coherent. If it be objected that it was strange that a man with Chesterton's libertarian principles should have approved of some of the methods which Pius invoked for suppressing modernism—censorship, secret delation, vigilance committees and the like—it can only be answered that Chesterton at that time was not much in touch with ecclesiastical circles and doubtless simply did not know what was going on.

But between that time and the present it is rather the Popes who have changed than their critics. Pius X thought that the terrible evil of modernism could only be suppressed by ruthless proscription. Chesterton had no natural liking for ruthless proscription. In his *Saint Francis* he contrasts Saint Dominic's weapon of the Inquisition with St Francis' weapon of loving kindness and sweet humility and admits without reserve that it was much better to cure heresy by Saint Francis' method than by that of Saint Dominic, if it were possible. In Pius X's time no Catholic was encouraged to think that the weapons of loving kindness could be effective. In John XXIII's time it is the weapon recommended to the Church. The way of anathema is rejected and the way of love recommended. Those outside the full Catholic communion are not utterly rejected. Rather is the Catholic reminded how large is their share of truth and he is bidden to cooperate with them in every way possible. There is no reason to doubt that Chesterton, had he been alive today, would, assured of the Pope's approval if he did so, have allowed full play to his natural genial kindness.

2

Magic and the Slade

Belloc was a political animal. To him the Church was to a large extent the political continuation of the Roman Empire. It was of course also much more than that, but nevertheless it is doubtful if with his natural scepticism Belloc would ever have been tempted to accept the Church at all if he had not been able to see it as an imperialism. He was essentially in agreement with Hobbes that the Church of Rome was the ghost on the tomb of the Roman Empire. He differed from Hobbes only in finding this a very noble ancestry. Chesterton on the other hand was not primarily a political tactician, still less an economist. All his opinions in these fields he accepted from Belloc. Thus they were to him but second-hand opinions. His primary interest was in the deeper truths of religion and Newman, in so far as he had a master in modern times, and behind Newman Saint Francis were there much more nearly his masters than Belloc. He was a Christian before he was a Catholic— not merely in the order of time but also in the order of thought. Such a mood as Belloc's life-long brooding over his failure to obtain a Fellowship of All Soul's was a mood incomprehensible to Chesterton.

That being so, it is necessary first to consider why Chesterton became a Christian at all. (He has told us the whole story both of his childhood, the troubles of his adolescence and of his subsequent conversion in his *Autobiography*. It is from that work that all the quotations of his own confessions in subsequent pages are taken.) He was not brought up as a Christian—or at least in any faith that he would afterwards have called Christian. His history was entirely different from that of Newman or that of any of the

Oxford converts of the nineteenth century, who were brought up in pious Anglican ways and then in later years reached the conclusion that the claim of the Church of England to be a branch of the true Catholic Church could not be sustained. Chesterton's father, the head of the auctioneering firm of Chesterton and Sons which still flourishes in such London boroughs as Kensington, was, according to Chesterton's account of him, a most delightful man. Chesterton records that he possessed many of the kindly characteristics of Mr Pickwick, differing from Mr Pickwick only in that he possessed a big black beard. He possessed also many of the characteristics which he transmitted to his son—a passion for toy theatres, a love of painting, wide knowledge of the central English poets, a burning passion for liberty. He differed from his son only in that he never had any kind of desire to make a professional use of those talents, preferring to make his living out of business and to preserve his accomplishments as private hobbies. He was a strong Liberal and an unquestioning believer in Progress. Chesterton in his *Autobiography* makes a characteristically amusing confession that, contrary to the general fashion, he had no tales of misunderstanding and cruelty to relate about his parents, that he received from them nothing but kindness and remembered them with nothing but gratitude. He wrote, 'I regret that I have no gloomy and savage father to offer to the public gaze as the true cause of all my tragic heritage; no pale-faced and partially poisoned mother whose suicidal instincts have cursed me with the temptation of the artistic temperament. I regret that there was nothing in the range of our family much more racy than a remote and mildly impecunious uncle; and that I cannot do my duty as a true modern by cursing everybody who made me whatever I am. I am not clear about what that is; but I am pretty sure that most of it is my own fault. And I am compelled to confess that I look to that landscape of my first days with a pleasure that should doubtless be reserved for the Utopias of the future.'

Chesterton's father was a man of the highest probity but it was with probity and conduct that, in his view of religion, he was almost entirely concerned. He was by belief a Unitarian—or very nearly a Unitarian. In the Victorian fashion he professed a high regard for the character of Christ but it was in fact only the general command to love his neighbour that he accepted from Christ. The incidental stories and paradoxes of the Gospels did not much influence him. Controversies about the exact nature of Christ seemed to him purposeless and meaningless. The Sacraments played no part in his life nor was there to him any special purpose in going to church. Chesterton and his brother Cecil were brought up to a régime that knew nothing of regular churchgoing. Their only visits to a church were occasional expeditions to hear long ethical sermons by such broad-church unitarian preachers as Stopford Brooke or R. J. Campbell. His father was of that Victorian liberal school of thought which, while having no liking for the vulgarity of assailing other people's beliefs, and while supporting the broadest tolerance, yet took it for granted that with the development of progress men would come to attach ever less and less importance to religious dogmas—to what Chesterton was later in his satirical *John Grubby* to describe as

> . . . Dogma, which, as is well known,
> Does simply hate to be outgrown.

It was in that atmosphere that Chesterton grew up. His very filial piety destroyed in him any youthful temptation to revolt against it. He went to school—first to a preparatory school called Colet Court and afterwards to Saint Paul's. That is to say, he was at a public school where the boys with whom he associated would be the sons of parents of comfortable middle-class origin, into whose lives the lives of the poor did not penetrate. On the other hand it was not an aristocratic school and it was one of the few public schools where the pupils were all day boys. He was thus unlike the average public school boy, who is separated from his parents for two-thirds of the year and encouraged to develop in independence of them. He was by general agreement an extraordinarily ungainly boy, quite incompetent at any athletic feat. He took no interest in games and under the régime of a day school seems to have been able to avoid them without difficulty. He was equally averse to any regular or disciplined work. Totally without regularity, he did what interested him and neglected what did not interest him. He neither gained nor wished to gain any high place in class. He was content to sit at the back among boys who were for the most part two years his junior—to be occasionally their butt. By rights he would have languished until the end of his career, in a lowly form, had not the High Master, as the Head Master there was called, given him a special promotion to the highest form, which at Saint Paul's was the Eighth, because of a prize poem which he had written. Prophetically enough, it was on Saint Francis Xavier, though in it he commemorated solely the courage of a heroic man and it contained no presentiment of the faith which he was afterwards to share with Xavier—rather indeed the reverse.

Chesterton's conduct was, if we may judge from his school reports that have been preserved, uniformly excellent. He was late in his physical development and was generally thought of, and respected by, the others as a boy of very puritanical principles. There is an anecdote of a boy who said of him, 'Chesterton, I am a boy of unprincipled debauchery.' Whether really debauched or not, this boy must surely have been pulling the leg of one whom he thought of as somewhat priggish. However that may be, Chesterton received the news with all seriousness and replied with gravity, 'I am sorry to hear it.' It is not strange that the records should tell us that Chesterton was a boy of strict principles. What is more strange is that they should tell us that he was a boy who was thought to take life with exceptional seriousness and to give no welcome to the introduction into it of a joke. His main interest in those days was neither in the class room nor in the general school life. It was in a curious little society which he and his friends called the Junior Debating Society. Chesterton was the oldest member of that little group, though by no means academically the most distinguished. Most of the rest of them went on afterwards to be scholars at Oxford or Cambridge. Chesterton never achieved any such honour. Yet he was able to exercise a strange mastery over them. He was always the Society's unquestioned president and it was by their confession the ambition of all of them to be the first in his favour—a favour which was beyond challenge attained by his greatest friend, E. C. Bentley. It would be interesting to know what some of the boys of Chesterton's own age made of this constant association with his juniors; whether he was condemned by them as a fool with little dignity. But there is, I fancy, no reminiscence from any such source. It is perhaps inevitable in the modern temper that a suggestion should have been made against him of a latent homosexuality. The accusation of vice or even of a temptation to vice would be ludicrous. He was at that stage of his life quite unsophisticated and undeveloped. That he was still in the stage where his affection went to juniors of his own sex rather than of the other is true enough but his letters, addressed always to the correspondents by the undiluted surname, show very clearly that whatever curious God might be at work within him he was wholly unconscious of its machinations. Yet is it certainly true that the Junior Debating Society did dominate Chesterton's life at that time to a very strange extent. He took its affairs with what in anybody would have appeared portentous gravity, and this was very unexpected gravity in him. He pondered its decisions almost as if they were divine edicts. He concerend himself about the behaviour of members and their possible expulsion as if he were excommunicating them from a Church, and even after the boys had all left school, after both Chesterton and others of them had become engaged to be married, they met together to dine and to exchange speeches in which the humour was somewhat self-conscious and the dominant note that of an esoteric society whose members were of a different sort from all other men.

Saint Paul's under its High Master, Walker, was a school famous for the scholarships that it won at Oxford and Cambridge, and, as has been said, most of Chesterton's school fellows won for themselves scholarships at the one University or the other. Such academic triumphs were not to come Chesterton's ill-organised way. Besides, he had betrayed a talent for sketching and the general expectation of the time was that his future would be that of an artist rather than of a writer—certainly rather than that of a scholar. While the others went to university he went to the Slade School to learn to be an artist, and it was there that he passed through a phase which it is not even yet very easy to understand but which is of a crucial importance in his development. Up till then, he had, it appeared, been content in a comparatively un-reflecting way to accept the easy optimistic faith which his parents had taught him. Life was good and getting daily better. Of its tragedies, of the miseries of the slums, of the teeming millions overseas in the subject nations, he in his comfortable middle-class Victorian environment knew nothing. During his boyhood a little sister had died. Otherwise no tragedy had come into his domestic life. At Saint Paul's he had found friendships and met with no great suffering. When he went to the Slade he was separated from those who had been his friends and he made no new friends of comparable importance. He was lonely. It was to the friends of his former life that almost all his letters are addressed. He lived in the memory of them. But apart from that he does not seem to have met with any great objective hardship.

Yet loneliness turned him in on himself and he passed through a phase of nihilistic introspection, pessimism and almost solipsism, the belief that we know of nothing but our own ideas and our own existence. *Cogito ergo sum.* But what reason have I to think that ideas correspond to any reality outside themselves? What do I know except my own ideas, and what reason have I to think that there is an existence outside my own mind? It is true that until I began to reflect I had imagined that the events of external reality were connected by a causal relationship. But may not this causal relationship be something which my mind has im-posed upon events? Is there any reason—if the word is not itself meaningless—to think that they exist in themselves? Is there in fact any reason to think that there is reason? It was along such lines that his mind then moved and it brought him at times, as he was afterwards to confess, whether with exaggeration or not, near to madness. Later, when he became a Catholic and was asked for the reason of his change, he used always to answer, 'To be absolved of my sin.' As Evelyn Waugh justly says in his *Life of Ronald Knox*, it is strange that a man of so transparent an innocence should have felt this as his special need. We know from Chesterton's own testimony that he was never even at this irreligious time a victim of the cruder sins. He wrote to his fiancée at the time of his engagement to express his thankfulness that he had never gone after strange women. He wrote of Oscar Wilde that he himself had never had the smallest temptation to Wilde's weakness. Yet he applied to himself—with what exact meaning it is hard to guess—Wilde's lines,

> Atys with the blood-stained knife
> Were better than the man I am.

Any man could see for himself that on the planes of humility, kindness, meekness or charity his standards were such as very few indeed achieved. What then exactly were these peculiar sins of that period of which he found it necessary so bitterly to accuse himself it is far from easy to see.

The answer, in as far as one can follow it, seems to run something along these lines. In schooldays he had accepted the external reality of the world and a code of honour with which to meet it without bothering himself about any metaphysical inquiry into its nature. Now in the solitude of the Slade he set out on a common road of idealist exploration. Impelled by his sceptical speculations, Chesterton in his drawing fell under the influence of the Impressionists—particularly of Whistler and Aubrey Beardsley. The artist, according to the Impressionists, should not attempt to draw things as they really are. Who knows what reality is? The most that he can hope to draw is the image of his own mind—his impression. Under these influences Chesterton came to draw, as he afterwards confessed, some very horrible pictures—so horrible that he came ever afterwards to have a strangely violent detestation of the Impressionists, almost as if they were a kind of satanist. What in detail these pictures were we cannot say. Was it simply that with his late adolescence he had imagined for a time that he was free from these desires with which others were affected, and that now that they came on him at this later date and in solitude he exaggerated their abnormality and exaggerated their wickedness?

He indulged, he told us, in these years a little in table-turning and dabbled in spiritualism and took from them not so much an impression that they were entirely fraudulent as that man soiled himself by indulging in them. Years later, in 1913, urged to do so by the insistence of Bernard Shaw, he was to write a play—called *Magic*. It was a well constructed play, but it met only with a moderate success and that no doubt mainly because of its subject, which was that of its title. A conjurer who had himself in youth dabbled in magic and become, like Chesterton, convinced of its evil, falls, under the taunts of a brash youth—an atheist convinced that all pretendedly preternatural phenomena are capable of a materialistic explanation—to the temptation of performing an act of pure magic and by it changing the colour of the light over the doctor's house. He is immediately convinced that in doing so he had been guilty of sin. In general, whatever may be the truth about preternatural phenomena, novelists or dramatists are ill-advised to introduce them into their stories because the laws of such phenomena are so ill-understood that, if they are introduced, there are no standards of probability by which the reader can judge the story. Thus when in *Perelandra* C. S. Lewis tells us how Merlin had made a road run uphill that normally ran downhill, our interest flags. Chesterton fully accepted this general rule. When he was president of the Club of Detective Story Writers he introduced into the oath of the detective writer a clause forbidding all such writers to allow their detectives to employ any preternatural aid in the solution of their crimes. Father Brown, soaked as he was in belief in the supernatural, is always careful to solve all his problems by purely natural intelligence. There is no doubt that many theatre-goers were put off *Magic* by its appeal to magic, and dismissed it therefore as silly and unreal. But *Magic* does not in the least introduce a magical trick to solve a secular conundrum. The conjurer offers no explanation by what means or incantations he has performed his trick. That is of no interest. He simply states without qualification that he has performed it by magic. The problem is not how magical tricks are performed but that magical tricks are evil. Chesterton was not introducing magic to solve a problem. He was writing about magic—writing about an evil of which, as he

29

believed, he had had personal experience, and exposing its ill effects on the soul through the conjurer's reticence. In what precise form he in his youth met with magic he, with his characteristic reticence, nowhere tells us. But he leaves us in no doubt that he believed that he had met with it and that, as with Macbeth, he appealed for help from beyond this world but refused to pay the moral price for that help; he received, indeed, what he asked for, but he received it in such a form that he would have done better to go without it.

When Chesterton turned with his extreme repugnance on Whistler and the Impressionist painters he turned at the same time on George Moore whom he saw among writers as the novelist most dangerously influenced by Impressionism. In his *Heretics* he attacked Moore with some harshness. It was therefore a great generosity of Moore when he repaid Chesterton's attack by highly praising his *Magic*. In a spirit of generosity that was not habitual to him, he wrote of *Magic*, 'I think of all modern plays I like it the best,' and only complained that the conjurer's love affair 'materialises him too much.' But the conjurer was to Chesterton entirely real and most material. *Magic* was not an exercise in whimsy-whamsy. It was an entirely real study of an experience which Chesterton thought entirely true.

3

The Wild Knight

Discovering magic, Chesterton was in his view discovering
something that was evidently real but also evidently evil. The
attempt to give a purely materialistic explanation of things always
seemed to him absurd. We only perceive matter through the mind
and he would have agreed with Descartes and Berkeley that the
existence of the mind was a great deal more evident than the
existence of matter. But equally he rejected the sophistry that
because spiritual forces were true they were therefore necessarily good. There were evil forces about in the world, but
evil could only be evil if there were behind it a good in contrast to
it. Evil was negative. If there was no good there could be no evil.
The God behind the gods must be good, the last word with
goodness. Existence itself was good. One's own existence was
good. He quoted in his *Autobiography* his grandfather's saying, 'I
should thank God for my creation, if I knew I was a lost soul.'
Other existence was good. The excitement of life arose from the
fact that there were other separate objects—not just a totality of
reality. 'God', he quoted from Coventry Patmore, 'is not infinite.
He is the synthesis of infinity and boundary.' Whether this is
exactly orthodox theology I do not know, but to Chesterton it was
always the double nature, man both good and evil which, as opposed
to either pantheists or materialists, posited a double nature in
reality—a God who was in nature but who was more than nature,
who was in a measure hidden behind nature, the Creator but a
Creator who permitted nature's apparent cruelties, a *Deus absconditus*. The good of the world proved that there was a God, the

evil of the world that He was not always easily apparent—that He had to be discovered.

Whatever Chesterton may have felt during his passing adolescent phase at the Slade, of course nothing could be further from the temperament of his nature than a Manichaean faith which held that love and desire and sex were in themselves evil. To the contrary, they were evil only when misused. In themselves they were good. 'Our God hath blessed creation, Calling it good,' as he was to write in *The Ballad of the White Horse*. He soon moved from an exaggerated pessimism to a perhaps exaggerated optimism. He turned from Whistler and Beardsley to Whitman and Robert Louis Stevenson. The refutation of solipsism was to be found not in any fallacy of logic. If a man chose to maintain his insane consistency, there was no way of proving to him that there was any other existence but his own. The refutation of solipsism was simply that it was impossible to believe it. Unless he was wholly mad, a man needs had to be as certain that he was not the whole of existence as he was that he existed at all. A man might know nothing but his own ideas, but at least even on the purely subjective analysis his ideas would fall into two classes: those of his imagination, which he called up for himself, and those which were forced on him, that is, those which he received by sensation from the external world. I can shut my eyes and imagine that I am looking at the garden or imagine that I am looking elsewhere, at my own pleasure. But if I open my eyes and look I have no alternative but to see the garden that is before me. Metaphysicians might dispute in what exact sense the external real world existed. Let their disputes be as they may. The important fact was that it did exist. It existed and, as Chesterton was able to find in his new mood, it was good. 'Dream; there is no truth,' said Yeats, 'but in your own heart.' It was not so. Walt Whitman was now his hero and he accepted with enthusiasm Whitman's paean of praise for the splendour of all reality. Life was good. There came

> far out of fish-shaped Paumanok
> Some cry of cleaner things,

as he wrote some years later, describing this transformation in his dedication to Bentley of *The Man Who Was Thursday*. Life, if it was to be enjoyed had to be accepted, as Stevenson taught him to accept it, as an adventure.

> Truth out of Tusitala spoke
> And pleasure out of pain.

The transformation of mind brought a transformation of Chesterton's manner of drawing. He turned fron the vague, indefinite, impressionistic form to the hard definite lines—from *La Belle Dame Sans Merci* to the caricature and the grotesque, which were to predominate in the illustrations that he was later to do for such books as Bentley's *Biographies for Beginners* or Belloc's satirical novels. 'It is the sacred stubbornness of things,' he wrote, 'their mystery and their suggestive limits, their shape and their special character which makes all artistic thrift and thought. The adventure is not an all-transforming enchantment, it is rather the answer of a challenge and one in which we have hardly the choice of weapons.' Things are as they are and neither the artist nor any other man has the freedom to call them otherwise. He was to write in *Orthodoxy* that 'If in your bold creative way you hold yourself free to draw a giraffe with a short neck you will really find that you are not free to draw a giraffe.' He praised Hans Andersen because he had brought reality into the fairy story, contrasting him in this, to his advantage, with Yeats. Hans Andersen, he said, 'may be said, to have originated a new kind of fairy story. Instead of dealing only with dragon-slaying princes and golden-haired princesses moving in a twilight land of terrible forests and enchanted castles, he told the histories of tin soldiers and ugly ducklings, of Christmas trees and old street lamps.' The transformation of Chesterton's mind caused him, as was inevitable to a man so full of theory, to turn from drawing to writing as his new medium of expression. Henceforth it is as a writer that we must mainly consider him. His first essays were in poetry. In 1900 he produced his first volumes, *Greybeards at Play* and *The Wild Knight*. *Greybeards At Play* was a slim volume in which nonsense verses were mixed with jokes against current artists and philosophers. He came to think that nonsense and satire should not be properly mixed and the dignity of laughter demanded that it be turned against a proposition—that it should not be merely nonsensical. Nonsense was the vehicle of the nineteenth century—of a static society. The society that was coming to birth was a society in motion and a society that required challenge. Life was too serious an affair to be left to nonsense writers.

Greybeards at Play met with no great success nor did Chesterton much value it. He did not include it in his collected poems nor mention it in his *Autobiography*. *The Wild Knight* was another affair and with it Chesterton's literary career was properly launched. *The Wild Knight and Other Poems* was the full title of the book and it reprinted some other verses that had appeared in *The Outlook* and *The Speaker*, of which the best known was *The Donkey*: this was the characteristic little Chestertonian piece of paradox by which the donkey, the most ridiculous of all the animals.

> The devil's walking parody on all four-footed things

was made to remember when

> One far fierce hour and sweet:
> There was a shout about my ears,
> And palms before my feet.

It is a poem that is stamped with the characteristic Chestertonian love of the paradoxical and the unexpected, but also with the equally Chestertonian indifference to pedestrian fact, for of course in the East the ass is by no means a figure of fun but a royal beast.

Apart from *The Donkey* there is one poem in which, with a typically Chestertonian whimsy, an unborn baby is described as expressing his longing to be born into a world so wonderful that its trees were tall, its grasses short with 'green hair on great hills,' its sea was blue and 'a fixed fire hung in the air.' How exciting, the boy reflects, it would be to be born into such a world if only such a world existed. But in general in the poems that were about living people, though the final triumph was always with happiness, the world that was described was by no means a world that contained nothing of suffering. To the contrary, there runs a morbid obsession with murder and gibbets which the student of the later Chesterton will find surprising but which gives full indication that he was at this time indeed a man who had struggled out of a world of sickness, but who had but recently struggled out of it. It gives us an inkling of the kind of perversions on which his mind had been recently dwelling—of what was to him the evil of life that he had now come to fight. It is a very different battle from the sort of battle against the healthy honourable atheist, Turnbull, with whom he was going to make the young Highland Catholic, MacIan, so often to cross swords a few years later in his *The Ball and the Cross*.

Yet our main concern is with *The Wild Knight* itself. What was it that caused Chesterton to step out of his mood of nihilism? He has himself told the story in one of his *Daily News* articles. The story is doubtless, as Chesterton's stories usually are, symbolic—that is to say, he concentrates into a single incident what was in fact a more general and more gradual experience. But the story as he told it was as follows. It appears under the title of *The Diabolist* in his book of essays, *Tremendous Trifles*, and is accompanied with an assertion that 'What I have now to relate really happened.' and he told it again in his *Autobiography*. According to the story, he had a conversation one day on a long flight of steps—probably the steps that run down to the quadrangle in front of the Slade School. The man with whom he was talking was a man who gloried in an evil life and was upbraiding Chesterton for his rigid, timid and boring respectability. Chesterton defended himself and his morality and pointed to the spark that was flying off a nearby bonfire and argued that to seduce a virgin was as if one were to quench a star. Things had their nature, and virtue consisted of respecting that nature. It was only the unnatural—the use of an instrument for a purpose other than that for which it was designed—that was evil. His companion argued that on the contrary the object of life was to collect as many experiences as possible. When we have used an object for its natural purpose, then, in order to obtain new experience, it was necessary to go further and to use it for an unnatural purpose. As for Chesterton's good and evil, he contented himself with saying airily, 'What you call evil I call good.' The student then went down the stairs. Chesterton followed him some time afterwards and, as he reached the bottom of the stairs, he saw him talking with some companions and heard him utter the words, 'If I do that, I shan't know the difference between right and wrong.' What this evil was at which even the evil man shuddered Chesterton tells us that he never learnt, never indeed even dared to speculate on. But he learnt from the episode two lessons—that there was indeed evil in the world but that even great evil could not quite escape the tug towards goodness. A time was to come some years later when Chesterton was to be criticised for a too exuberant optimism, when Professor Kettle in Ireland was to rebuke him for a fatuous pretence of finding good in everything and to ask whether the notion of a little child dying of an incurable disease was so jolly and funny and could properly be greeted with a mere roar of laughter. Whether there was ever a time when such accusations could justly be levelled against Chesterton we shall later consider, but certainly they could not justly be levelled at this time of his first entry into the literary world. Then, at any rate, he was not blind to the evil of the world. It was on the contrary the existence of evil which first led him to the appreciation of goodness.

A number of incidental poems in *The Wild Knight* are quite frankly a little difficult to understand. The young Chesterton piled up words upon words and paradox upon paradox and it is difficult at the end of them to be quite certain what it is that he is intending to say. He had not yet become the master of lucidity into which he was later to develop. And if this criticism be valid of the incidental poems it is equally valid of the title poem, of *The Wild Knight* itself. It requires very careful following and at the end of that following one cannot be quite certain that one has even then got all the points. Also, in great contrast to any of Chesterton's later works, it is quite untouched by any humour or light-heartedness. Its strange story is roughly as follows. The *Wild Knight* is a Don Quixote figure travelling through the world on his dedicated quest—on his quest for the love of God to which he has vowed himself, of the truth of which he has no doubt but of which he has never yet seen visible evidence. He comes to an old house within which is a chapel, lit by candles, in which a service is going on. Outside, sitting alone above the door astride the bracket of the porch is Captain Redfeather. Captain Redfeather is the Whitmanesque man who has accepted with gusto all the good things that this life has to offer.

> I have drunk to all I know of,
>   To every leaf on the tree,
> To the highest bird of the heavens,
>   To the lowest fish of the sea.
> What toast, what toast remaineth,
>   Drunk down in the same good wine,
> By the tippler's cup in the tavern,
>   And the priest's cup at the shrine?

The priests come out of the chapel and abuse Redfeather for his blasphemy. He replies by attacking them as the ministers of repression.

Then when the priests have departed there comes out of the house the beautiful Lady Olive, a totally good and Christian lady. Captain Redfeather falls instantly in love with her and, falling himself in love, is at once confronted with the challenge of hate. If what is lovely is good, what is unlovely is bad, and there is hate in the world. His paean to general and absolute goodness everywhere appears to him to have been naïve and superficial. Yet how can a good God have made hate? In particular there is within the house, as Lady Olive tells him, the wicked Lord Orm. Lord Orm is an evil man who has attempted unsuccessfully to seduce Olive. He is like Shakespeare's Richard III—'myself alone'—above, as he considered, both good and evil. He is not metaphysically a solipsist. He does not deny the existence of other beings, but to him nothing outside his own ideas is of any importance. He is only interested in collecting experiences and sensations. He has attempted to seduce Lady Olive not even

37

out of lust, let alone love, but simply to satisfy his curiosity in the experience, to discover what it is like—as the modern vulgarism would put it, for 'kicks'. Redfeather is horrified and challenges him. It is Redfeather's belief that even in the most unprincipled of men there is a final breaking point—a relic of virtue in him which will not allow him to refuse a challenge. He who is content to receive any other accusation is not content to be called a coward.

> I have seen men go mangier than the beasts,
> Eat bread with blood upon their fingers, grin
> While women burned—but one last law they served.
> When I say 'Coward', is the law awake?

But Orm cares not what others think of him, cares nothing if they think or call him a coward. Why should he care? And, when he refuses the challenge, Redfeather is reduced to impotence. If Orm refuses the challenge, then, as he says,

> I am stronger than the world.

Redfeather could kill him in a fair fight. He cannot strike him if he is unresisting.

> And yet—and yet you do not strike me dead.
> I do not draw—the sword is in your hand. . . .
> Now look on me—I am the lord of earth,
> For I have broken the last bond of man.
> I stand erect—crowned with the stars—and why?
> Because I stand a coward—because you
> Have mercy—on a coward.

He is, as he says in his soliloquy,

> Perfectly free and utterly alone,
> Free of all love of law, equally free
> Of all the love of mutiny it breeds.
> Free of the love of heaven, and also free
> Of all the love of hell it drives us to;

Not merely void of rules, unconscious of them;
So strong that naught alive could do him hurt,
So wise that he knew all things, and so great
That none knew what he was or what he did—
A lawless giant—

in fact Richard III. He takes out his title deeds and sets them on fire. The light flares up. At that moment comes in the mad Wild Knight. To the Knight a flame, which more nearly than anything else in this world appears to become something out of nothing, is is the very symbol of creation, the evidence of a creating God. Seeing the light flare up, he thinks that he has at last found God, and seeing Lord Orm standing there, he hails him as God. But God is the one being that, for all his complacency, Orm knows that he cannot be. Even if he is the devil the devil cannot create. Furious at what the Knight had in his simplicity thought to be a recognition but what Orm accepts as an exposure, he turns on him. Orm's act of violence in its turn frees Captain Redfeather to draw his sword. He can now use violence against one who has himself used violence and turns on Orm. They fight and Orm is killed.

There are some complications, some loose ends that are not comprehendingly tied up in *The Wild Knight*. It is intelligible enough that the crazy Knight should see in flame a symbol of creation and therefore evidence of God and should hail as God Orm who had lit the flame. But why, save to suit Chesterton's dramatic purposes, Orm should wish to burn his title deeds is by no means clear. Was it to assert himself as a sort of twisted Melchizedek without father nor mother truly 'myself alone'? Nor is it clear why Orm, having received with complacency from Redfeather every insult and treated it with scorn, should bridle into fury at the Wild Knight's ascription to him of divinity. One can easily enough see why he knew that the ascription was not true. But why did he mind so much whether the Knight believed that it was true or not?

However, our concern is not so much with literary criticism as with an evaluation of what Chesterton was thinking. For that purpose *The Wild Knight* is a work of crucial importance. It shows very clearly what was the point to which Chesterton had at that moment moved out of the nihilistic dreams of the Slade. On a purely metaphysical plane the case for solipsism is, as we have argued, incredible, and at the same time irrefutable. We do know nothing but our own ideas—and that is the end of it. We may have free ideas which are created by our own imagination and forced ideas which it is common to say were imposed on us by external experience. But of neither do we know anything except what we have learnt in our own experience. And if the solipsist chooses to face the world, if world there be, with an attitude of total nescience and say 'All I know are my own ideas. Where the ideas may come from I have no means of knowing,' there is no answer to him. But solipsism sets not only a metaphysical but also a moral problem. If our ideas are of two sorts in that some come from the imagination and some at any rate claim to come from external reality, they are equally of two sorts in the moral order. I have impulses. Some of them appear innocent and no voice within forbids me to obey them. Others appear guilty and to obey them an act of dishonour. The solipsist may argue, as Lord Orm argued or Chesterton's diabolist of the Slade, that the notions of honour are an illusion which a man has invented and imposed upon himself in order to provide him with a false notion of a purpose in his life. Impulses are merely impulses. It cannot be that some are right and some are wrong—that one owes an account to some being beyond oneself, since, says the solipsist, he has no evidence that such a being exists. Yet the difficulty of such arguments is that since the solipsist allows no reality to anything but his own ideas, it is not easy to see by what test any idea of experience can be dismissed as an illusion. If all knowledge is derived from experience, then we must face it than an ultimate sense of honour is as certain a fact of experience as a man's sense of his own existence. The Richard IIIs of this world might do the best that they could to kill their consciences but even with them as with the diabolist and Lord Orm, conscience asserted itself at the last. Like the cheerfulness of Dr Johnson's lawyer friend Edward, it was always breaking out. There was some point beyond which even the wickedest of men would not allow himself to go. The conclusion to be drawn from that was not indeed a conclusion of easy roystering optimism such as that of Captain Redfeather in the early verses of this poem. There was plenty of apparent evil in the world. There was plenty of misuse by man of the gifts which God had given him. Man used fire, which was given to him to purge or to warm, in order to destroy. But somehow, in the mysterious battle which the *Deus absconditus* had condemned fallen man to fight, the final truth was with faith and the final victory was with good.

Those who profess to reject God and to deny obligation always betray themselves by using such words as 'ought' which their principles give them no right to use. Indeed, without such a constant appeal, neither thought nor language is possible. Such a man as Bertrand Russell divides his time between asserting that there can be no right or wrong and abuse of those who differ from him for their wickedness. As Samuel Butler said, the controversy is between those who believe in God and those who call Him by another name. Superstition is often strongest in those who profess atheism. The need to profess a belief is so strong in man that, as Chesterton said, 'He who does not believe in God will believe in anything.'

Now it is clear that all this is tight arguing. But it does not in itself involve any appeal to the authority of Christ or any acceptance of his Divinity. Chesterton himself in his *Autobiography* has made it quite clear that at that stage of his life he would not have been prepared to make any such admission. Both in *The Wild Knight* and in his *Notebooks* of that period he was coming increasingly to use biblical and Christian language. In *The Wild Knight* there is a poem of a *Christian Lullaby*, from which, standing by itself, the reader might have deduced that he was at that time a pious and orthodox Christian. But we have his word for it that the problem with which he was at that time wrestling was the problem of sin and that he wrestled with that problem not because he had been told about it in the manuals or the catechisms but because he had come across it as an experience in his own life.

[4]

The First Acceptance

If Chesterton so often used Christian language and imagery it was not because at that time he thought that the Christian claims were historically true so much as that he thought that its language symbolically corresponded to the reality of the problems of life— at any rate of his life. At this period he was not so much a Christian. Rather he thought—though he would never have used such language—that Christ was by anticipation a Chestertonian. In order to understand Chesterton's attack on this age-old and all important difficulty of the existence of evil in a world that was by definition the creation of a good God, we must set side by side three of his works, each of a very different kind from the others and each separated from the others by a considerable space of time—*The Wild Knight*, his *Browning* and *The Man Who Was Thursday*. While it is true that in these early years in which he was not yet ready to accept the divinity of Christ he was increasingly turning to biblical language, it was the apocalyptic rather than the ethical sayings of Christ to which he turned and in general the Old Testament rather than the New. Of the books of the Old Testament that which was the main influence on him was the book of Job, for it was there that he found this problem of evil more frankly confronted than anywhere else in literature. The pessimist deduces from the evil which he experiences the conclusion that the world is an evil place. Chesterton after perhaps a passing mood of pessimism at the Slade had refused to accept this conclusion. Mere personal experience refuted the pessimist. If there is much evil in this life there is also in any normal man's experience much good. Life, save to those who are afflicted with exceptional calamities, is not on balance an evil. If accepted on the terms on which it is offered, it is happy, nor does it make sense to say that God has created an evil world. Why should He? Evil is a limitation and God by definition is unlimited. Like Dr Johnson, Chesterton accepted the goodness of God because of 'the absense of any reason for His being other'.

Yet clearly Johnson's argument for the goodness of God through the absence of any reason for His being other only relieves us of one difficulty by involving us in another. If there was much good in the world, yet as certainly as a matter of experience there was also much evil. There were the wicked actions of men and, if the existence of original sin was paraded to account for all the world's evil, what of the natural calamities which brought evil even though they were in no way the consequence of any man's sin? Chesterton's first answer—on the whole the answer of *The Wild Knight*—was simply, like Job, an assertion of faith in God's goodness and in the ultimate victory of good. 'I know that my redeemer liveth.' 'Though he slay me yet will I love him.' If we knew all we would understand all. As things are at present we cannot hope to know but we must believe by faith. Why Lord Orm is as he is *The Wild Knight* does not consider. He is only concerned to demonstrate that even in a wicked man there does come an ultimate breaking point at which wickedness surrenders and admits the rights of honour. As the diabolist said, 'If I did that, I should no longer know the difference between right and wrong.'

The Wild Knight appeared in 1900. During the next years Chesterton was engaged on a paper, *The Speaker*, writing vigorously against the Boer War. After the war he became a regular columnist for *The Daily News*, which for the first time established him as a well-known public figure. In 1901 he collected some of the essays which he had contributed to *The Speaker* and published them under the title of *The Defendant*. They are in essence a defence of high spirits and of particular objects as opposed to his more usual essays in generalisation. He was by then in full reaction against the pose, as he thought it, of the previous decade in which aesthetes pretended that boredom was an evidence of intellectual superiority, when, as he was to write in the dedication to Bentley of *The Man Who was Thursday* a few years later,

> Like the white lock of Whistler, that lit our aimless gloom
> Men showed their own white feather as proudly as a plume.

'In our time,' he wrote in *The Defendant*, 'the blasphemies are threadbare. Pessimism is now patently, as it always was essentially, more commonplace than piety.' Just as the joke, as Aristotle said, can only be funny if it is surprising, so the blasphemy can only shock if it is thrown into a world where people are generally pious and well behaved and as a habit shrink from speaking frankly. As soon as blasphemy becomes common it becomes pointless and boring and, when it ceases to be amusing, it is examined fairly on its merits and found not even to be true. The answer to the solipsist argument could not absolutely demonstrate that there was existence outside oneself. It could not demonstrate that particular things exist. But Chesterton in the robust Stevensonian optimism into which he was by now moving was concerned to assert that not only did a God exist but also that God was not a mere pantheist totality of reality but a creator of particular things and that the world could only be enjoyed if we recognise each thing for what it is, love it for what it is and use it as its purpose designed it to be used.

> The world is so full of a number of things
> I am sure we should all be as happy as kings—

said Stevenson, embarking on his 'great task of happiness'.

In *The Defendant* Chesterton embarked upon the defence of trivialities despised by the highbrows, such as penny dreadfuls, detective stories, slang and the like—showing with exuberant high spirits, or at least purporting to show, that each of them, if accepted for what they were, had their place in the scheme of things. It was not very serious but it was good fooling. It was important in the development of Chesterton mainly because it was not serious—the first evidence of his new discovery that laughter and ridicule were weapons that should properly be harnessed to the service of truth. Up till then the enemies of Christianity had annexed to themselves a monopoly of jokes. They could laugh at Christians. It never occurred to them that Christians might laugh back. Not of course for a minute would Chesterton admit that when he used laughter against the secularist he was indulging in a mere trick of debate. To the contrary, to his contention laughter was in the very stuff of truth and true religion, and there could be no truth that was wholly solemn. 'No artist,' he wrote, 'will deny a unique good in mediaeval art; a power of the Gothic for fusing the grotesque with the divine. Such craftsmen found, as it were, a special clay that could be moulded in one piece into angels and apes. I do not say that ancient stoics or modern sceptics have been unable to smile or to be serious. I do not say that the Praying Boy is not praying; or that no dignity belonged to that stone on which was written *Deo erexit Voltaire*. I say that the Greek and Gallic stones were not graven like the Gothic stones; had not that special spiritual energy and even gaiety that can be seen in any world-old waterspout sticking from the roof of Lincoln or Beauvais. For the gargoyle is really typical of the mystical utilitarianism of the Gothic, of something which got poetic good out of a gutter and turned a vision into a thing of beauty. Similarly I do not say that pagan and secular gaiety are not as beautiful, but I do say that they are not as gay.' The Christian claiming laughter for his creed was merely reclaiming what was intrinsically his right.

In the next year, 1902, Chesterton produced a similar reprint of essays that had appeared in newspapers—reprinted but slightly rewritten and improved—entitled *Twelve Types*. Where *The Defendant* had been concerned to emphasise the uniqueness of things, *Twelve Types* was concerned with the uniqueness of people —with character sketches of such people as Alexander Pope, Walter Scott, Saint Francis of Assisi, Rostand and Charles II. It was not quite clear why he called the book *Twelve Types* since the essential point about all those characters was that they were unique and not mere members of a class to be easily labelled.

Chesterton also at this time wrote the first of his biographies—on the artist G. F. Watts. Watts is not today an artist of any very great fame and Chesterton's book not perhaps very much read. He used Watts very largely as a weapon in his reaction against the Impressionists, praised the brave definitions of his outlines and propounded the theory that the business of art was neither to give a mere photograph nor a merely subjective impression but to speak of the world in a special language of its own, neither indifferent to its subject nor slavishly copying it but, as he put it, 'not above taking hints from the book of life with its quaint old woodcuts.'

Eight years were to elapse before he attempted another biography of an artist—his *William Blake* of 1910. This, written in maturity, was the more successful book. Writing for the same series as that of *Watts*, he was under obligation to his brief to write of Blake the engraver and the painter, rather than of the poet, and he obeyed his brief, with, for him, surprising fidelity. He makes no attempt in that book to adapt Blake's vision to his own. His only essay in interpretation is to suggest that Blake, precisely because he lived in an age which had surrendered itself too completely to rationalism, compensated by indulging in mystic visions, but, he argues, alike in his poetry and his painting Blake was at his best when he was least under the influence of his visions.

It was in 1903 in the middle of his journalistic work that Chesterton produced his *Browning*. The commission came to him from John Morley to write such a book for the *English Men of Letters* series which Morley was then editing. The invitation was a considerable compliment to a rising young author, the issue of it to the credit of Morley who with his somewhat bleak positivist faith cannot have been very sympathetic to the intellectual quips and excursions either of Browning or of Chesterton. Morley was a man who believed in bluntly saying what he thought was true and what he did not believe could be known, and leaving no one in doubt about his intentions. The vague probing speculations and intellectual twists which Browning loved and which attracted Chesterton to him were not Morley's taste. Whether Morley liked what he got was not, I think, ever revealed. It is certain that there were many who did not like it. Anyone who was looking for the conventional Victorian biography with lists of careful dates and

accurately verified quotations most certainly went away dis-
appointed. Chesterton had an almost whimsically perverse
aversion to accuracy. He prided himself on rarely quoting a date
and never verifying a quotation. He argued that if he quoted from
memory that was proof that he really lived in the company of an
author as opposed to the pedant who had merely looked up the
quotation for the occasion. It is hard to feel that this contention
was wholly justified, and with a little more carefulness in his work,
he would have given it greater force without any risk of his falling
into pedantry. Yet that was how he was and how until the end he
obstinately insisted on remaining. The *Browning* was the first
advertisement which he gave to the world of such a quirk and there
were those who resented it. 'An impudent fraud' was a frank comment on it. Some argued quite simply that he was a man of no
scholarship who should never have been given a place in such a
company of scholars as the authors of the Home University
Library. Others suggested that his inaccuracy and his shapeless
style were products of the deliberate pose of a young man who was
mainly anxious by this false originality to flutter the dovecotes
and to get himself talked about. All publicity for the man on the
make, it was said, is good publicity. If one is not capable of doing
anything extraordinarily good, then it is better to do something
extraordinarily bad if only thus can one get oneself talked about.

While it is reasonable enough to criticise Chesterton's methods
it is clear that this last explanation was wide of the mark. There
was never anyone who cared less about the mere vulgarity of
publicity than he did. His tactics, whether justified or not, were
deliberate. Browning had at that time been almost captured by
somewhat fantastic *Browning Societies*—pedantic persons who met
together in learned groups and read one another dry papers,
elucidating the meanings of his obscurer sentences, straightening
out his syntax and tracking down his allusions. Chesterton felt
that these worthy old fogies were missing the wood for the trees.
Browning was above all a poet, a man capable of beauty, a man
who, when he used the grotesque, did so for a purpose; a man of
humour; a man who had something to say on the actual purposes
of life—not a man who was setting a puzzle for a literary magazine

or to tease a schoolboy in an examination paper. He insisted that Browning was a poet—indeed almost the only poet in English literature who never wrote anything but poetry—and he was also a man who had something to say. Nor could the one be separated from the other. For with Browning, as with everybody else, the style was the man and one could not comprehend the matter of the writer without also attending to the manner. Browning wrote in verse because verse is the medium through which the writer conveys that there is truth beyond that which he is capable of expressing, that the ultimate reality is not to be found in syllogisms and propositions, that 'all things go out into mystery,' that

> our mark must exceed our grasp,
> Else what's a heaven for?

He wrote often (though not always) in grotesque verse adorned with far-fetched, cacophanous and almost barbaric rhymes because such was reality—a reality of unassorted, separate unique persons and objects—not of obedient types and regiments, 'train'd to stand in rows and asking if they please.' It was a wild world on which God had impressed his order. The very defects of the world, as he argued in *Old Pictures in Florence* and elsewhere, were an argument that this world was not everything. It was 'blessed evil' here which caused us to look for goodness in its true home, whither we would not otherwise have been tempted to turn our eyes. Yet Browning did tell stories about people and in *The Victorian Age in Literature* Chesterton was to call him 'rather one of the Victorian novelists than wholly one of the Victorian poets'.

The particular truth about the mystery of evil, which Chesterton professed that Browning had taught him, was that wickedness was indeed a reality which it was foolish sentimentality to deny, but that even the wickedest of men had a side of goodness in him which would be in the end revealed. Man had such a double nature. His lower nature might often conquer, but it was his higher nature that was his truer self. We pay tribute to our recognition of that when we say to a man, urging him to do a good action:

'Be yourself, be a man.' We do not say in rebuke to a greedy crocodile: 'Be a crocodile.' When a man fails at such a test he is, we think, lessening his own personality. It was Browning's achievement, thought Chesterton, that he was a kind of cosmic detective who walked 'into the foulest of thieves' kitchens and accused men publicly of virtue.'

The first question that one obviously asks is whether this was a fact, an accurate description of what Browning in fact did. Browning possessed an exuberant personality and he created for us not only his *Fifty Men and Women* but on his various occasions a very large number more. He would indeed have been a desiccated artist if all his creations had been mere puppets who danced in obedience to a single formula, and there are many of his creations in which no trace of virtue lurking behind a mask of wickedness is to be found. Some, like the Grammarian or Pippa Passing, are just plainly good and need no excuse. Pippa passed scattering happiness all round her by her goodness and high spirits. Others, like Guido in *The Ring and the Book*, are plainly bad. The Pope may pray that 'Guido see one instant and be saved', but there is no hint of an inkling of such repentance in Guido himself. Chesterton interpreted *The Ring and the Book* as a manual of free speech—arguing that this was a new form of art when every sort of witness was allowed to have his say. Truth to the liberal Browning was a many-faced beast and, if every one's tale is told, it is likely that it will emerge that more is to be said for the defendant than had at first been thought. There may be many poems of Browning of which this is indeed the lesson. It is curious to choose *The Ring and the Book* as the example of it: there, the unquestioning verdict—made only the more certain by the accumulation of witnesses—is that Guido was absolutely and totally guilty.

The monk in *The Spanish Cloister*, far from concealing love behind his hatred, rather conceals hatred behind his professions of love. The Bishop, ordering his tomb in Saint Praxed's church, has indeed a kind of pagan geniality behind his worldliness which wins for him a certain mood of sympathy, but his ambition from his tomb to

> hear the blessed mutter of the Mass
> And see God made and eaten all day long,

shows, under whatever mask of geniality, so utter a lack of comprehension of the religion to which he was supposed to have devoted his life that one can hardly call it virtue. In several places, most notably in *The Statue and the Bust*, virtue is depicted not as obedience to a law so much as the courage to act at 'the great hour'—somewhat irrespective of the quality of the act—a morality more reminiscent of that of Shaw than of that of Chesterton.

> The sin I impute to each frustrate ghost
> Is the unlit lamp and the ungirt loin

Indeed there are places where Browning is only concerned to denounce wickedness as wickedness in the tones of the most conventional of moralists, like

> Dante who loved well because he hated—
> Hated wickedness that hinders loving.

It is true that in *Mr. Sludge the Medium*, Djabal in *The Return of the Druses*, and *Fra Lippo Lippi*—bad men who nevertheless almost in spite of themselves discover some surprising relict of sincerity at the bottom of their souls—we find what might be called examples of the Chestertonian formula in Browning's extraordinary fecundity of creation. Doubtless one could find it elsewhere than in the examples given, but it must be doubted if we can fairly say that it is a general formula that illuminated all Browning's work. Of the critics of Chesterton as a biographer the more superficial were content to complain of the absence of dates and the inaccuracy of quotations. Deeper critics had a deeper complaint. Their complaint was that Chesterton, even when he pretended to do so, did not really discuss or describe the man about whom he was pretending to write. He was always really describing his own ideas, from time to time throwing out a passing remark to explain—truly or falsely—that his subject happened to agree with him. There was some truth in this criticism—particularly when it was applied to his writing as a young man. Thus we can see that it was not altogether clear whether Browning did ever firmly hold this theory of evil. It was far more clear, if we look at *The Wild Knight*, and *The Defendant* and the *Twelve Types* that it was a theory to which Chesterton was gradually feeling his own way.

There was a similarity of origin between Browning and Chesterton. Both were Londoners, Browning from Camberwell and Chesterton from Kensington—of comfortable middle-class families—Chesterton's father an auctioneer and Browning's a clerk in the Bank of England. Both fathers were cultivated, well-bred men who had no ambition to make art or literature their profession but encouraged their sons in them. Both were of a liberal political tradition. Both were of Nonconformist and almost Unitarian origin who started life with a certain bias against both the Church of Rome and the Church of England. Neither went to a university. Each found in marriage the crowning happiness of his life. Both found their way to religion through the adventures of their own minds. In Browning's work it is always Christianity which wins all the arguments and yet, strong as is the Christian case as he puts it, can we be quite certain, we feel at the end of all his arguments, that the Christian events actually happened in history? Browning's old Jewish *Rabbi Ben Ezra* is allowed to come to as full a conception of the love of God as any of his Christian characters.

So in the same way at that time Chesterton often spoke in Christian language. There are poems like *A Christmas Carol* in *The Wild Knight* which the reader would have said was certainly the work of a fully believing Christian. But by his own confession Chesterton was at that time one who would answer unhesitatingly 'Yes' to the question 'Has it your vote to be so if it can?' He would not yet have been quite ready to say certainly that it was so. It was doubtless this similarity of origin and belief which was to some extent responsible for Chesterton's interest in Browning.

Among Browning's bad men in whom nevertheless he contrived

to find some good, Chesterton rather curiously names Bishop Blougram. I do not think that he can have read *Bishop Blougram's Apology* very carefully at that time nor would he perhaps have written thus later in life. He quotes an anecdote in which in answer to Gavan Duffy's challenge Browning admitted that Bishop Blougram was indeed modelled on Cardinal Wiseman but hotly denied that it was in any way an attack on him. It was, he said, a defence. As a matter of fact, whatever suggestions Browning may have got from Wiseman, whom I do not think that he ever met, Blougram was certainly in a number of material respects very different from Wiseman. A Roman ecclesiastic in England in the middle of the last century with the Ecclesiastical Titles Act only a few years behind him was by no means a man who enjoyed the worldly comforts and esteem which he ascribed to Blougram. He by no means enjoyed his easy income. Though Wiseman was a man of learning of a sort, it was entirely the learning of the seminary. He could not have ranged over history and literature as Blougram did. For Blougram, like Browning himself, was a man of wide experience and reading who thought truth was many-sided and to be culled from a broad variety of experience. To Wiseman, as to the great majority of nineteenth-century Catholic ecclesiastics, the answers were to be found only by looking them up in a seminarian's text-book. Browning had sympathy with a dogmatism that enlarged experience like that of Newman but he had no sympathy with a constricting or narrowing dogmatism. Wiseman was a buttoned man and it is inconceivable that he would have dined tête-à-tête with an unimportant young journalist of the type of Gigadibs—let alone that he would have talked to him thus indiscreetly.

But, however that may be, it is strange that, having noted in Browning this capacity to unearth virtue from beneath the apparent absence of it and having noted Browning's own assertion that the poem was a defence of Blougram, Chesterton should yet describe Blougram as 'a vulgar, fashionable priest, justifying his own cowardice.' For the whole point of the poem is that Blougram does not admit Gigadibs' accusations of worldliness but consents, for the sake of argument, to argue on them and to refute Gigadibs

in his own terms of reference. Blougram does not admit that he
is worldly or that he does not really believe what he professes.
He merely argues that if, as the agnostic Gibadibs asserts, there
is no truth, then there is no reason for preferring good to evil, no
standard by which one man can condemn another. One might as
well in that case do and say whatever is most comfortable. Gigadibs
complains that the ugliness and wickedness of the world makes it
difficult to accept religion and a good God. Bishop Blougram
admits the difficulty but turns the argument the other way round.
Equally the goodness and beauty of the world makes it difficult not
to accept religion and a good God.

> Just when we are safest there's a sunset touch,
> A fancy from a flower-bell, someone's death,
> A chorus-ending from Euripides—
> And there's enough for fifty hopes and fears,
> As old and new at once as nature's self,
> To rap and knock and enter in our soul,
> Take hands and dance there, a fantastic ring,
> Round the ancient idol, on his base again—
> The grand Perhaps.

So

> All we have gained then by our unbelief
> Is a life of doubt diversified by faith
> For one of faith diversified by doubt.
> We called the chess board white—we call it black.

Chesterton's strange misreading is to assume that these arguments
were all the arguments with which Blougram sustained his faith,
though Blougram has explicitly explained that he is there arguing
not on his own premises but only on those of Gigadibs—concerned
not so much to justify his own faith as to show that Gigadibs had
on his terms of reference no right to object to such arguments.
As for his own beliefs, 'For Blougram he believed, say, half he
spoke.'

Chesterton's *Browning* appeared in 1903. In the next year he published *The Napoleon of Notting Hill*, in 1905 *The Club of Queer Trades* and *Heretics* and in 1906 his *Dickens*. In 1908 appeared *The Man Who Was Thursday*. *The Club of Queer Trades* is a *jeu d'esprit* which does not throw any special light on Chesterton's opinions and which, in so far as it demands consideration, can be most conveniently considered in the company of Father Brown and the detective stories. *The Napoleon of Notting Hill* is an exposition in fantasy of Chesterton's political opinions and we will return to it in a subsequent chapter. *Heretics* falls most naturally into the company of *Orthodoxy*. In *Dickens* there is good deal of social and political theorising that will again be most conveniently considered in another place; but it is pertinent to notice in passing how, widely different as they were as men, Chesterton was to some extent attracted to Dickens by the same reasons as those for which he was attracted to Browning. Chesterton had a great passion for the particular in detail whether in character, in landscape or furniture. As Dowson wrote

> For detail, detail most I care—
> *Ce superflu si nécessaire.*

He was not, to be frank, abnormally observant of such detail himself and his admiration for those who did notice it was to some extent an example of *lucus a non lucendo*. He was almost unbelievably irresponsible about accuracy, almost in principle refused ever to verify a quotation, invented a non-existent line for *Mr. Sludge the Medium* in his *Browning*, and in his *Dickens* sought to explain Dickens' family troubles by the theory that he fell in love with the whole of his wife's family and by mischance married the wrong one. Kate Perugini, Dickens' daughter, pointed out that at the time of Dickens' marriage to her mother her three aunts, Mary, Georgina and Helen were aged fourteen, eight and three respectively. Chesterton wrote in his book that every postcard that Dickens wrote was a work of art. A critic pointed out that Dickens died on June 9, 1870 and that the first postcard appeared on October 1 of that year.

Yet, whatever he liked most about Dickens, by his own confession, was what he called Dickens' 'Mooreeffocishism.' Mooree-ffoc is coffee-room spelt backwards and refers to the sign on the windows of the coffee-room which the young Dickens read backwards as he looked out into the London fog from the coffee-rooms of his youth and saw the London world outside. Dickens, to Chesterton's mind, was as a man what he had been as a boy, the master of fantasy seen through a window. Looking at life thus, he looked at it, though in a very opposite interpretation, as it was to be looked at a few years afterwards by that very different Victorian, Lewis Carroll. For Dickens looked through a window, where Carroll only looked into a looking glass.

Again, whatever his own capacity for detail Chesterton always disliked the man who talked in sweeping generalisation about the universe, and he preferred the man who noticed the particular things that came under his nose. He disliked the pantheist who pontifically announced that God was one. God was indeed one but He had created many things. Even He himself was indeed one God but three persons. Monotheism was a true faith. But the faith of the man who was merely monotheist and no more—the Jew or the Mahomedan—was a bleak faith in contrast to the exuberance of the Christian creed. So, in considering Browning, Chesterton had justly rebuked those who argued that Browning was merely a thinker expounding his abstract theories. Browning was an artist—a man painting his pictures of his scenes and characters and decorating them in bewildering and exuberant detail. So with Dickens, Dickens' thinking, in the technical sense in which Browning thought, was almost non-existent. His plots were not of great importance. His political ideas were not very coherent. He is immortal as a great creator of character and it is the scenes of Dickens in all their detail which are indelibly imprinted on the mind. No more than Browning was he a sentimentalist who denied and shut his eyes to the existence of evil. But he attacked life with such a vigour that even evil was a better thing than non-existence. It was the spirit with which Chesterton's grandfather used to say that he would thank God for existence even if he knew that he was to be a lost soul.

During these years, as we have seen in *The Wild Knight*, in

Browning and in *Dickens*, Chesterton was then reacting from the pessimism of the Slade to a passionate and exuberant affirmation of the splendour of existence. There was of course a certain danger in this doctrine of the value of 'blessed evil'. It is a commonplace of all theology that on the metaphysical plane evil does not really exist. Things appear to be evil because our vision is no more than a partial vision. If we would see the whole picture of God's plan we would see that what, seen by itself, appeared to be a blot, in fact fitted into the total plan and found there its place. But this, if it be true, can only be true if we can believe that the existence of this world is not the whole of existence, that there is another world where the rough places will be made even. For it is obvious that in this world, taken by itself, there is much injustice. Browning was well aware of this. As he made *The Patriot* say of the future life where he would be repaid, ' 'Tis God shall repay. I am safer so.' But Chesterton had not up till that time written much about the future life. The young, though they may know as a notional fact that they are destined one day to die, yet for practical purposes think of themselves as immortal and, of any project of the future, take it for granted that they will still be there to participate in it. So Chesterton's danger in the exuberance of his optimism was that he was tempted to say that all was always for the best in this, in itself, the best of all possible worlds. It was to that Leibnitzian temptation that he addressed himself in this next, most strange work, *The Man Who Was Thursday*. *The Man Who Was Thursday* is a story—one might call it a work of fiction. One could hardly call it a novel. Chesterton indeed in his sub-title called it A Nightmare and, if the word nightmare carries too evil a connotation, it certainly contains all the lack of consequence, the sudden transfer of scene, which one experiences in a dream. It was, said Monsignor Knox in his funeral panegyric on Chesterton in Westminster Cathedral, 'an extraordinary book written as if the publisher had commissioned him to write something rather like the *Pilgrim's Progress* in the style of *The Pickwick Papers*.' The story of the book is that all order in society is apparently threatened by a gang of desperate anarchists. Of these anarchists each by a peculiar whim is called after a day of the week. Gabriel Syme, the hero of the book, is really a detective. He joins the gang under the name of *The Man Who Was Thursday* with the intention, as the modern phrase puts it, of infiltrating into it. He discovers in his colleagues, one after another, as he first imagines, qualities which are indeed the enemies of order. He discovers first the man who is merely conventional and has no reality of personality at all—Baron de Worms. He discovers then the coldly scientific man who would banish all poetry from existence—Dr Bell. Then he discovers the man drunk with the love of power who would destroy order for the mere love of physical killing—the Marquis de St. Eustache. Then there comes the man who wants not so much to kill the body as to dominate the mind—who wants power at all costs and demands submission. One after another he discovers that these apparent anarchists are really men living behind a disguise. The disguise is torn off and behind it are revealed the features of a simple decent detective.

With their exposure, Syme is left to face the last and most awful of his fears, the fear that there is no reality, that all is mask—the fear, as he puts it, of the Impressionist: 'the thing which the modern world calls Impressionism, which is another name for that total scepticism which can find no floor to the universe.' After Syme has uncovered the four first pretended anarchists as no more than detectives, there only remains, as they believe, two among the days of the week—Monday, the secretary, and Sunday himself—who are genuine anarchists. The detectives are chased in a wild nightmare chase by a vast and increasing half-mob, half-army across the northern French coast. Everyone turns mysteriously into their enemies. It is in the end discovered that this army was raised by Monday and that Monday himself was also a detective who was chasing and who had raised an army against the five in the belief that they were genuine anarchists. The last confusion is cleared up. They discover not only that they are all detectives but that it was Sunday, himself, who in mysterious interviews had recruited them all to the anarchist company, knowing that they were detectives. Sunday now alone remains, and there is a still wilder chase of Sunday by the other six through the streets and the neighbourhood of London. Sunday jumps madly from cab to fire-engine, from fire-engine to elephant and from elephant to balloon. The story is illuminated by pure buffoonery. All ends at last in a strange council in a garden with the other six sitting on thrones and Sunday in their midst.

What does all this mean?

It means up to a point that those who call for anarchy do not in the last resort want anarchy but are merely calling for certain remedies, which may have virtue in themselves, if accepted on a decision of balance, but which, unbalanced by their contraries, would be far worse evils than any evil that they remedied. Yet behind the question how far particular remedies should be introduced into an ordered system, there still remained the ultimate question: Is order itself right? Chesterton had turned against the old *fin de siècle* praise for boredom in which 'Science announced nonentity and art admired decay.' With Browning and Dickens, Stevenson and Whitman, he had come to admire the exuberance of explosive energy. But, if energy was goodness, was it not then wrong that any order of rules and regulations should be allowed to restrain it? Should it not be allowed absolute and anarchist free play in an unrestricted system? In other words, if God was in nature, was it not a blasphemy to interfere with that nature? Should not our motto be rather the motto of Rabelais' Abbey of Thélème, '*Fais que voudras*'—do what you will?

In this book the representative of this untrammelled nature was Sunday, the captain of the gang. When all the members of the days had been found to be detectives, they still thought that Sunday was a genuine anarchist. They still lived in terror of him. All assembled in a final climactic council to hear Sunday's exposition. Sunday expounded to them, to begin with, a pantheist worship of nature— of the life of total impulse. 'You can take him to stand for nature,' as Chesterton himself later explained in an interview, 'as distinguished from God. Huge, boisterous, full of vitality, dancing with a hundred legs, bright with the glare of the sun and at first sight somewhat regardless of us and our desires.' But there is an obvious and prosaic difficulty in a gospel of the canonisation of mere impulse, and that is that impulses often conflict with one another. One man's impulses conflict with another man's and—

even more difficult—a man's own impulses conflict with one another. As Shakespeare says, what is 'past reason hunted' is also 'past reason hated.' To praise the life of impulses is not to solve the problem of life but merely to bring us face to face with it. Pantheism was not so much false as insufficient. God was indeed in everything. The Holy Ghost was at work in every creature of this world. But there was not only the Holy Ghost who inspired. There was also God the Father who created. There was a God behind the gods, and the life of nature was good in itself but only good in so far as it was itself regulated by a higher code. Does Sunday understand this? Is he merely nature or is he God behind the mask of nature—the *Deus absconditus*? He is challenged at the end of the book and reveals himself by his answer: 'Can ye drink from the cup that I drink of?'

Shortly after the appearance of *The Man Who Was Thursday* a book appeared, of which it was subsequently discovered that Chesterton's brother, Cecil, was the author, in which Cecil Chesterton described and criticised *The Man Who Was Thursday* as a book of mere optimism—an assertion that everything in the world was good. Such an interpretation is a misunderstanding. It is derived only by failing to notice Sunday's final challenge— a failure as serious as Chesterton's own failure to notice the concluding line in which Bishop Blougram qualifies his belief in the arguments which he has been using. Ronald Knox in characteristically whimsical fashion prophesied that in a hundred years' time textual critics would be arguing that the passsage containing Sunday's confession of faith was a passage introduced later by unscrupulous priests into an essentially pantheist docu- ment. But of course in reality *The Man Who Was Thursday* was a clear confession of faith. 'I hazard a guess,' wrote Monsignor Knox in his essay on Chesterton in *Great Catholics*, 'that the moral of *The Man Who Was Thursday* reflects a moment in Chesterton's life when his religious beliefs had taken clear shape; when he had made his soul.' Yet, if so, Chesterton's first clear confession of faith was made in a characteristically roundabout way.

Chesterton's progress in faith had, it will be noted, up to the present been entirely personalist. There are indeed in his argument incidental allusions to biblical quotations, but his case derives not from any appeal to or acceptance of the authority of Christ—still less of the authority of priests—but entirely from his own experiences. 'Even in the earliest days,' he wrote of Lord Orm and the Wild Knight in his *Autobiography*, 'and even for the worst reasons I already knew too much to pretend to get rid of evil. I introduced at the end one figure who really does, with a full understanding, deny and defy the good . . . I put that sentiment into that story, testifying to the extreme evil (which is merely the unpardonable sin of not wishing to be pardoned) not because I had learnt it from any of a million priests I had never met but because I had learnt it from myself.'

The Coming of Orthodoxy

A couple of years before *The Man Who Was Thursday* Chesterton had written his *Heretics*. It is an amusing book, that was more amusing at the time of its publication when the heretics attacked were all men prominent in the public eye than it would be today when some of them are somewhat forgotten. In places, as so often in Chesterton's criticism, he seemed to choose what he wanted to pick in his subject and overlook what did not suit his thesis. Thus with some justification in that book he complained that Kipling in his imperialism was a man who loved discipline but had no local patriotism for a place. He overlooked *Puck of Pook's Hill* and

> God gave all men all earth to love,
>   But since our hearts are small,
> Ordained for each one spot should prove
>   Beloved over all.
> Each to his choice, and I rejoice
>   The lot has fallen on me,
>   In a fair ground
>   In a fair ground,
> Yea, Sussex by the sea—

so similar to his own

> For every tiny town or place
> God made the stars especially

in praise of Belloc's Sussex.

61

At its appearance *Heretics* considerably enhanced Chesterton's fame. In *Heretics* he took one after another the leading publicists of the day—Shaw, Kipling, Ibsen, Wells, Joseph McCabe and others and attacked their gospels. But it raised the inevitable question—asked by Shaw and Wells and G. S. Street—'If they are heretics, what are they heretics from? What is this orthodoxy which Chesterton opposes to them?' In his book Chesterton gaily defined a heretic as 'a man whose view of things has the hardihood to differ from mine' and, if that was all there was to it, if orthodoxy was simply my-doxy and heterodoxy was simply somebody else's-doxy, then it was not a very meaningful word. Had Chesterton left his criticism in this negative form it would perhaps have been our task to attempt to construct from his negations a picture of his positive beliefs. But in fact Chesterton very readily replied to the complaints of Shaw and Street that it would be time for them to consider whether they were heretics when Chesterton had produced his own orthodoxy by following up *The Man Who Was Thursday* with a book of precisely that title which performed precisely that service. We therefore can turn to the positive book and need not consider in great deal the negative.

By his own confession the writing of *The Man Who Was Thursday* had its own considerable influence on the development of Chesterton's mind. It was in his dedication to it that Chesterton wrote to Bentley: 'We have found common things at last and marriage and a creed, And I may safely write it now and you may safely read.'

Bentley once told me that Chesterton here ascribed to him a far more definite creed than any that he in fact possessed, but even Chesterton himself was then, as he confessed, 'more foggy about essential and theological matters than I am now.' The anarchy that was threatened in *The Man Who Was Thursday* was political anarchy. The crimes that were there debated and advocated were those of political assassinations—of the Czar and the French President. A more common form of anarchy, both then and even more today, is sexual anarchy—the anarchy of those who preach that their sexual freedom should be unregulated and that a man has a natural right to satisfy all his impulses, as also has a woman.

Such a gospel both then and now is often preached under the strange name of paganism. It is imagined that before Christianity came into the world pagan man lived this care-free, happy uninhibited life, that Christianity appeared and introduced (or according to some versions Saint Paul introduced, perverting the true teaching of Christ) an evil masochistic asceticism which has brought misery to mankind. The modern man according to this theory had only to reject Christianity and to return to this life of natural freedom. Yet, it is obvious that there must be some code of a sort, even if it be not precisely the traditional code of Christianity. It is obvious that there must be some code, for if all is left to mere natural impulse, the male will ask for much more sexual licence than the female has any wish to grant. So things must be regulated on some principle if only for the sake of peace and comfort. Today the modern man has indeed to a large extent rejected Christianity and returned to his life of natural freedom. But as one looks around the world it is not easy to believe that he is the happier for having done so. This is an age indeed less trammelled by religious taboos than any that has preceded it, but it would seem paradoxical to deduce from that an argument against religion. Surely rather the contrary is the reasonable deduction. For, being the least religious of ages, it is also to all appearances the most unhappy.

Yet such is the end of the story. We are here concerned with its beginning, and, whatever may be seen at its end, we are here concerned with what Chesterton said at its beginning. In many ways the most interesting of the essays in *Heretics* is that on Lowes Dickinson, a Fellow of King's College, Cambridge, a member of that brilliant group of young men there who in the years before the First World War set up their standard of revolt against traditional morals—a revolt the wisdom of which Keynes, the most distinguished of them, was by the end of his life to come in *My Early Beliefs* gravely to doubt. The theory of Christianity as the inventor of asceticism is plainly unhistorical. It is the natural instinct of man not merely to want to satisfy his desires but also to hate himself for being a slave to them. As Shakespeare put it—to quote him once again—what is 'past reason hunted' is also 'past

reason hated', and similarly man's pre-Christian history is filled
not only with stories of sexual inordinance but also with stories
of inordinate revulsion against it—dedication to virginity, orgies
of castration as among the priests of Attis described by Catullus.
There have of course been acts of unhealthy excess among Christians but the influence of the Church has not been to encourage
but to oppose such excesses. As Chesterton once said to me in his
later years, 'Christianity has not invented asceticism, it has
controlled it.' It was his belief that in its early years the Church
had to fight a battle against the pre-Christian world's sexual
obsession—an obsession which showed itself both in too great
hatred as well as in too great addiction—and it was only by the time
of Saint Francis of Assisi that it could say that the battle had been
won and could without anxiety bid its children give themselves
to the love of natural things. Whatever may be the truth about the
mediaeval Church, Chesterton was certainly right in rebuking
Lowes Dickinson for his belief that the life of the pagan was a life
that was free from sexual taboos or that happiness could easily be
attained merely by repudiating religious discipline.

It so happened that among the 'heretics' with whom Chesterton
crossed swords in the book Robert Blatchford was not included,
though he was incidentally mentioned in the essay of Joseph
McCabe. But in fact Blatchford was in those years Chesterton's
most persistent opponent. Blatchford was a very decent old man,
not really an opponent worthy of Chesterton's steel, but Chesterton never refused a challenge and was too humble a man to
reserve himself only for worthy opponents. Blatchford, an ex-
sergeant major, was a vigorous professional atheist, who promulgated his attacks on religion in a paper called *The Clarion*.
Chesterton, who always maintained that he himself was converted
to Christianity mainly by arguments used against it by its opponents, used this characteristic weapon of paradox against
Blatchford in a little composite book called *The Doubts of Democracy* to which he contributed an essay. Blatchford had extracted
from such works as Frazer's *Golden Bough* the argument that there
were many stories similar to the Christian stories to be found in
the beliefs of many peoples in many parts of the world. This, said

Chesterton, is surely an argument for the truth of the Christian story. If it be true that God is trinitarian, that a Divine Incarnation is in the predestined nature of things, that God will die and rise again, it is surely only to be expected that men everywhere should have had vague intimations of those truths even before they happened, that there should have been a certain groping feeling that something of the nature of an Incarnation was required to make sense of things, that they should have told one another mythological tales which said: 'These are how things must be, otherwise they do not make sense'—even before the event took place. Then, those who received the news could at last say with assurance, 'This is how things are.' Or again, if it was true, as Blatchford claimed, that over the years there had all too often been violence and injustice done in the name of religion, what did that prove? Violence and injustice are of course in themselves evil, but the fact that people resort to them in a cause does not surely prove that that is a false cause. It proves that it is a strong cause. People have often resorted to violence and injustice for the sake of love. This does not prove that there is no such thing as love. It proves rather that love is a very strong force.

> Likelier the barricades shall blare,
>   Slaughter below and smoke above,
> And death and hate and hell declare
>   That men have found a thing to love.

Chesterton's final quarrel with Blatchford was over determinism. There are two sorts of people who deny human free will—the materialist and the deist. The materialist says that all is matter. There are no laws except the chemical and physical laws. Man is but a machine. There is, as Professor Ryle puts it, 'no ghost within' and man obeys the laws as much as does any other machine. To such a man there is very little to be said except that he is making arbitrary assumptions. Today, in an age which is more inclined to think that mind is the master of matter than that matter is the master of mind, such views seem strangely old-fashioned. Fifty years ago they were up to date. Yet, whether in fashion or out of fashion, what is important is the logic of the argument. There is not the beginning of proof that man is no more than a machine, as Blatchford alleged, and, if we know nothing but our own ideas, then—even though we cannot explain exactly how—we nevertheless have as certain a conviction of possessing some sort of freedom as we have of our own existence.

The deist's determination is more difficult. If there is an all-seeing, all-knowing, unlimited God, then how can there be any freedom outside his jurisdiction?

> The ball no question makes of Ayes or Noes,
> But here and there, as strikes the Player, goes
> And He who tossed you down into the field
> He knows about it all—He knows—He knows.

Nor indeed can it be denied that our own mind can only think in terms of causes, and, if the causal train runs through all existence, then it is not easy to see where there is room for freedom, since a free choice of its nature implies the undetermined. Yet this only proves that determinism is the condition within which our mind works. It does not prove that that is how things are, and there is at the end perhaps little to say except the cogent dicta of Dr Johnson, 'All argument is against it but all experience is for it,' and, 'Sir, we know our wills are free, and there's an end on't.' The consciousness that we do possess some sort of freedom is a condition of our existence. Use reason to attack this consciousness and you use it to undermine all existence.

It was on the first materialist plane that Blatchford attacked freedom. He explained the alleged degradation of the poor by pointing to their miserable circumstances and arguing that in such circumstances they could not help themselves but be degraded. Chesterton claimed that such an argument stripped all human nature of its dignity—that, on the contrary, the man whom we admire was the man who overcame circumstances and conquered obstacles. Argue that circumstances could not be overcome and you were arguing that man was not a man.

Blatchford was not, as we have said, one of the named characters

of *Heretics* but he was quoted in the essay on Joseph McCabe—
an unfrocked priest who had turned very violently against religion
and bitterly attacked it. McCabe was certainly as responsible as
any other of Chesterton's challengers for the *Orthodoxy* which
appeared later in 1908. *Orthodoxy* is one of Chesterton's central
works—one of the works most essential for an understanding of
the development of his mind. For it contains his first unequivocal
assertion of his belief in the historical validity of the Christian
claims. He had for some years come to think that Christian
doctrine offered the only satisfactory answer to man's dilemmas—
that it held the only key that could unlock the gate. But was this
because it contained ultimate, revealed truth brought down in
literal physical form from heaven to earth? Or was it rather that
the wisest of men throughout the ages had worked out their
answers and then, to give them authority, had ascribed to them a
divine origin—a sort of Platonic *hen gennaion pseudos* (Plato's
one noble lie)? In his early books it was often not quite certain
which he believed. Indeed by his own confession he did not quite
know himself. In *Orthodoxy*, in answer to the challenge of Shaw and
Wells, he finally nailed his colours to the mast—or perhaps we
should rather say, to the Church.

Yet, if *Orthodoxy* is one of Chesterton's most central works, and
if the whole book is essential for one who has not read Chesterton's
other works and wants as good a comprehension as possible of his
mind, he who is acquainted with the book that preceded it need
not necessarily delay on its first chapters. For the first two-fifths
of the book are negative and destructive. They are devoted to a
restatement of the modern heresies with which he had already
dealt and to showing how the spirit of destructive rationalism led
back inevitably to total nihilism, to solipsism, and even to the
denial of self—how that which questioned everything must
necessarily in the end come to question even itself. The semi-
logical materialist argues that there can be no freedom because
everything moves in obedience to immutable laws. But the logical
materialist, like Hume, argues that if there is nothing but matter
then there can be no laws since the laws themselves are not matter.
All that we can say at the best is that we have observed that ninety-

nine times when the ball has been struck by a billiard cue it has rolled along the table. Laws can of their nature tell us only of what has happened and therefore of the past. They cannot tell us with certainty that the ball will therefore roll again if it is struck the hundredth time. There can be no 'therefore.' The word begs the question.

Yet, if man is to live at all, some way must be found to break out of this prison of solipsistic insanity. The critical argument is familiar enough to those who have followed Chesterton's earlier works. The interesting pages in *Orthodoxy* are those of the second half in which he professes to show how orthodoxy offers the escape, and the only possible escape, from this prison. He sets out the five propositions on which his thinking had come to be based. First, he asserts, 'this world does not explain itself.' We may in agnostic fashion assert that we cannot possibly know what is the explanation of it. But a confession of ignorance is not an explanation. 'All things,' as Saint Augustine said, 'go out into mystery.' It is not less a mystery because we are ignorant of the answer to it. Secondly he asserts that the world must have a meaning. It is the very condition of our thinking and our being that we should believe that there is some purpose in things. A man may assert in words that he does not believe in any purpose in things, that there is no good or bad, that it matters nothing whether he does things well or ill, but he who uses such language in any sense that matters does not really believe what he says. We cannot help ourselves but believe that life has a meaning and the only issue is whether we believe this because it is really true or whether this is an invention of our own imagination which we impose upon reality in order to save ourselves from despair. But why should we have this feeling of a need for a meaning in things if such meaning has no reality? If we cannot believe in meaning we cannot believe in anything and are forced back to that solipsism in which it is in itself impossible to believe. On the other hand, if there is meaning, then there must be a Meaner. What could meaning mean if it was not a meaning to Somebody? Thus Chesterton comes to an acceptance of God on personalist grounds substantially similar to the position of Newman or Kant who deduced a belief in God from the existence of conscience rather than from the traditional arguments about a First Cause. The argument from the First Cause is not in itself convincing. If everything must have a Maker, then who made God? Thirdly, the world, as we look at it, is clearly beautiful but not perfect. It is good—on the whole. It is enjoyable—on the whole. One should enjoy the enjoyable. But it is absurd to deny its defects. Fatuous Panglossians who pretended that evil does not exist were merely silly. Chesterton in later life used often to quote with pleasure the parody of Coleridge, invented by his friend, Philimore:

> He prayeth best who loveth best
> All things both great and small;
> And streptococcus is the test,
> I love him best of all.

Indeed, by a parodox, to Chesterton's contention the existence of evil in the world was the refutation of atheism. If the world had been wholly good it might have been possible to argue that God was entirely contained within it. It was 'the blessed evil' in it which proved that God was beyond it. To the pantheist God is 'in all things as if he were in a box.' To Chesterton God was an artist, the Creator who had created the world as a work of art.

Therefore if there was such a thing as goodness a good God must have made it. If there are defects, or apparent defects, in His creation, there must be an explanation for them. Two explanations are possible—that what appears to be evil and ugly may only appear to be so because, looking at this world, we are only looking at a part of reality; or that evil is the result of human sin. There is a further existence beyond this world and, when we see the whole reality, we will see how what, seen by itself, appears a defect, is, in its place in the total picture, good. But, though this Bolingbrokean principle of 'partial evil, universal good' was a part of the explanation of the problem of evil, it was of course by no means the whole explanation. At the most it could explain the evil that was in no way the consequence of sin. There was evil in the world which was in no way the consequence of human sin. Nevertheless there was human sin, and of its reality Chesterton had no doubt. As he was to explain in his interview about *The Man Who Was Thursday*, to which reference has already been made, he had no doubt at the time he wrote that book that 'there was a final adversary' and that you might 'find a man resolutely turned away from goodness.' Now if there was both good and evil in Man, two conclusions necessarily followed. From the existence of good it followed that there must be a good God, and from the existence of evil, that this good God must in some manner be shut away from Man—that He must be what Newman called a *Deus absconditus*—that Man knew that there was a God but had an imperfect vision of Him. He had an imperfect vision of Him because within himself he had both good and evil instincts—instincts that were God-directed and instincts that were directed away from God—and to say this meant only, in other words, to say that Man was born in sin, to enunciate the doctrine of original sin. The Christian said that Man was born in sin because the first man had fallen. It is indeed not clear how it could have been that an Adam who was born without sin can yet have fallen to temptation nor, even if he did so, why all subsequent generations should have to suffer because of his transgression; but, whatever the explanation of original sin, however incomprehensible it might be that a good and perfect God might create men who were thus capable of sin, the certain fact was that He did so. However myth and history might be mixed in these early tales, the story of the fall did not seem to Chesterton inherently improbable. Whether or not there was a fall in the past it was quite certain that there was original sin here and now. Original sin was, according to his assertion, the one doctrine of Christianity that was quite certainly demonstrable.

His fourth assertion was that, if the existence of good proved the existence of God, the fact that God had created him a creature of a good world made it reasonable that he should wish to thank that God. Man, as Disraeli put it, was 'a creature born to worship'. Worshipping was a part of his full nature. It is true that there were men who neglected their duty of worshipping: but though the colour-blind man or the man who is tone-deaf does not cease, for that, to be a man, yet he is, if he cannot thus see or hear, something less than fully man. Fifthly, Chesterton here repeats what is essentially the point of Kant and Newman, that we derive our knowledge of God from the existence of conscience within us in an essentially similar but characteristically gracious fashion. Kant believed in God because he felt that there must be someone to whom he owed his duty. Chesterton believed in God because he felt that there must be someone to whom he gave his thanks.

Now all these conclusions Chesterton reached, as he says, from his own cerebration. As will be noticed they are conclusions advanced, as they are advanced in the fourth chapter of *Orthodoxy*, on their own intrinsic merits. There is no appeal to Christ or mention of Christ's name in the development of the argument. 'All this I felt,' he wrote, 'and the age gave me no encouragement to feel it. And all this time I had not even heard of Christian theology.' Chesterton, it must be remembered, came from an essentially different background from that of most of the English religious leaders of his or of the previous age. Whether in maturity they accepted Christianity or rejected it, they had been brought up to it. They had been brought up in the tradition of a Church and in maturity either abandoned the Church of England for agnosticism, remained in it, went over to Rome or otherwise as the case might be. In any event they were always arguing against an Anglican background—arguing as if Anglicanism was the creed that a man was expected to hold and which, according to his choice, he must either defend or reject, duly justifying his rejection. Browning, almost alone among the Victorian thinkers, grew up in an undogmatic Nonconformist home and discovered doctrines for himself by his own reasoning rather than accepting in maturity the teaching of childhood. Chesterton came to dogma by the same road.

It might of course have been argued that the very fact that Chesterton had been able to discover much of Christian teaching for himself was evidence that that teaching was not of divine origin and that the revelation was neither true nor necessary. If Chesterton could think of it all for himself, what need of God to reveal it? The very fact that he had not come to these problems through the seminary text-books of a formal Catholic education enabled him to come to them with a freshness of mind that would have been less easy to a cradle Catholic. Later in life he was to prove himself, according to Gilson's envious confession, the greatest of all amateur students of Saint Thomas Aquinas. But at this date he probably knew little of Saint Thomas. He did not approach the problem of the existence of God or the Divinity of Christ by setting out formal demonstrations of their truth. He reached his conclusions rather as Newman had reached them and, before Newman, Bishop Butler, the eighteenth-century Anglican theologian, had reached them, by an accumulation of probabilities. In the preface to the American edition of *Orthodoxy* Chesterton compared the intention of that book to the intention of Newman's *Apologia*. There is no single irrefutable proof of the Divinity of Christ, he argued. If there were such a proof, how could it be that some learned and sincere men were to be found unable to accept it? There are no learned and sincere men to tell us that the three angles of a triangle do not make two right angles. In the final analysis, if we would accept Christ we must make a venture and accept a bet. If it were not so, what place would there be for faith? 'Has it your vote to be so if it can?'

So we look at the strange expectation that something more must be coming or else things do not make sense that is to be found in the greatest of the pre-Christians—in Plato or Virgil or Isaiah—in the Messianic longings of the Jews and their mysterious survival under every sort of inducement to mongrelise their blood among the surrounding peoples and lose their identity as all their neighbours did. Does not their very survival in some degree prove the truth of their claim to be the Chosen People? We look at the record of Christ's own life. It may be that secondary miracles are the consequence rather than the cause of faith. The evidence that He walked on the water or fed the Five Thousand is not sufficient, if we did not for other reasons accept His claims, but can the central miracle of the Resurrection be so easily disposed of? If He did not rise again from the Tomb, where was He after Easter Sunday morning? If He were still in the Tomb, if a mistake of identification had been made, why did not the Jews or the Romans lead people to the Tomb, show them the Body and expose the whole story? If it be said that the disciples stole His body away, what motive had they for doing so? They clearly, of all people, least expected that there would be any Resurrection. Had they stolen it, what motive had they to stick to a story of total fraud under the sufferings of torture and martyrdom that were to await them? The four Gospels are there. They are in any event remarkable documents—remarkable if they contain an historical record of truth. But, if they contain nothing but falsehoods, who were these strange crook-novelists who invented them—so utterly unlike any other documents of their own or any other time—and if they were false for what purpose were they invented? The teachings ascribed to Christ—the Sermon on the Mount and His other sayings—have survived the ages and been the comfort of the suffering of two thousand years, alike to those who have accepted the full Christian teaching and to those who have been unable fully to accept it. The magic of Christ's words— or at the least of the words ascribed to him—are undoubted facts of history, facts more strange almost if the sayings were invented than if they were genuine. What account can be given of their secret? As Rousseau—a rather strange witness in such a case—said '*L'inventeur y serait plus étonnant que le héros.*'

Or again during the tumultuous years of the early Church there were doubtless many who failed under the threats of persecution. What is surprising in that? What is rather surprising is that so many did not fail—resisted to death rather than abandon their faith. It is easy to say that fanaticism will always produce martyrs. But the early Christians not only produced martyrs, they invented the very notion of martyrdom. It was not merely that pagan Romans had not the courage to witness to their faith. The very notion that any religion could be so uniquely true that a man could have an obligation thus to bear witness to it was unknown to them. If subsequently those who rejected Christianity have sometimes died for their rejection it was from Christianity that they learnt the very notion of such a rejection. So throughout the centuries of Christian history the notion that faith is something for which men ought to be willing to die has been kept alive. Chesterton was no simpleton who imagined that all Christians were automatically good, and all non-Christians automatically bad. He was to write later of

Bad men who had no right to their right reason,
Good men who had good reason to be wrong,

73

and of

> Borgia and Torquemada in the throng.

Yet on the whole Christian civilisation was an achievement un-paralleled in history and most of the accusations against it were to his mind simply untrue. Where Christianity's enemies asserted that in priest-ridden lands men were miserable, he asserted that in such lands they were exceptionally happy. Where Christianity's enemies ascribed to their religion the incompetence and the fecklessness of the Irish, he asserted that it was their religion alone which had given to the Irish the courage and the competence to defeat their more powerful English enemies.

Opinions will of course differ as to how much weight to attach to this or that of Chesterton's accumulation of arguments. Some will perhaps dispute altogether some of his assertions about recent history, for he was always, it must be confessed, selective in the historical instances that he quoted and those which he overlooked. Would Jews for instance, with the traditions of the Maccabees behind them, admit that martyrdom for a faith was a wholly Christian invention? But his conclusion did not turn on the accept-ance of any one particular example but on his catalogue of the surprising facts pointing in the same direction and, taken together, leaving no alternative from them but to believe that the direction in which they pointed was the truth.

Chesterton's own thinking had brought him to say of the Christian truths, 'Things must be like that or they do not make sense.' Christ, accepted, gave him the assurance. 'I speak with authority and they are like that.' As Browning wrote in *Christmas-Eve and Easter Day*,

> And thence I conclude that the real God-function
> Is to furnish a motive and injunction
> For practising what we know already.

The humanist said that all that was required was that we love our fellow men. There was no need to seek out a metaphysical, logical reason why we should do so. But who does love all his fellow men? We love perhaps a very few people, in the sense that we identify our wills with theirs. To the vast majority the most that we can offer is a recognition of their rights, a reluctance to do them an injustice —something that comes very far short of love. Saint Francis of Assisi perhaps loved all men. Of whom else can we say it? It is not easy even for the Christian to love all men. But the Christian at least has a motive for doing so which the non-Christian has not got.

Orthodoxy was a work of Christian apologetics. It was of course in no sort of way a work of Roman Catholic apologetics. Another fourteen years were to elapse before Chesterton was to become a Roman Catholic. Nevertheless his method of argument was one which naturally carried him towards Catholicism and away from Protestantism. The Protestant invokes Christ to sit in judgement on the Church. He accuses the Catholic of preferring the Church to Christ. But Chesterton's apologetics even at this time of course refused to admit this dichotomy between Christ and the Church. The evidence of Christ strengthened the case for the Church. The evidence of the Church strengthened the case for Christ. One believed in each because of the other. There was no dichotomy between them. Nor was there any dichotomy between reason and authority. He had used reason, in of course the large illative Newmanian sense, not in the sense of mere syllogistic propositions, and it was reason that had led him to accept revelation and authority. But, if God had revealed Himself to Man, it was only reasonable that Man should learn from him things that he had been unable to discover for himself, and Chesterton, having discovered for himself and independently so much of Christian truth, was with all logic, ready, having accepted authority, then to accept from it details that he had been unable to see for himself, hoping that he might one day be able to see them. He instanced virginity—an interesting choice as it provides refutation, if further refutation was needed, of Mrs Cecil Chesterton's absurd suggestion that his marriage was never consummated. Again man, convinced of the existence of God, may most logically turn and say 'If there is an omniscient and omnipotent God, what purpose can there be in praying to Him?' and it is a little curious that extreme Protestants, who reject as mumbo-jumbo the antics of ritualism and sacramentalism, should not burke at the much deeper mystery of prayer; but it is also reasonable for him, looking to the universal custom of mankind, to say, 'If I cannot understand prayer, since so many others through the ages have understood it, the defect must be in me.' There is no exact evidence at what date Chesterton took up with the habit of prayer, in which he had almost certainly not indulged in his youth; but it is most probably at about this time, and he took to it in the first instance not because he altogether understood it but because in humility he thought that he should do what holy men and women had always done through the ages. Through praying he might come to see a meaning in prayer, which he could not hope to see from the outside.

Chesterton accepted religion as a result of an accumulation of evidences and in similar fashion he accepted Christ because on examination of all other faiths he discovered that they did not, as at first sight appeared, contradict Christ, but on the contrary that Christ said all that they had said, and had always something more to say beyond it. 'Who is Christ? What think ye of Him?' There must be some explanation of Him. The difficulties of accepting His extraordinary claims were indeed formidable but the difficulties of rejecting them were even more formidable. Christ, he found, was not only Man but the total Man—the man in whom was summarised all the wisdom of mankind. He wrote in *Orthodoxy*:

'That a good man may have his back to the wall is no more than we knew already, but that God could have his back to the wall is a boast for all insurgents for ever. Christianity is the only religion on earth that has felt that omnipotence made God incomplete. Christianity alone has felt that God to be wholly God must have been a rebel as well as a king. Alone of all creeds, Christianity has added courage to the virtues of the creator. For the only courage worth calling courage must necessarily mean that the soul passes a breaking point—and does not break. In this indeed I approach a matter more dark and awful than it is easy to discuss; and I apologise in advance if any of my phrases fall wrong or seem irreverent touching a matter which the greatest saints and thinkers have justly feared to approach. But in that terrific tale of the Passion there is a distinct emotional suggestion that the author of all things (in some unthinkable way) went not only through agony but through doubt. It is written, "Thou shalt not tempt the Lord thy God." No, but the Lord thy God may tempt Himself, and it seems as if that was what happened in Gethsemane. In a garden Satan tempted Man, and in a garden God tempted God. He passed in some superhuman manner through our human horror of pessimism. When the world shook and the sun was wiped out of heaven, it was not at the crucifixion but at the cry from the Cross; the cry which confessed that God was forsaken of God. And now let the revolutionists choose a creed from all the creeds and a god from all the gods of inevitable recurrence and of unalterable power. They will not find another god who has himself been in revolt. Nay (the matter grows too difficult for human speech) but let atheists themselves choose a god. They will find only one divinity who ever uttered their isolation; only one religion in which God seemed for an instant to be an atheist.'

6

Shaw and All That

Chesterton brought into adult life in his first years the spirit of Saint Paul's Junior Debating Society. He argued with vigour but without rancour and some of his warmest personal friendships were with men with whom he most deeply wrangled. Of no one was this more true than of Bernard Shaw. Their unending controversies in paper after paper were among the main journalistic events of the first years of the century. It began with an argument about Shakespeare but extended thence to almost any subject under the sun. Shaw was one of the thinkers whom Chesterton took to task in *Heretics*. He was one of those, as we have said, who challenged Chesterton to justify his charge of heresy by expounding his own orthodoxy, and it was neither unexpected nor unreasonable when Chesterton followed up his *Orthodoxy* by a book specifically on Bernard Shaw. It was not among his best books of literary criticism because he knew Shaw too well in the flesh to give to his writing the detailed study which he gave to Dickens or Browning. The book has little to tell us about Shaw's plays. It is almost entirely concerned with Shaw's views.

Shaw and Chesterton for all their differences in philosophy had a certain similarity of manner. Both delighted in what it was the fashion to call paradox—that is to say, in standing truth on its head and astonishing the reader by saying the verbally unexpected. Dean Inge, who did not like Chesterton, described him as 'that obese mountebank who crucifies truth head downwards.' Every word except the word 'obese' could equally have been applied to Shaw. It was therefore natural that Chesterton should defend Shaw and perhaps exaggerate his devotion to truth. It is true that one can make a case for it that there was a lifelong consistency in Shaw's opinions which can powerfully be contrasted with the oscillations of parliamentary politicians. One can prophesy with confidence, Chesterton said, what twenty years hence Shaw will be saying. Who would venture to prophesy what Mr Asquith will be saying? But of course the task of the writer on this field is somewhat easier than that of the politician. The writer can say what it pleases him to say. The politician, if he wishes to accomplish anything, has always to be looking to see whether the majority will support him. Shaw had the advantage in preaching his gospel that he was in no danger of being called upon to put it into practice. But to say that he was more sincere than the average politician was not very high praise. I doubt if he was as blazingly sincere as Chesterton claimed. He liked jokes and paradoxes and, like Belloc, 'partly wrote to give you pain.' There is surely at least a degree of truth in Gilbert Murray's counter-judgement that 'When he was faced with a problem, Shaw's concern was not to think what it was true to say about it but what it was funny to say about it.' Shaw would have replied—indeed did reply in *The Quintessence of Ibsenism*—that it is a waste of time to throw novel ideas at people in serious form since they then rejected them simply because of their novelty. The only way to get such ideas considered was to soften the hearers up by first presenting them as jokes. 'All my serious revolutionary propositions began as huge jokes. Otherwise they would be stamped out by the lynching of their first exponents.' This was a principle of Shaw as indeed it was to a large extent also a principle of Chesterton.

Maisie Ward asserts that the great accusation which both Shaw and Chesterton levelled against the Victorians was that in all their estimates of national prosperity they never thought to make allowance for the condition of the poor. The very language which called prosperous a nation whose poor were in such dire want proves the justification of this charge. Yet, of course, when Maisie Ward says—and truly says—that Shaw and Chesterton dedicated themselves to the battle for the poor we must remember the peculiar way in which they conducted that battle. They did not fight as Ben Tillett or John Burns fought, leading a strike of dockers and pleading their cause in public in Trafalgar Square. They were writers whose writings were very little read by the poor and circulated almost exclusively among the middle classes. Maisie Ward tells us—and very truly tells us—that Chesterton was as little of a snob as any man that ever lived. He was willing to talk to anyone whom he met and the notion that he was the superior of another because of a social advantage would have been unthinkable to him. But in fact those who frequented his house and his company were almost entirely men of middle-class origin like himself. He wrote a pleasant essay about the two barbers in Beaconsfield to whom he used in turn to go to be shaved. But it is clear from the essay that the possibility can never have occurred to him that either of the barbers would ever read it.

Chesterton's basic criticism of Shaw was that he was a puritan. To the average middle-class Edwardian a puritan was a man who respected the traditional taboos of society and laid rather more emphasis on their importance than did his fellow citizens. Therefore, as Shaw went out of his way to mock at all society's institutions, it seemed to the Edwardians natural to accept his own description of himself as anti-puritan and to dismiss it as a characteristic paradox when Chesterton said that he was a puritan who had written not as he himself advertised, *Three Plays for Puritans* but thirty-three plays—all of his plays—for puritans. Yet in truth Chesterton on this point was plainly right and more nearly guilty of a platitude then of a paradox. Shaw was obviously a puritan in the plain straightforward sense of denying himself the pleasures of the flesh. He was a vegetarian, a teetotaller, a non-smoker. It is true that he believed in free divorce but that was not at all because he was a romantic who believed that all was well lost for love. It was rather because he thought that romantic love was so unimportant and contemptible an interruption of the real business of life that it and marriage did not deserve to be taken seriously. A typically Shavian moment is that in *Caesar and Cleopatra* when Caesar, about to leave Egypt, knows that there is something that he has forgotten to do but cannot for the moment remember what it is, and then at the last recollects that he has forgotten to say goodbye to Cleopatra. Shaw was the enemy of all local loyalties. He objected to the family. He objected to national patriotism. Such petty loyalties were all limitations which impeded a man from giving himself to the only worthy service—that of all mankind. He objected to Shakespeare because Shakespeare's exuberant delight in lush words for their own sake seemed to him an indecency. His favourite author was Bunyan who ruthlessly subordinated his language to his purpose. So with religion. Shaw was, of course, not a Christian and had no real right to use Christian phraseology at all but it pleased him at times to use the language of Catholicism and to pretend that he offered a truer Catholicism than that of the Pope. 'If,' Shaw wrote of Belloc, 'he could be induced to believe in some sort of God instead of that wretched little conspiracy against religion, which the pious Romans have locked up in the Vatican, one could get some drive into him.' And he spoke of 'the Pope and other ghastly scarecrows'. It must, of course, be remembered that at that time Pius X was on the papal throne and the campaign against modernism at its height, and it was not altogether easy for one outside the Catholic Church to recognise the lineaments of true Catholicism in Pius' policies of delation, repression and secret 'vigilance committees'.

But, however that may be, it is obvious enough that, whatever the personal bonds between them, the philosophies of Shaw and Chesterton were almost the direct opposites of one another. These local loyalties which Shaw denounced as petty and cramping, were to Chesterton the very stuff that made a man a man. As Alfred was made to say in *The Ballad of the White Horse*

> When all philosophies shall fail,
>   This word alone shall fit;
> That a sage feels too small for life,
>   And a fool too large for it.

> Asia and all imperial plains
>   Are too little for a fool;
>   But for one man whose eyes can see
>   The little island of Athelney
>   Is too large a land to rule. . . .

> So were the island of a saint;
> But I am a common king,
> And I will make my fences tough
> From Wantage Town to Plymouth Bluff,
> Because I am not wise enough
> To rule so small a thing.

To Chesterton it was the pursuit of the romance of love which alone gave life its creative value. By Shaw's bleak doctrine of *élan vital* Man was condemned to follow out the dictates of his will and, through its action, to create. But the fact that he derived incidental pleasure in doing so was almost an indecency to be concealed and, as far as possible, denied. As Chesterton wrote, 'Shaw follows the banner of life, but austerely, not joyously.'

Shaw inherited from Samuel Butler, whom Chesterton oddly enough does not mention in his study, and from Bergson, who more oddly still Shaw hardly mentions, the doctrine of the *élan vital* which taught that the will was the great creative force in life. Chesterton naturally agreed with him in so far as he repudiated materialism and determinism and championed the freedom of the will. But the Christian view of the will, which was of course Chesterton's view, was that we have indeed within us these conflicting impulses, and that of these impulses some are God-sent and some are in opposition to God's purposes. Our free will gives us the power to choose between them and it is our duty to choose the good

> Our wills are ours—we know not how—
> Our wills are ours to make then thine.

Thus life is indeed a conflict but the conflict is within us—the conflict between ourselves as we are and ourselves as we are destined to be—and if repeated failure in ourselves or in those around us sometimes tempts us to fall into a Swiftean mood of *saeva indignatio* and despair of the human race, we can reflect that Man is unlike other creatures not in that he is perfect but in that he alone has a notion of perfection—an idea that he ought to make himself something other than he is. When he is tempted to despair of human beings, apparently so feeble as often so unlovable, he can reflect in the words that Chesterton put into the mouth of Johnson in his *Judgement of Dr. Johnson*, 'These are they for whom their omnipotent Creator did not disdain to die.'

Now Shaw also believed that man's life was a life of internal conflict, but with him the conflict was not between right and wrong, between obedience to a divine law and disobedience to it. It was a conflict between a man's fundamental creative purpose and the incidental temptations of a merely passing whim, and on such a conflict a number of comments suggest themselves. First, the great artists and discoverers and governors doubtless have within them- selves an overriding creative purpose, and the vast majority of men have neither the ambition nor the power to transform the world. They are quite content to live according to the conventions of society and have no higher ambition than to be worthy of them. For them

> The trivial round, the common task,
> Will furnish all we need to ask.

Shaw's philosophy allows no value to the lives of such men and women—the vast majority of the human race. They were no more than lobby-fodder. 'I have never had any feelings about the English working class,' he wrote 'except the desire to abolish them and replace them by sensible people.' Great riches in a modern capitalist society could only be obtained as was shown by Broad- bent in *John Bull's Other Island* or by Undershaft in *Major Barbara*, by a strange combination of self-deception and half- witted concentration on the inessential—or such was at least his opinion until in his very old age and in the decline of his powers he became, in his absorption in a millionaire's complaint about the size of his supertax, almost exactly the sort of creature that he had spent his life in satirising. It was almost like the men turning into pigs at the end of Orwell's *Animal Farm*. As Roy Campbell truly wrote, 'We become that which we fight.' In contrast Chesterton's conception of the common man as the 'dreadful image' of God— indeed Saint Thomas Aquinas' conception that there are as many

separate types of excellence as there are separate individual souls
—was both deeper and nobler.

Apart from that, it makes sense to say that the will is free and
that it is a man's duty to identify his will with the will of God. But
it is not very easy to see what is especially admirable in a will that
is free but which owes no allegiance to anything beyond itself.
What was this distinction which Shaw drew between the creative
will and feeble desire save the protest of a puritan against the
indulgences that he did not happen to find attractive? If the test was
persisting and energetic purpose that refused to accept defeat from
obstacles, it was indeed true that nothing great was ever achieved
save through such energy and courage; but it was equally true that
energy and courage have often been used for very evil purposes.
The saints have all been courageous and energetic men but it is far
from true that all courageous and energetic men have been saints.
It is as plausible to argue with Lord Acton that 'all great men are
bad men.'

'The golden rule,' said Shaw, deriving his precept from Ibsen,
'is that there are no golden rules'. Against this Chesterton raised the
banner of absolute values. But in truth the argument between them
was up to a point an argument about words. Catholic teaching has
always insisted on casuistry—on what it is today the fashion to call
'situation ethics'. The general rule, for instance, is 'Thou shalt not
kill.' But there are special circumstances—if you are defending
yourself or others against a would-be murderer, if you are a soldier
fighting in a just war—when it is no sin to kill. The general rule is
'Thou shalt not steal,' but there are special circumstances—if you
are starving and penniless—when it is no sin to steal. In that sense
certainly the golden rule is that there are no golden rules, and it
must be remembered that this argument between Shaw and
Chesterton took place in the first decade of this century during the
rule of Pius X. Most people would today agree that the theologians
of that decade overstretched themselves in trying to define on paper
the exact circumstances under which this or that action was permis-
sible and that it is wiser to leave broader judgements to be interpreted in particular cases by the individual conscience. But the
objection to Shaw was not that he was a casuist but that he was at

fault in his general social principle. At times, as, for instance, in *The Showing Up of Blanco Posnet,* he invoked a principle that was entirely Christian—and, when he did so, needless to say was proscribed by the Lord Chamberlain for being anti-Christian. At other times he appealed to a principle of the omnipotence of will which justified a man in overriding the interests of others provided that he was anxious enough to do so. The Catholic saint to the eulogy of whom he was not unwilling to give himself—of course many years after this controversy—was Saint Joan. But Saint Joan is depicted by Shaw as devoting herself to the cause of French nationalism—a cause which on Shaw's cosmopolitan principles was a very petty and worthless cause. Saint Joan is praised, however, not because she pursued a sensible purpose but because she pursued a purpose intensely.

Change in itself, argued Shaw, was good. 'The law of God is the law of change,' he wrote in the preface to *Back to Methuselah.* He gave no reason why this should be so, and it is by no means easy to see why it should be so. We have to take it simply on Shaw's word, and it is reasonable to reply that if in the end we are to be pressed back upon authority then we prefer an authority with higher title deeds than those of Shaw. For, if the law is the law of evolution, then Man must in the end be destined to become something more than Man—Superman as Shaw and Nietzsche called him. The pictures of the dreary Ancients in the last act of *Back to Methuselah* do not encourage us to think that the company of the Superman will be much of an improvement on the company of Man, but there Shaw could fairly plead that he, a man, could not be expected to know what the Superman will be like any more than the Christian on this earth can know in detail how the future life in which he so firmly believes will be arranged. 'It is enough for Lilith that there is a beyond.' Yet the main difference between Chesterton and Shaw at this point is that Chesterton believes in Man—fallen man indeed—Man with all his faults, but one who is capable of redemption and who will be redeemed. Shaw does not believe in Man— does not believe that Man is capable of redemption. He is only capable of abolition. To Shaw the problems (what problems exactly?) can only be solved when Man is abolished and another creature, the Superman, substituted in his place. Since we live here and now, in the company of Man, that inevitably meant that Shaw for all his personal geniality, looked on his fellow human beings with an inhuman loveless pity. He advocated a general equality of incomes (except of course for writers who would get a great deal more) not because he greatly wished to benefit the poor but because, by settling such problems in a rough and ready way, he hoped to keep the wretched little creatures quiet. The generosity of Chesterton was lacking in him.

It also meant to Chesterton's mind that God incarnate in Christ was incarnate in a creature that was something less than the ultimate creature. It would have been interesting had Chesterton lived on into the age of Teilhard de Chardin to have seen what he made of Omega Point or what Teilhard made of *The Everlasting Man*.

That Shaw was a greater master of dramatic technique than Chesterton; that Chesterton was a poet while Shaw was unique among men (so Chesterton contended) in that he never wrote a line of poetry; that Shaw was the more meticulous and businesslike in his ways; that Shaw, though his position was ultimately irrational, used reason most brilliantly as an incidental weapon; that Chesterton, though deeply rational in his conclusions, was pictorial and romantic in his manner; and that Shaw had a keen ear for music while Chesterton was tone-deaf: all these are true, but not strictly pertinent to our present purpose. On the plane of thought it was certainly Chesterton who was by far the deeper thinker—a man of 'colossal genius' as Shaw confided with characteristic generosity to T. E. Lawrence.

Shaw's Fabian and socialistic principles did not arise self-evidently from his general view of life. To the contrary, Samuel Butler, from whom he learnt the doctrine of creative evolution, was in politics a strong conservative who believed that it was the duty of those who had independent incomes to protect them and to live off them. And between the two it might well be argued that a theory which asserted so strongly the uselessness of the average man might naturally be expected to be anti-democratic; and indeed in his later life Shaw did seem to prefer totalitarian dictators like Mussolini or Stalin or kings like King Magnus of *The Applecart* to democratic politicians. Even in his younger days he espoused socialist and apparently liberal principles not because he wished to benefit the poor so much as because he wished to organise them—to tidy up their untidiness. He thought, as we have said, that the poor ought to be abolished. Orwell was quite right in his suspicion of a type of intellectual Socialist whose only desire was to rearrange the poor and Chesterton quite right in saying that Shaw's Fabian dialectics trampled out the last ashes of the French Revolution.

Bernard Shaw of course advocated on paper the most drastic changes in society but in practice he lived without difficulty as an ordinary comfortable member of it and was never at all tempted to involve himself personally in any revolutionary activity—any more than was Chesterton. This was a general characteristic of the age—of the age before 1914—an age in which one might debate but in which nothing was ever expected really to happen. Chesterton noted it of the Victorians in the last of the major books of criticism which he wrote before the First World War—in his *Victorian Age in Literature* which appeared in 1913. To this book the Home University Library which had commissioned it paid the curious compliment of publishing it with a foreword which explained that it was 'not put forward as an authoritative history of Victorian literature,' but as 'a free and personal statement'—a compliment which they did not pay to any other volume in that series. As has been already stated, Chesterton's assertion in that volume was an assertion that the Victorian age was essentially an age of letters—an age of men who said much but did little. In that he contrasted the English with the French, the men of action and energy. It is certainly true that, whatever else we may say of them, the French of the Revolution and of the Napoleonic wars were men of energy. Whether the Frenchmen of the years after 1815 merited the line in Chesterton's *Secret People* which speaks of

The strange, fierce face of the Frenchmen who knew for what they fought

or whether it was not rather Matthew Arnold's

that madhouse France from whence the cry
Afflicts grave heaven with its long senseless roar

is as it may be; but certainly the notion of the Englishman as essentially a man of rhetoric, in contrast to the practical Frenchman, gave Chesterton an opportunity for a display of arguable paradox not dissimilar to that in which Shaw indulged in his *John Bull's Other Island* when he contrasted the English, Broadbent, the victim of words, with the Irish Doyle, the brutal master of them. Yet the age of Victorian England was, to Chesterton's view, an age when a few Darwins and Huxleys might indeed issue their challenges of agnosticism, or a Newman might recall the age of a more intense faith; but he saw it as an age in which the great majority, like Matthew Arnold, accepted the institutions of Christianity without believing its doctrines, or, like Trollope, accepted the institution without even thinking whether they really believed the doctrines.

It is odd that this book of Chesterton which had on every page of it evidence of deep reading—for Chesterton had truly been brought up by his father on the works of the great Victorians—yet does not mention Arthur Hugh Clough, surely the arch-apostle of Victorian incapacity to act. Perhaps it was a sign that Chesterton, for all his persisting reluctance to act, had at the last with *The Man Who Was Thursday* finally made up his mind to turn his back on solipsistic scepticism, and with *Orthodoxy* to commit himself to Christ; he no longer had patience with the very explicitness of Clough's havering, with his continual oscillation between the two great alternatives of 'He is risen' and 'He is not risen.' At the least it is certain that while dealing in detail and sympathetically with the hesitations of other great Victorians, he has no words to give us about Clough—neither in that book nor, so far as I can recollect, anywhere else in his works.

In this book Chesterton noticed what is indeed a curiosity of Victorian England: that it was the only period in all history when a writer, such as Dickens, called on to write *A Christmas Carol*, would invent a new Christmas story of his own with no mention in it of the Babe of Bethlehem. It is, he wrote, another curiosity of the Victorians that while they did not as a rule explicitly repudiate the supernatural, yet it appeared little in their writings, and when it did appear, as in Henry James' *The Turn of the Screw* or in Stevenson's

Dr Jekyll and Mr Hyde, it usually appeared in an evil form. In so far as there was a possiblity of supernatural intervention in the affairs of men, this was to them much more likely to be an intervention of the devil than of God. Matthew Arnold described God in somewhat typically mid-Victorian verbosity as 'a force not ourselves making for righteousness'. But in reality to the average Victorian it was 'we ourselves' who worked for righteousness. It was man who was the instrument of progress and bringing it inevitably to be, and God, if He intervened at all, was likely to intervene to prevent it. When the Victorians described imaginary secular societies of the future, as with William Morris in *News From Nowhere*, these societies were always much better than the present—in contrast to the modern utopians who, as in *1984* or *Apes and Essence*, look forward to a very much worse future.

This inaction of Victorian man and, as a consequence of it, the predominance among Victorian novelists of women, who are by nature more interested in noting the detail of the accepted pattern than in planning a universal philosophy, Chesterton ascribes—a little surprisingly—to the decline in Victorian times of the military spirit. It is true that physical fighting is one of the forms of action, but it is only one form and not—one would have thought—for a Christian a form to be very highly recommended if it could in any way be avoided. Yet Chesterton, though the least physically violent of men in his own life, always allowed fighting and duels to play a large part in his stories—in *The Napoleon of Notting Hill*, *The Wild Knight*, *The Ball and the Cross*, *The Man Who Was Thursday* or *The Ballad of the White Horse*. He described as 'a touching *cri de coeur*' Stevenson's petulant demand, 'Shall we never shed blood?' It is all a little odd. We must of course remember that *The Victorian Age in Literature*, like *The Napoleon of Notting Hill*, *The Ballad of the White Horse* and the rest of these books, was written before 1914 and that before 1914 men had not yet come to guess what the horrors of modern war could be. Yet before 1914 Britain had been involved in plenty of wars. Those wars, when they had been fought in Europe, had usually been fought against the French, or they had been fought overseas in the pursuit of imperialist expansion. And as Chesterton, with his admiration of the French Revolution and Napoleon, thought that Britain in the early wars of the century was fighting on the wrong side, and as he detested the imperialist adventurers of the end of the century, it is a little surprising that he should have praised the military spirit so highly and should, it seems, have reflected so little on the probability that soldiers, should they be sent to war, would be sent to fight on the wrong side. It was only 1914 which brought a war in which he could believe that Britain was indubitably right and which 'closed up his quarrel with his sires.'

Chesterton was, as we have said, for all his pretence of lack of scholarship, in fact a most deeply read man and particularly so in Victorian literature. It is common enough that the writers with whom we most easily live are those with whom we became familiar in the late 'teens or early twenties and only the few among us, as we grow older, retain the appetite to remain acquainted with those who have more recently come into fashion. Chesterton was a victim of this common habit, but, while he talked most easily of the Victorian writers, he had by his maturity and after the writing of *Orthodoxy* come to say very different things about them from what he would have said in his youth.

A Liberal himself, Chesterton was content to notice of the great Victorian writers that they, too, were by and large Liberals, men demanding the removal of certain obvious abuses, quietly confident that those abuses would in fact before long be removed. But he also noted another curiosity about them. Such a man as Matthew Arnold was content mildly to notice and welcome the decreasing power of dogma and to decry the vulgarity of the age. Ruskin denounced ugliness. Carlyle preached the virtues of silence in twenty volumes, as Dean Inge put it. Dickens satirised the follies of the Circumlocution Office and exposed the miseries of the poor. Certainly the Victorian writers by no means shared the complacency of which the age was so often accused. But, though they preached reform and were glad enough to welcome its coming as long as it did not come too quickly, they in fact did very little to help its coming. They were by no means the men to go out and fight upon the barricades. They thought, rather, that they had done something and had indeed done all that they could be expected to do when they had written their book or their article and posted it to the printer. Indeed, far from supporting drastic action, they shrank back in horror from any prospect of it. *Barnaby Rudge* and *A Tale of Two Cities* showed Dickens as far more afraid of the mob than *Oliver Twist* had ever shown him in favour of reform, Dickens, wrote Chesterton in *The Victorian Age in Literature*, 'had no plan of reform, or, when he had, it was startlingly petty and parochial, compared with the deep, confused clamour of comradeship and insurrection which fills all his narrative.' Carlyle, after all his praise of action, escaped the necessity for personal action by his convenient theory that God was always on the side of the big battalions and that might, merely by being might, proved itself to be right. Froude thought the same. Matthew Arnold shrank ¡back from the 'ignorant armies' that 'clash by night' and called in the name of Culture for a National Church 'which will still survive as established long after people have ceased to believe in any of its dogmas'—a body uncomfortably like the Churches that have been favoured by Hitler and other totalitarians. Carlyle and Ruskin supported Governor Eyre's brutalities to the Jamaican Negroes. Ruskin, Chesterton said in an epigram which Dean Inge afterwards purloined without acknowledgement, 'seemed to want all parts of the cathedral except the altar.' Tennyson with his parochial Victorian middle-class English ideas, 'could not think up to the height of his own towering style.' 'He had much more of expression than was wanted for anything that he had to express.'

The Victorians thought that progress might continue—was indeed almost certain to continue—that this or that detail of life might be altered and improved, but they never thought that there was any possibility of the whole shape of the world being altered. Newman and Browning alone of the great Victorian thinkers, each in his very different way, allowed their thought to lead them to a total refashioning of life, and Chesterton, whose admiration for Newman was throughout these years steadily growing, noted how in him, unlike the others, thought led so very definitely to action. Yet indeed at this stage, even when he praised him, he misunderstood and underrated Newman. 'Newman,' he wrote, 'took down the iron sword of dogma to parry a blow, not yet delivered, that was coming from the sword of Darwin.' Most students of *The Idea of Development* today would surely say that in it Newman did not so much refute the idea of evolution as show that it was only to be expected.

Yet Chesterton does not at this stage seem to have derived from Newman any lesson that he felt the need to apply to himself. The truth is, of course, that Chesterton was a man abnormally fertile of ideas but he was also, as we have said, a man reluctant to act. He all too easily, like his Victorian subjects, thought that he had done something about a problem when he had merely written about it. So it is a curiosity that both in these years, when he had come to call himself an Anglo-Catholic, and in later years, when he had come to call himself a Roman Catholic, although he was always ready to write, to lecture and of course to think about his faith, he was never a very frequent church-goer. 'What but religion could induce us to do this?' he said, heaving himself reluctantly out of bed in order to go to church. He noticed of his wife at the time of his marriage that she, in contrast to almost everyone else whom he had met, actually practised a religion. He noted and he applauded. In a manner he imitated, but he never imitated with abandon, and in later Catholic years he found embarrassment in such practices as Confession or Communion—an attitude perhaps more appropriate for a Jansenist than for a full Catholic. In all his writings there is no piece about the Blessed Sacrament—only the passing line in *The Ballad of the White Horse* about how Our Lord 'broke Himself for bread.'

A consequence of Chesterton's lack of a strong desire that his ideas be put into practice was that all his works of fiction are unashamedly fantastic. To the first of such fictional extravaganzas—*The Napoleon of Notting Hill*—we shall return later when considering his political ideas. All that it is necessary here to say is that the political idea—the notion that men are happier when they give their loyalty to a small unit rather than to a large one—is a perfectly serious, sensible and tenable idea, but the exploitation of it in *The Napoleon of Notting Hill* is without apology fantastic. So again we have already considered *The Man*

Who Was Thursday. Whatever is uncertain, the certainty remains that the stability of society will not be threatened by seven anarchists calling themselves after the days of the week, who are in fact all detectives in disguise. Nor is there any probability that there will be a real chase of such men by bourgeois citizens over the fields of Northern France. It is the same with his next work—even more defiantly an extravaganza. *The Ball and the Cross* is the story of two men: a pious, simple-minded Catholic from the Western Isles of Scotland, the defect in whose philosophy was that he had absolutely no sense of humour, and an atheistic London journalist. They decide that their ideas are so flagrantly in contradiction to one another that nothing remains for them but to meet in a duel and fight it out to the death.

The story of *The Ball and the Cross* records how these two adventurers travel over the world, continually trying to fight their duel with one another and continually being frustrated by people to whom the notion of actual devotion to religion or to irreligion is quite incomprehensible—by a Tolstoyan, by a Nietzschean, by a Protestant, by a good citizen and above all by the police. They finally take refuge in a house that turns out to be a lunatic asylum, presided over by Satan. All those with whom they had come into contact are also incarcerated there so that all evidence that they had ever existed might be destroyed. Liberation comes at last when one of the unjustly interned inmates of the asylum burns it down. Satan, or Lucifer, is worsted and in the burnt relics of the asylum the two swords of the two contestants—Turnbull and MacIan—are found lying upon one another in the shape of a cross. The name Turnbull had a curious attraction for Chesterton as a fighting name. He gives it here to his fighting atheist as he had already given it in *The Napoleon of Notting Hill* to the owner of the curiosity shop who turned out to be a military genius.

It were absurd pedantry to list all the improbabilities which realism could find in the extravagances of this book. Its only reality, like the reality of *The Man Who Was Thursday*, is that of a dream, and there is a particular contradiction by which in some pages MacIan is spoken of as a wholly simple-minded Highlander who had never before seen London or any sophisticated society, and in other passages is made to draw elaborate parallels between the membership of the Catholic Church and the membership of the Athenaeum Club, or to discourse about French literature. But the broad lesson was that these two men represent the two absolutes of faith and unfaith. Lacking any point of contact and yet thinking truth important, they fancy that they have no alternative but to fight it out: this puts them into contrast with the Laodicean society around them, which neither sees point nor possibility of either believing or not believing. It is self-evident that in sober fact it would be quite impossible for a good man, having walked and eaten and debated over the days with another good man, at the end of it all still to think that it was his duty to kill him; and indeed the suspense of the story is somewhat marred by the certainty that neither of the duellists will in the end kill the other. It is clear that the world in which they move is a mad and an evil world and that at the end of it Lucifer must somehow be put under foot and expelled from it, even though it is not very easy to give the story an ending without in some way causing Turnbull to be converted from his atheism, which would reduce the dignity of the story. The story is not worked out quite clearly: there is one curious lapse in it—the too rapid transition from a world of sane high spirits to a world of Orwellian nihilism. For the most part it is written in the usual Chestertonian spirit of bonhomie and, as always in Chesterton, swords, though they are the weapons of death, are brandished in high spirits and with little risk that they will kill anybody. The story is a riot of euphoria—except for the few pages in which the incarceration of Turnbull and MacIan in solitary cells in the asylum is described. Suddenly we find ourselves there in a world of *1984*, and Lucifer's plan to make Turnbull and MacIan into non-beings, by destroying all the evidence of their existence, has about it a curious echo of George Orwell. Orwell objected to the irresponsibility of *The Napoleon of Notting Hill* in which Chesterton imagined that men could fight one another in civil war without suffering degradation of their characters. I wonder if he ever read *The Ball and the Cross*. Or, if he did, would he have said that Chesterton wrote of such atrocities, never imagining that there was any serious possibility that they would happen, but that we have lived on into a totalitarian world in which the menace of them is all too actual?

The Ball and the Cross was published in 1909. *Manalive* followed it not long after in 1912. It has the same characteristic of extravaganza. Back in his earlier days, just after he had left the Slade School, Chesterton, as we learn from his Notebooks, had had the notion of describing the adventures of a fictional Eric Peterson who was to be led through experiences of horror, solipsism and nihilism only to discover at last that the final novelty which he accepted and by which he was to be rescued was traditional truth. But, returning to these notes in 1911, he recognised that he had already described such experiences in fiction in *The Man Who Was Thursday* and defended the answer to them of tradition in *Orthodoxy*. He therefore turned his invention to a more light-hearted purpose, rechristened Eric Peterson Innocent Smith, and involved him in the bizarre topsy-turvy adventures by which he rediscovered his love of his home by going round the world in order to return to it, and recaptured his love of his wife by eloping with her again and again under a number of aliases. Innocent Smith, who exultantly accepts the soubriquet of Manalive, had, when an undergraduate, challenged the Master of Brakespeare College, Cambridge, a pessimist and a disciple of Schopenhauer, who asserted that life was not worth living, and threatened to call his bluff and shoot him. The Master, thus threatened, confessed his desire for life; and Innocent Smith dedicated himself to the task, for which he is blown around the world by an unrelenting gale of wind, of stabbing the spirit broad awake by continually rediscovering the familiar through coming to it in a new way. He proved that, far from being mad, he alone was sane in a world of lunatics and, like Browning's Pippa, he injected romance into the dry-as-dust in whom it had been dead.

In the course of his adventures Innocent Smith deals a number of swinging blows at various enemies of the sane and balanced life who chance to cross his path—financiers, Socialists, Irish melancholics, French and Russian revolutionaries, an aristocratic lady, and above all a Chinese priest who is rebuked for turning a church into no more than a museum. It is all excellent and high-spirited fooling—the most light-hearted of all Chesterton's serious books—but all that it is necessary to say for the moment is that, however cogent the arguments which Chesterton can think up for behaving in such a way as Innocent Smith, he would certainly never have dreamed of behaving in such a way himself. The very notion of Chesterton attempting to go round the world unaccompanied by his wife is unthinkable. He wrote about going round the world, but in fact he remained at Beaconsfield. In all Chesterton's fiction there are always men fighting one another with weapons and men moving with incredible rapidity from place to place. Chesterton himself moved little and with difficulty.

Many years later, of course, and after the war Chesterton took what was to him incomparably the most important positive action of his life and joined the Roman Catholic Church. But the overwhelming importance of this step tended to make him even more than before treat minor social inconsistencies as whimsical and attractive comicalities. For instance in 1927 he carried out a project that had long been in his mind and wrote a play about Dr Johnson—*The Judgement of Dr Johnson*. He was often compared by critics to Johnson, though there were others who argued that it was Belloc rather than Chesterton who was the real re-incarnation of Johnson; and some—Bernard Shaw for instance—a little surprisingly compared Chesterton to Rabelais. However that may be, Chesterton's admiration for Johnson's clear and sturdy thinking was undoubted and he wrote an excellent play about him, to which we will return on a later page. One of the incidents in it was an incident to whose possibility he had already adverted many years before in a passing essay. He imagines Dr Johnson giving an eloquent lecture to the company on the importance of good manners, while not noticing at all that at the same time he was knocking over and breaking one after another of his hostess' cups. I remember him being entertained to luncheon by a young undergraduate admirer and, offered cigars, absent-mindedly helping himself to three and putting them into his pocket. Then, recollecting himself and his manners, he commented, 'This is what cads do' and, turning to his wife, demanded, 'Give me money!' There was doled out to him the pocket money which was to see him through the business of the afternoon.

This book is concerned with a study of Chesterton's mind—not with his life—and the mind of a writer is obviously for the most part to be discovered from his writings. But, just as a certain amount had to be said about his parentage and his school days, so it is not possible to dismiss Chesterton's religious development without saying something about his wife. For whatever part his own independent thinking may have had in bringing him to his religious position, there is no doubt, and it is on his own confession, that a large share of the responsibility was his wife's. He married her in 1901. It was a marriage of complete happiness. Chesterton surrendered entirely to her the management of all the practical affairs of his life and numerous anecdotes bear witness to his total dependence on her. I remember one day standing with him on the first floor of a hotel and saying 'Will you walk down the stairs or shall we take the lift?' 'My wife will come and she will decide,' he replied.

But we are concerned with her religious influence. It was in a way remarkable that she should have this large influence, for she was not a woman of especially outstanding intellectual power nor were her religious opinions of any especial originality or profundity. But of her influence there can be no doubt. It was a triumph of sheer goodness. Chesterton, as we have seen, accounted for it by saying that she was the first person whom he had ever met who actually practised a religion. The religion that she practised was that of Anglo-Catholicism, and it was soon after their marriage that Chesterton definitely enrolled himself as an Anglo-Catholic. (I once asked the pub-keeper at Beaconsfield whether Chesterton was often seen at church, and he replied, 'Clever men like that do not need to go to church.' For all I know, the pub-keeper was an Anglican, had merely observed that Chesterton did not attend the Anglican church, and was

G   97

unacquainted with the fine distinction which led him to another place of worship. But I could not help reflecting how pained Chesterton would have been to have heard such a verdict.) Though neither then nor later as frequent a church-goer as one might have expected, he was always ready to obey a summons to the platform and was a frequent speaker at meetings of the English Church Union—the Anglo-Catholic society. The members of it—and in particular Conrad Noel, a strange aristocratic, Socialist, Sinn Fein parson of Thaxted in Essex—were his warm friends and warm friendships continued even after his change of allegiance. The modern ecumenism, however, which is so anxious to find the good in all faiths and to search out the beliefs which members of all denominations hold in common was unattractive to him.

It was Isaiah Bunter

> Who sailed to the world's end,
> And spread religion in a way
> That he did not intend

he wrote of a missionary who had been, or was alleged to have been, eaten alive by cannibals.

> And many a man will melt in man,
> Becoming one, not two,
> When smacks across the startled earth
> The kiss of Kikuyu

he commented, the Kikuyu conference being a conference, much talked upon at the time, where it was proposed to allow joint Communion between persons of different denominations.

During his Anglo-Catholic years he wrote in *Orthodoxy* and elsewhere much in favour of the Christian tradition and much in favour of a position that was in general Catholic; but he never wrote to explain why a man ought to be an Anglo-Catholic rather than a Roman Catholic. In those years when he associated with Anglo-Catholic friends and when, so far as the record goes, he was not as yet thinking in any way of changing his allegiance, almost everything that he wrote was as acceptable to the Roman Catholic as to the Anglo-Catholic—so much so indeed that many who did not know the details of his life would often say that he was a Roman Catholic.

The man who apparently even in these years made the deepest impression on Chesterton was a Catholic priest—Monsignor O'Connor, later to play so great a part in his life, to receive him into the Catholic Church and to earn his niche in literature as the prototype of Father Brown. Monsignor O'Connor was the parish priest at Keighley in Yorkshire. He and Chesterton met when Chesterton was lecturing there in 1904. They got into conversation one evening and the next day walked together over to Ilkley to visit a friend. On the walk Chesterton advanced certain theories about certain perverted practices. (Characteristically enough, he never revealed exactly what those practices were. It pleased Shaw to reply to Chesterton's gibe that he, Shaw, was a puritan by asserting that Chesterton was the modern Rabelais. But Chesterton was in fact very unlike Rabelais in at any rate one respect. He instinctively recoiled from describing physical processes— from 'detail of the sinning and denial of the sin.') He was surprised and impressed to discover how deep was the knowledge which Monsignor O'Connor had acquired of those practices through the confessional. Arriving at Ilkley, Chesterton found there two pleasant young Cambridge undergraduates who were passing through on a walking tour. They discussed Monsignor O'Connor, spoke of him with kindness but agreed that they could not approve of a 'cloistered' life, shut off from the evil of the world. Chesterton was characteristically amused at these young men, so utterly innocent of the world, so complacently confident that they knew more about it than the wise and infinitely more experienced priest. He conceived the idea of writing some detective stories in which the priest might turn the knowledge that he had acquired of human nature in the confessional to the detection of criminals. That, for the moment, was all—all that he conceived of doing as a result of his experience.

7

The Chesterbelloc

It was Shaw who coined the portmanteau word Chesterbelloc. Though the word came to be frequently used, it was, as is the habit with such creations, most frequently used inaccurately. Those who used it thought that Shaw was saying that there was total identity of opinion on all subjects between Belloc and Chesterton—so much so that it mattered nothing which of them was speaking since there would be no difference at all in what they were saying. Of course Shaw never suggested anything of the sort. To the contrary it was his opinion, as expressed in *The New Age* of February 8, 1905, that 'Chesterton and Belloc are not the same sort of Christian, not the same sort of pagan, not the same sort of Liberal, not the same sort of anything intellectual.'

It was obvious enough that, even where there was identity of opinion between them, there was an almost total contrast of artistic manner. Chesterton was exuberant, romantic, careless of form. Belloc was classical, strict and contained, and what Shaw intended to convey by his portmanteau word was that the two were very different from one another. Of the two he preferred Chesterton, though he had a regard for Belloc and no hostility towards him, even if a certain doubt about his sincerity. He thought that Chesterton, when he wrote in his own personality, as in his religious and imaginative speculations, was, as he put it to T. E. Lawrence, a man 'of colossal genius'. Shaw was not himself a Christian and not himself a humble man, but he rightly saw that humility was the fundamental Christian virtue; he wondered at it, and admired a man of Chesterton's capacity genuinely humbling himself, as he was aware that he did. In Belloc he found humility less evident—to say the least. Belloc had the more dominating character and on certain topics had, as it were, captured Chesterton and dictated to him opinions that were not Chesterton's own in fields in which Chesterton was not competent. Of such were, Shaw thought, Chesterton's political opinions, and in particular his theory of distributism. With that theory Shaw greatly disagreed and he regretted that, as he thought it, Chesterton under Belloc's influence had surrendered to it. Chesterbellocisms were, in Shaw's connotation, those opinions which Chesterton expressed but which he had not discovered for himself, but which had been dictated to him by Belloc.

There is no question about it that Shaw's contention was basically correct. Chesterton was, when he first impinged upon the world, a conventional Liberal—as indeed at that time was Belloc himself. Chesterton's opposition to the Boer War had taught him to champion local loyalties against large imperialisms. His Christian faith taught him to denounce any political system which denied respect to any soul that was subject to it. No man must be treated as a means. It was this that he meant when he praised 'democracy', rather than any particular system of voting or election. But he was not a man who naturally either knew or cared how political constitutions, and still less how financial systems, worked. He would have had little notion how to set about floating a company. Indeed, as evidenced by a famous anecdote, he did not even know how to buy a pair of pyjamas. When he arrived back from a lecturing tour having lost his pyjamas, and was asked by his wife why he had not bought a new pair, he asked pathetically, 'Are pyjamas things that one can buy?' Similarly he would have had little notion how to organise a political campaign. When in his youth he went canvassing with Charles Masterman and they decided between them each to take one side of the street, Masterman, when he had gone down the whole of his side, found Chesterton still arguing vigorously at the first house on the other side. On all details of political programmes—the servile state or the methods of distributism—Chesterton was very confessedly the disciple of Belloc and said obediently what he was told. It was the same with his views on foreign politics.

There is a fairly clear distinction between Chesterton's opinions that were derived from his own reflections and those which he received from Belloc. It is worth while trying to plot out the two territories. Chesterton was brought up, as has been said, as a conventional Victorian Liberal, a disciple, indeed almost a worshipper, at the shrine of Gladstone. Of Gladstone's death he wrote

> We never saw you like our sires
>   For whom your face was freedom's face,
> Nor knew what office-tapes and wires
>   With such strong cords may interlace;
> We know not if the statesman then
>   Were fashioned as the sort we see,
> We know that not under your ken
>   Did England laugh at liberty.
>
> Yea, this one thing is known of you,
>   We know that not till you were dumb,
> Not till your course was thundered through
>   Did Mammon see his kingdom come.
> The songs of theft, the swords of hire,
>   The clerks that raved, the troops that ran,
> The empire of the world's desire,
>   The dance of all the dirt began.
>
> The happy jewelled alien men
>   Worked then but as a little leaven;
> From some more modest palace then
>   The soul of Dives stank to heaven.
> But when they planned with lips and leer
>   Their careful war upon the weak,
> They smote your body on its bier
>   For surety that you could not speak.

Chesterton's first irruption into political life was as a writer for *The Speaker* in opposition to the Boer War. One could not father on Belloc any responsibility for that opposition to the war as such, for Chesterton had not met Belloc at the time that he began to write. They only met as a result of their agreement in that opposition. Against the Boer War they stood on the same side. They also shared there what to some modern eyes might appear to be the same blindness. The modern young man, when he thinks about South Africa, thinks most naturally of *apartheid* and of the white treatment of the blacks. To Belloc and Chesterton the only problem of South Africa was the problem which white, Dutch or English, should rule there. The only possible defence for a creed of imperialism was that the British Empire, like the later Roman Empire, should be a supranational organisation preventing impartially the exploitation of one race by another and imposing justice for every individual as such. The imperialists sometimes pretended that the British Empire was such an organisation. One had only to look to Ireland to see that it was nothing of the sort. The imperialists raised a great protest about the alleged murder in the Transvaal of a British subject called Edgar and sought to make out of him a Don Pacifico. But Chesterton was amused to note that they never dared to publish his picture and the reason why they did not dare was that he was a black man. To the imperialists, for all their boasts of equal justice, it was manifestly absurd that a white man should be asked to lay down his life for a black man and they did all that they could to conceal the evidence that that was what was happening.

But it is even more important to note that this seemed equally absurd to Chesterton. The question, which of the two white races would be kinder to the black, did not bulk either to Chesterton or to Belloc as of major importance. When later the Conservative government brought in indentured Chinese labour to work in the Rand mines, Belloc and Chesterton joined with other Liberals in protest, but they did not raise any protest when, in order to procure a Union of South Africa, Asquith accepted a restriction on the voting rights of blacks and coloured in that country. Belloc's attitude towards racial imperialism was later shown in his *Modern Traveller*: here he exposed the rascality of the white exploiter of the negro, but spoke of the blacks as children whom it was indeed unscrupulous thus to exploit without conscience, but whose claims to freedom were not to be taken seriously.

> Cain Abolition Beecher Boz
> Worked like a nigger which he was

and in the last resort the white man could comfort himself:

> Whatever happens we have got,
> The Maxim gun—and they have not.

Yet we must remember the dates of which we are speaking. If it was a defect in Belloc and Chesterton that they did not much advert to the claims of racial equality half a century ago, no more did anyone else at that time on either side of the controversy.

If they were on the same side in their support of the Boers it is nevertheless important to understand that they were on the same side for slightly different reasons. To Belloc the Catholic Church was an imperial system, the inheritor of Rome. He had in him a strong vein of scepticism, and could well understand those unable to admit that any directing voice had been given to man to guide him in his faltering ways. He wrote in some bitterness

> The world's a stage. The trifling entrance fee
>   Is paid (by proxy) to the registrar.
> The orchestra is very loud and free
>   And plays no music in particular.
> They do not print a programme that I know.
>   The cast is large. There isn't any plot.
> The acting of the piece is far below
>   The very worst of modernistic rot . . .
>
> The scenery is very much the best
>   Of what the wretched drama has to show.
>   Also the prompter happens to be dumb.
> We drink behind the scenes and pass a jest
>   On all our folly; then, before we go
>   Loud cries for 'Author' but he doesn't come.

But, sympathetic with scepticism, Belloc had no sympathy at all with those who pretended to find any alternative voice of revelation other than that of the Catholic Church. 'We Catholics,' he wrote, 'may doubtfully admit some sceptics to be our equals but none others.' Therefore the Boers with their Old Testament Calvinistic religion were people wholly outside his sympathies. He had for them, as he wrote in *The Cruise of the Nona*, 'a contempt'. His opposition to the war was not that he liked the Boers but that he intensely disliked the exploiting capitalists—largely German Jews as he alleged—who were using the excuse of the imperial cause to establish themselves as the masters of the Transvaal:

> I have said it once and I say it again
> There was treason done and a false word spoken,
> And England under the dregs of men
> And bribes about and a treaty broken—

and in his bitterly satiric lines of protest against the noble lord who had accused him and his friends of not honouring the military virtues he wrote of

> Tall Goltman, silent on his horse
> Superb against the dawn,

and

> The little mound where Eckstein stood
> And gallant Albu fell,

and of

> The little empty homes forlorn,
> The ruined synagogues that mourn
> In Frankfort and Berlin:
> We knew them when the peace was torn—
> We of a nobler lineage born—
> And now by all the gods of scorn
> We mean to rub them in.

Chesterton at this stage of his life had no bias against Protestantism, nor any feeling that the functions of a priest were essential for true religion. To the contrary, in *The Wild Knight* the priests had been portrayed as the obstacles to a good life. In his poem in praise of the American part in the Spanish-American war—a poem for which he afterwards apologised—he wrote

> Ere priest or tyrant triumph
> We know—how well we know—
> Bone of that bone can whiten,
> Blood of that blood can flow;

and he, in distinction from Belloc, wrote of the Boers in Africa that they were 'a sleepy people without priests or kings', and called for friendship between 'the two kindly nations'—the Boers and the British.

In *A Song of Defeat* he recorded:

> And the peace of a harmless folk was shattered
> When I was twenty and odd years old.
> When the mongrel men that the market classes
> Had slimy hands upon England's rod
> And sword in hand upon Afric's passes
> Her last Republic cried to God.

Quite frankly he did not know very much about the Boers. He never went to South Africa. But to him the Boer way of life was a way to be preserved and defended for its own sake—not merely in order to prevent the victory of yet more evil forces. While others were against the war because they were against all war or against the Uitlanders, Chesterton almost alone was defiantly in favour of the Boers.

Chesterton was an enemy of imperialism. He liked small units because they were small. Belloc was a soldier of imperial Rome. He wanted a strong central government and had little objection even to despots—whether to a king or a revolutionary dictator.

He objected only to the British imperialism because it was the rule of an anonymous plutocracy.

When the Boer War was ended and interest in the particular fate of the Boers abated Chesterton had the whim of stating his philosophy of nationalism in a more generalised form and, in tune with the high spirits of his youth he did it in fictional form— in the first of his fictional extravaganzas—*The Napoleon of Notting Hill*. *The Napoleon of Notting Hill* is a novel cast in the future— eighty years, to be precise, after the 1904 in which it appeared. He imagines that men have by then lost all faith and accept without enthusiasm a dreary rule of cosmopolitanism simply because they can see no alternative to it. Kings were then chosen by lot— the only truly democratic form of selection as Chesterton argued. If rulers were elected, only a very peculiar sort of person would prove a successful candidate. The lot alone asserted that any citizen was capable of ruling and ensured that power would be entrusted to the ordinary, average man. The King of England of that day was one Auberon Quin, who had had the whim of introducing colour into the life of London by giving each of the boroughs its own city guards, its own walls, its own suburban tocsins and the like. To Auberon Quin the notion was no more than a passing fancy, adopted for amusement and to kill the time, but it was taken up with immense seriousness by a citizen of Notting Hill, called Adam Wayne, Notting Hill's Lord Provost; he burned with a true love for Notting Hill and called its citizens to arms against the neighbours of Bayswater and Kensington, who wished to pull down one of its streets, Pump Street, for road development. War breaks out between the suburbs. Notting Hill is victorious so long as it is content to defend its own freedom, and only meets with defeat when it passes on from nationalism to imperialism, and attacks and attempts to dictate to its neighbours.

There are a number of comments to be made on this amusing extravaganza. The first obviously is that it is not intended to be serious in its details. Whatever the future may hold neither Chesterton nor anybody else can have imagined that there is likely to be a revival of suburban London patriotism on a scale sufficient to make the men of Notting Hill lay down their lives in battle against the men of Pimlico. Street battles in London or any other city are all too likely in the temper of the modern world but they will not be battles on the issues of Adam Wayne's choosing. Nor can anyone who has seen the modern experiences of Berlin and Jerusalem imagine that it is a humane or a romantic plan to drive a frontier through the middle of a city. It is amusing, if in some ways a little pathetic that, when Chesterton in *The Resurrection of Rome*, written towards the end of his life, looked at the Swiss Guards round the Vatican, he wondered at first what it was of which they reminded him; and then he reflected that they reminded him very exactly of the halberdiers of Notting Hill in his *The Napoleon of Notting Hill*. The Vatican City was in those days the only state on earth that at all resembled the little states of Chesterton's fantasy. But if the Swiss Guards are almost creatures of a Chestertonian fancy, still even they have in recent times been sentenced to extinction by the Pope himself.

Yet, if *The Napoleon of Notting Hill* is totally unreal in its details, it has proved far from unreal or uninfluential in its essential teaching. It was the favourite book of Michael Collins, the Irish leader, who derived from it an inspiration for his Irish nationalism. When the Irish delegates went to meet the British Cabinet to negotiate for the Irish Treaty, Lloyd George, hearing of Michael Collins' literary taste, presented a copy of *The Napoleon of Notting Hill* to each member of his cabinet in order that they might the better understand Collins' mind. What benefit these exceptionally unimaginative men derived from the study, how much in particular Lord Birkenhead and Walter Long, whom Chesterton had so brilliantly satirised, enjoyed negotiating with one of Chesterton's disciples, who can say?

Whether Chesterton and Michael Collins were right in the gospel that they adopted is a further matter. The cause to which they professed to devote themselves was the cause of individual freedom. That is a coherent and intelligible cause. 'No man,' said William Morris, 'is good enough to be another man's master;' and it might be argued that governors should be allowed to interfere with the lives of the governed only as little as possible because of the inevitably corrupting force of power—because of 'God's scorn for all men governing', as Chesterton put it in his poem on the Secret 'People of England which never had spoken yet.' And it is obviously true that the gigantic units, whether of politics or of industry, are often callously indifferent to the freedom of their subjects. But is not tyranny as often found in small countries and in small business firms? Is there, for instance, more individual freedom to-day in the Republic of Ireland than in larger states? And is there any tyrant worse than Goldsmith's 'petty tyrant of the fields' if his power is unchecked? Is not the gossip of the village sometimes more cruel than any public opinion of a nation? What is surely important is that power should be under constant challenge. This is more important than whether the units are large or small. In agriculture Chesterton appreciated the value of a king who was strong enough to prevent the tyranny of the squire. Might there not be something of a case for an imperial government strong enough to prevent the tyranny of the champions of small nationalism?

Yet, even if we concede Chesterton's right to champion the small unit, there remains a further problem. It is one thing to love Notting Hill. It is quite another to think that one can only show one's love by fighting and killing. Chesterton dedicated the book to Belloc and in his dedicatory poem he wrote

> And when the pedants bade us mark
>   What cold mechanic happenings
> Must come; our souls said in the dark,
>   'Belike; but there are likelier things.'
>
> Likelier across these flats afar
>   These sulky levels smooth and free
> The drums shall crash a waltz of war
>   And Death shall dance with Liberty;
> Likelier the barricades shall blare
>   Slaughter below and smoke above,
> And death and hate and hell declare
>   That men have found a thing to love.

It is, as we have noted, extraordinary, considering how pacific a man Chesterton was, that book after book of his should be filled with stories of men fighting one another either in battle or in duels with swords. One of his great heroes, Stevenson, lay in bed wasting away with the consumption that was to bring him to an early grave, crying out 'Are we never to shed blood?' almost at the time when he was spitting up blood in his sickness. In his books he compensated for his inability to live a full physical life. They are filled with the arms and battles that he never saw. So Chesterton, the least athletic of men, to whom it was almost a torture to go for a walk along the street, filled his books with men rushing over the countryside and confronting one another in battles.

> Who will write us a riding song
> Or a fighting song or a drinking song?

he was to ask in *Wine, Water and Song*. One could imagine him writing a riding song. It would be less easy to imagine him riding. What is so strange about *The Napoleon of Notting Hill* is not so much that he makes his characters fight one another as that it never occurred to him that this civil war would interfere with the normal tenor of life. In the middle of the battle the buses still run punctually to time, drawn by obedient horses. There are no motor cars in his London of 1984 and no guns are fired in its battles, which are entirely fought with sword and halberds. One looks in these days on the pictures of the pall of smoke rising over American towns that have suffered race riots to remind oneself what civil fighting is really like. Odder still, neither in *The Napoleon of Notting Hill* nor in any other of these early books of Chesterton does it seem to have occurred to him that killing would have any effect on the characters of the killers. They emerged from their battles exactly the same sort of decent, kindly people that they had been at the beginning. In much the same way Kipling in *Kim* can describe men as living the life of a secret society without any suspicion that such a life of secrecy and deceit would degrade their natures.

The answer is, of course, that all these books were written before 1914—written in a world in which we all flattered ourselves that civilisation was a state that had been finally achieved and that no conceivable calamities could seriously damage that achievement. The fifty years since 1914 have shown us how unjustified was that assumption—how very brittle is the crust of civilisation that protects us from the reversion to total barbarism. Chesterton wrote *The Napoleon of Notting Hill* in 1904, proclaiming that he was narrating events that were to happen in eighty years time—that is to say, in 1984. There is no exact evidence that Orwell had this coincidence in mind when he chose the title of his own book. But, whether intentional or not, Orwell's book, in which the death of freedom brought with it the death of every decency even down to the proverbial honour among thieves, was certainly a protest against the irresponsibility of Chesterton's forgetfulness of the great lesson: he who draws the sword will perish by the sword, and violence, when once employed, cannot easily be quenched. It is hard, as one looks at the tale of current violence, not to sympathise with Orwell's impatience.

What is most curious about *The Napoleon of Notting Hill* is that in it, alone among Chesterton's books, there is no reference to religion. There is hardly a hint of what either Adam Wayne or Auberon Quin believed on ultimate matters. There is no description of what may have been brought to Notting Hill by any religious developments during the eighty years between the writing of the book and the date of its supposed events.

The Napoleon of Notting Hill was the first of Chesterton's political books, but it only dealt with a small part of what was to become Chesterton's full political programme. The novel was only concerned with the gospel that the unit that demands men's loyalty should be a small unit. There is nothing in it of the notion of widely distributed property with which Chesterton in later years was to be deeply concerned. At that time, as has been said, Chesterton was still the loyal and regular Liberal he had been brought up to be. He had indeed differed from a certain wing of his party—the Liberal imperialists of Asquith, Grey and Haldane—over the Boer War, but the leader of the party, Campbell Bannerman, was as strongly opposed to the war as was Chesterton himself, if for slightly different reasons, and in any event once the war was over differences about it were no longer a main cause of division. He met the 1906 election as an entirely loyal, unswerving Liberal and greeted the Liberal victory with the swinging lines of the *Election Echo*. He wrote in contempt of the defeated Conservatives:

> Fear not these, they have made their bargain,
>   They have counted the cost of the last of raids,
> They have staked their lives on the things that live not,
>   They have burnt their house for a fire that fades.
>
> Five years ago, and we might have feared them,
>   Been drubbed by the coward and taught by the dunce;
> Truth may endure and be told and re-echoed.
>   But a lie can never be young but once.
>
> Five years ago and we might have feared them;
>   Now when they lift the laurelled brow,
> There shall naught go up from our hosts assembled
>   But a laugh like thunder. We know them now.

The law, he still thought, was the law of progress. Things had been getting better and better and should be helped to get even better yet. Politics meant primarily turning out the Conservatives and putting in the Liberals. There was nothing within him at that time of that bitter tang which was to cause Belloc to write:

> The accursed power that stands on privilege
> (And goes with women and champagne and bridge)
> Broke; and democracy resumed her reign
> (Which goes with bridge and women and champagne.)

His loyalty was the more unquestioning in that his friend, Belloc, stood at the election as an entirely regular Liberal candidate for a constituency in Salford and was elected. Yet, from his first arrival at Westminster, Belloc found himself at odds with his party. He quarrelled with them first about what he alleged to be their breach of faith over Chinese slavery in South Africa. The Liberals at the election had been loud in their denunciations of the wickedness of the Conservatives who had brought in indentured and, as they claimed, essentially slave Chinese labour to work in the Rand mines. Having used that cry to win them their victory, they showed in office—so Belloc alleged—no intention of bringing the scandal rapidly to an end. He quarrelled also with the unwillingness of the leaders of the party to agree to any publication of the financial accounts of the funds of the political parties. It was an almost open secret that at the time honours were bestowed in return for contributions to the party funds—though not on the gigantic scale on which they were to be sold later by Lloyd George. Belloc thought that the accounts should be published so that the public might know what was happening. Neither of the party machines had any such desire and they managed to circumvent Belloc's demands.

In general Belloc and his friend, Cecil Chesterton, Gilbert Chesterton's brother, soon reached the conclusion that the whole party system, as it was worked, was a gigantic fraud. The two front benches were really in collusion with one another to keep the system going, the two taking it turn and turn about to be in office. Between them they arranged mock debates and saw to it that none of the real scandals of the system were ever exposed. To what extent the thesis of Belloc and Chesterton was true is a nice point. It is certainly true that at that period the social intercourse and family relationships between members of the two front benches were very close—much closer than was commonly understood by the public. The book that Belloc and Cecil Chesterton wrote about *The Party System* describes the inter-relationship most wittily by a comparison with the relationships of the Montagues and the Capulets in *Romeo and Juliet*. 'We are not surprised,' they wrote, 'at Romeo loving Juliet, though he is a Montague and she a Capulet. But if we found in addition that Lady Capulet was by birth a Montague, that Lady Montague was the first cousin of old Capulet, that Mercutio was at once the nephew of a Capulet and the brother-in-law of a Montague, that Count Paris was related on his father's side to one house and on his mother's side to the other, that Tybalt was

Romeo's uncle's stepson and that the Friar who married Romeo and Juliet was Juliet's uncle and Romeo's first cousin once removed, we should probably conclude that the feud between the two houses was being kept up mainly for the dramatic entertainment of the people of Verona.'

Belloc, in a letter to Maurice Baring, reduced this fantasy to a devastating actuality. 'On Thursday,' he wrote, 'is the big division which will wind up the session, I suppose; the division which will give the resolution of the Commons defying their brothers-in-law, stepfathers and aunts' lovers in the Lords. Thus Geoffrey Howard will defy Lord Carlisle while the more dutiful Morpeth will acquiesce in his father's power. Kerry will similarly support the privilege of Landsdowne but Fitzmaurice (oddly enough) will be of an adverse opinion. Alfred Lyttelton will think the power of the peers reasonable; not his sister's husband, Masterman, who will however be supported by his wife's first cousin Gladstone; while the Prime Minister will not find his brother-in-law, Mr Tennant, fail him, nor need he doubt Mr McKenna, since he had married the daughter of the Tennants' chief friend. Oddly enough, however, while Pamela Tennant's husband will support the Government, her brother Mr George Wyndham, will not find it possible to agree with them. His stepson, the Duke of Westminster, has privileges not to be despised, and it is curious that that young gentleman's wife's step-nephew, Mr Winston Churchill, should be found in the Liberal ranks. However it is some compensation to this member that his aunt is the mother-in-law of the Tariff Reform League in the person of Lord Ridley, called by the vulgar Fat Mat.'

Now, it is certainly true that there have been many periods in British history when there has been no clear dividing line of principle between the political parties, and it is quite arguable that that is how things most usually are. Yet the strange thing is that the years immediately before the 1914 war, when Lloyd George's schemes of compulsory insurance were introducing a wholly new principle into British legislation, when Ireland was drifting into civil war and leading members of the British Unionist party openly supported the Orangemen in their threat of armed rebellion—these were years when, more than ever before or since in British history, the proposition that here was no great dividing line between the parties was least tenable. Belloc brought to British politics a swashbuckling, Gallic, Dantonesque spirit which longed for violence and the clash of arms. It was arguable that, if deeds corresponded to words, that was how British politics should be. It was at least as arguable that the British people did not wish it to be like this; that they were wiser than Belloc in not wishing it to be like this; that they knew very well that party politics were a game, played as they were played, to keep them amused; that the system could only work if the two parties were to a large extent the same, agreed in preserving the general nature of society, whichever of them was in power, and were only concerned to tinker at details. They might pretend in their speeches to a total opposition to one another, but if the pattern of society was really to be changed from top to bottom every five years, if each party was to think the other so wholly evil that it was prepared to resort to violence to prevent its accession to power, all ordered society would be impossible. It was arguable that the system, as it was worked, was in fact a great deal more sensible than Belloc would have had it be. Or was Belloc a prophet before his time? Although his assertion that the party system was a fraud seemed in his day a wild paradox, today a very large proportion of the British public take it almost as a platitude, and anyone who professes a passionate loyalty to the one party or the other is looked upon almost as an eccentric.

Yet, however that may be, our concern here is not so much whether Belloc was right or wrong as with his influence over Chesterton which was most certainly immense. It was a field on which Chesterton was not naturally at home. It was not to his temperament to follow the ups and downs of politicians' manoevres. Personal ambition was an emotion that he hardly understood. He lived in the world of general ideas. It was from Belloc that he accepted the doctrine of the unreality of the party game. We can follow the movement of his mind. In *Heretics* in 1905 he was still willing to profess himself without qualification a loyal Liberal. Three years later in 1908 he tells us, in *Orthodoxy* that, though he still believes in liberalism, he can no longer believe in Liberals. It was in 1911 that *The Party System* of Belloc and Cecil Chesterton appeared, but Belloc had before that already made his disillusion clear. He stood at the 1906 election as a regular Liberal. At the January election of 1910 he stood as an Independent, inevitably, of course, as a result paying his own expenses. At the November election of that year he did not stand at all.

In the year before, Chesterton had given his statement of the political position to which he had come in his *What's Wrong With The World*. It had been his original intention to publish this book under the title *What's Wrong* with a question mark. It was his publishers who persuaded him to change the title. It is not quite clear why they did so and almost certain that the judgement was a mistake. The addition of the words 'With the World' is cumbersome and meaningless. The excision of the question mark spoils the point of the title. It makes it appear that Chesterton was laying down the law about everything in the world and explaining how all should be put right. That was not at all his intention. The book was rather the book of a puzzled man who observed that the high hopes of beatitude, which the French Revolution had held out to mankind, were not being fulfilled, and was wondering why. What was wrong with the world was almost exactly what a year before he had explained and refuted as Bernard Shaw's diagnosis of what was right with it. His two challenges were to the gospel of progress and to the totalitarian belief that it was only the whole of society which was of value and that the individual only existed as a link or part of society. The first part of the book is what he calls 'methodological'. The trouble about purely pragmatic solutions, with their rejection of speculation about ultimate reality as worthless and irrelevant, is that we cannot reasonably say what institutions will work for Man until we have first decided what Man is. The basic institution of human life, Chesterton comes to assert in Chapter Six, is the family. All other institutions, as for instance the state, are manmade. Man does not decide by a social contract that it is for his advantage and that of his neighbours that he should recognise some person as his mother and that she should recognise him as her son, as he decides to recognise some person as his monarch. He cannot depose his mother, if he dislikes her, and elect someone else as his mother in her place. As a result, it is the duty of the state to support the family. If in the name of progress it attacks the family for the sake of its greater freedom, it is exceeding its functions. Of course there have been, and there are, such beings as cruel and tyrannical parents, and special rules must be made for special cases. But, because the family is a natural unity, tyranny among parents is less probable than tyranny among governors. To call in the state to redress the tyrannies of parents as a general policy is a folly. For there is every probability that you will then be calling in the greater tyrant to redress the evils of the lesser tyrant.

So the normal way to grow up is as a member of a family. The man or woman is first a child before becoming man or woman, and is brought up by his or her parents. Then, when he grows to maturity, he marries and in his turn brings up a family of his own children. As a child he was supported by his parents and as a parent he supports his own children and, in order to support his children it is essential that he should have a reasonable income and highly desirable that he should have a little property. For the man with property can support himself by his own labour as a free man. He who has only a wage or salary is dependent on the good will of others and therefore less free.

Thus it was that in *What's Wrong With The World* Chesterton for the first time enunciated his theory of the desirability of a wide distribution of property, with which his name was later to be so closely connected under the not very euphonious title of distributism. He had still many more lessons to learn and many more discoveries to make before that gospel took any final form, but *What's Wrong With The World* was important for its adumbration. The adumbration was important because, whereas in *The Napoleon of Notting Hill* there had been no trace of religious influences, the insistence on the importance of widely distributed property—as against either the capitalist theory of the concentration of all effective property into the hands of a few rich men, or the socialist theory of the concentration of all property into the hands of the state—had been a doctrine laid before the world by Leo XIII in his encyclical *Rerum Novarum* in 1891. There is not much explicity about religion, and still less explicity about the Catholic religion, in

117

What's Wrong With The World. He indeed especially says that it is not a religious book. A man might easily read it without being aware that religious influences were playing their part in the development of Chesterton's political and economic interests. But, if so, he would be missing an important truth.

If the family was the basic unit, it was inevitable that certain of the teachings current in society about the treatment both of children and of women should come under review. The uninhibited critics of the society of two generations ago—such as Nietzsche and Shaw —had sought to solve the problem of the patent incompetence of the men of their generation to deal with the world's problems by proclaiming: 'If man cannot solve his problems, then abolish man. Breed another creature—the Superman—to take his place.' The more modest critics, not going quite as far as that, were content to think that they could improve Man so as to make him competent by the magic machinery of education, which throughout history had been regarded only in so far as it was the servant of religion, but was now canonised as an alternative to it. As each insoluble problem presented itself, men told themselves—as indeed they very frequently still do tell themselves—that it could be solved when a new generation had had a little more education. Education, thus employed, obviously was, and was intended to be, the enemy of the family. What it meant was that the children should be taken away from their parents and incarcerated in institutions where they were taught to believe and to do things different from what they had been taught by their parents to believe and to do. Now Chesterton, as we have seen from his memories of Saint Paul's, was by no means one of those who had an unhappy childhood and who delighted in later years in recounting the brutalities that he had there suffered. He had enjoyed himself well enough there. He had not taken much trouble about the lessons which did not interest him. But nevertheless he had emerged from school, not indeed encumbered with academic distinctions but at least endowed with a certain knowledge of Greek and Latin and grateful that this knowledge had been imposed upon him. He thought that the modern notion that it was the business of education to 'draw things out' of the pupil, to encourage him in self-expression was as false in fact as it was in linguistic derivation; and, when in later life he saw such experiments not merely being discussed but actually being applied in American schools that allowed themselves to become the disciples of Dewey, he thought it even more false than he had previously imagined. The business of the teacher was, he thought, to teach—to impart information. He dismissed the controversy about dogmatic teaching with a characteristic quip. 'A teacher who does not teach dogmatically,' he said, 'is simply a teacher who does not teach.' No one who thinks about it at all can be impartial about the claims of the Christian religion. Either one must think them true or one must think them false. If you think them true and you are asked to talk about them, then you must inevitably want to say that they are true and to teach as much.

Perhaps he a little oversimplified. But in general his position on education was conservative. The old theories on education seemed to him more sensible than the new. But his main concern was not with what was taught in schools or with how it was taught but that its importance should not be exaggerated. 'All this talk about education,' said Canon Demant, 'is a proof of our decline.' Chesterton would have agreed. Being an egalitarian, he was on the whole opposed to the public schools. In a democratic society children should not be barred off from playing with one another. But the evil of the public schools was less than the evil of the ill will that would be created by their abolition by an all-powerful state. The real lessons, the important lessons, that a child learnt were the lessons that it learnt from its parents. A school might add a few useful little details to that original instruction but if the school set itself up as a rival in any way to undo the teaching of the parents it became a very evil place.

Naturally enough Chesterton's reassertion of the rights of the family caused him also to reconsider the teaching of the age about women. The fashionable progressive theory was that women had through the ages been kept in unjust subjection to men and that the great feminist movement would at last bring to them the equality to which they had a right. To Chesterton this was mainly nonsense. To him the family was the unit. In order to make a family, both husband and wife had a part to play. Which was the more important part was a largely meaningless question. The condition of happiness was that they should respect and recognise each other's differences—that the men should be manly and the women womanly. Therefore he had no sympathy with the feminist suffragette movement which was so much in the air in England before 1914. The demand of women for their so-called rights seemed to him no more than a demand of some women to be allowed to behave like men—to compete against men at the things at which men were their superiors. They were not likely to make much of a success of these manly jobs and, engaging on them, they were more likely to lose their influence over men in their own field—in those tasks of personal influence in which they traditionally excelled. The suffragette movement, argued Chesterton and his brother, was a false movement. The great majority of women had no interest in feminism. It was a fad of a few upper-class women with too much money and too many servants. Cecil Chesterton satirised the movement with the cry of 'Votes for Ladies'.

Now women have got their vote and have been granted entrance into most professions, though even yet they have not fully succeeded in capturing the citadel of Equal Pay. Not many of them have met with much success in their new adventures. The number of women Members of Parliament has never been more than a handful. If the women who have had public careers have, more often than not, been women of some means, that does not indeed prove that Cecil Chesterton's gibe about feminism as an upper-class movement has been justified. The explanation is simpler. It is rather that in the nature of things the woman whose husband cannot afford servants has no alternative but to stay at the kitchen-sink, whatever might be her preference. Among the first suffragettes it might be true that the majority of working-class women were not interested in the movement. It was not at all true that there were not some working-class women such as Mrs Kerry who were most keen suffragettes.

The Chestertons have certainly proved themselves right in so far as they argued that most women were not interested in feminism, in votes for women or in careers. It does not necessarily follow from that that they were right to fight the movement. It may, if you care to argue so, be best that all people should belong irrevocably each to his or her sex—that the man should be utterly manly and the woman utterly womanly. But for better or worse, that is not how all people are. Psychologists since Chesterton's time have had a good deal to tell us about the intermediate sex—about how men have some feminine traits, and women have some masculine traits. The eccentric have even on occasion managed physically to change their sex. The suffragettes said that all women should be treated as if they were men. The Chestertons said that no women should be treated as if they were men. Both overlooked that most women doubtless cared little about feminism but that there were a few women, unbalanced, if you wish, who were condemned to frustration and unhappiness if they were not allowed to compete with men in men's careers. It is arguable enough that on balance Chesterton's generalisation about the two sexes was wiser than the generalisation of the progressives. But he was wrong to generalise so sweepingly as they; and, rightly appealing to tradition, he made insufficient allowance for the way the customs of these relations had changed from age to age with the changing generations. He thought with confidence that he was speaking for the Christian tradition when he spoke against feminism. He would perhaps have been surprised to find in a new age Pope John XXIII in *Pacem in Terris* committing the Church to the support of feminist claims. 'The part that women are now playing in political life,' wrote the Pope, 'is everywhere evident. This is a development that is perhaps of swifter growth among Christian nations but is also happening extensively, if more slowly, among nations that are heirs to different traditions and imbued with a different culture. Women are gaining an increasing awareness of their natural dignity. Far from being content with a purely passive role or allowing themselves to be exploited, they are demanding both in domestic and in public life the rights and duties which belong to them as human persons.'

What's Wrong With The World, though it contains perhaps the first clear exposition of Chesterton's social and political principles, is not one of the most interesting of his books to modern readers because so much of it is concerned with personalities and passing controversies of the day. The air and the newspapers were then full of suffragettes. We do not today so greatly care if women have votes or not because we do not so greatly care about votes. It is clear that the poor at any rate are showing themselves much more violently critical of the education that is offered them than they were in Chesterton's day. In general, wise institutions are, in his contention, institutions that respect traditional relations, and folly is shown when it is believed that the new upstart can be treated as the equal of the inheritor of traditions. In perhaps the most unfortunate of all his prophecies he asks whether, for all the rhetoric that was then in favour, any inhabitant of Europe could really think of an Australian as his equal. 'If ever we were in collision with our real brothers, and rivals,' he wrote, 'we should leave all this fancy out of account. We should no more dream of pitting Australian armies against German than of pitting Tasmanian sculpture against French.'

Soon after the 1906 election, Chesterton, under Belloc's influence, began to lose his original faith in the Liberal party. He shared Belloc's indignation that after the loud promises of the election campaign so little was done to bring Chinese slavery to an end. He shared Belloc's indignation that the party battle, as it was fought, should, as they thought, be so largely a sham battle, defended by its champions as that minimum acceptance of the rules which was necessary to make the system workable. But above all he shared Belloc's indignation at the acceptance by the Liberal Government of the principle of compulsory insurance of workers against unemployment and sickness which was finally to be embodied in Lloyd George's national insurance schemes and form the basis of what is known as the welfare state. Under the full theory of laissez-faire it was the business of every man to find a job for himself and to earn from it whatever wage it was possible to extract out of free bargaining. Those who could not find a job or who were too ill to perform it did not get a wage. The state had sufficient pity to provide a workhouse into which they could go and to provide them with sufficient food to preserve them from absolute starvation. But beyond that it took no responsibility for their fate. Lloyd George's plan was that the workman himself, his employer and the state should each make a compulsory weekly contribution out of which a fund would be formed on which they could draw in case of illness or unemployment.

Belloc denounced such schemes. According to his contention the whole difference between a free man and a serf was that the free man was paid in cash and the serf was paid in kind. The worker, according to Belloc's contention, should be given a decent wage and then left to choose for himself how he met his necessities out of it. He saw in the process that was going on the beginnings of a return to a system of slavery. In 1913 he developed his full thesis in his book *The Servile State* which was to become in many ways the text-book of the distributists. *The Servile State* was not a book against socialism. It did not argue, as many people often argue today, that all property and power under socialism will pass into the hands of the state and that the rest of us will become slaves to the bureaucrats. On the contrary it argued that socialist projects of wholesale nationalisation will prove too difficult to be workable— that therefore a compromise will be accepted by which the owner of an industry will be allowed to remain in possession of his property provided he accepts responsibility for keeping his workers in tolerable conditions. The worker will be paid increasingly in kind rather than in cash and, tied to his firm as the mediaeval serf was tied to his land, *ascriptus glebae*, he will lose his freedom of movement and his freedom to withdraw his labour and will become increasingly a slave. The only remedy to the process was to restore the system of general property instead of the system by which all effective property was vested in the hands of a few capitalists. 'If we do not restore the institution of property,' he wrote on the title page of his book, 'we cannot escape restoring the institution of slavery; there is no third course.'

To what extent Belloc's analysis was accurate, to what extent developments have been along the lines which he foresaw, whether his use of the striking word 'slavery' was justified or whether it was to some extent used to attract attention by startling, those are questions to which we will return later. The important point for the moment is that Belloc's exposition of the problem was entirely accepted by Chesterton and that henceforth in his distributism he always joined his acceptance of the desirability of a wide distribution, which he had derived from Leo XIII's *Rerum Novarum*, to his acceptance that the alternative was a return to slavery which, whether true or not, could not lay any claim to ecclesiastical authority. He, following Belloc, was of course always careful to explain that he used the word 'slavery' not in the rhetorical sense to describe any system of great evil but in an exact sense, to describe a system in which one man controlled the labour and property of another. He accused the Leverhulme soap factory of being a 'slave compound' and was threatened by them with an action for doing so, but they called off the action when he explained his exact meaning. They appeared to think slavery in this precise sense to be a rather good thing.

More important for the moment was the personal story. Ever since his days at Saint Paul's Chesterton had always seen life as to a large extent a high-spirited debating society. His life was filled with debates on principles with men from whom he differed deeply but with whom he remained on most friendly personal terms. His works of fiction tell of friendly quarrels among his characters. Belloc's temperament was different. His differences of opinion always tended to take on a sundering, personal quality. So, too, did those of Gilbert's brother Cecil. Now among the new Liberal members who entered Parliament in 1906 was Charles Masterman, with whom Chesterton had associated in his days with the English Church Union. Masterman was at first considered as one of the Bellocians and joined with Belloc in the first battles which he fought in that Parliament. In particular he voted for the Right to Work bill, introduced by the Labour party in 1908. But he was also a friend of Lloyd George. In 1909 he accepted the Chancellorship of the Duchy of Lancaster in the Government and later in that year under the discipline of the whips voted against the same bill which he had previously supported. A few months later at the beginning of 1910 there was a general election and Masterman was defeated. He was defeated again at two by-elections in the following months and had to resign from the Government. He was not to get back into Parliament until 1923 and then only for a very brief period.

That the Conservatives should have attacked him and exulted over his defeats was of course only in accordance with the rules of the party game, but his defeats were at least partly caused by the fact that Belloc and Cecil Chesterton attacked him with extreme bitterness and through what they called the League for Clean Government turned out and heckled him at his meetings. They sang a somewhat absurd song to the tune of 'God rest you merry, gentlemen' which ran

God rest you merry, gentlemen; let nothing you dismay.
I fear that Mr Masterman will never go away.
He's lost his seat in Parliament but draws his weekly pay,
    Oh, tidings of comfort and joy.

It is true of course that Masterman somewhat changed his tune when he accepted office. Everyone does. It is inevitable. No sane man in his independent opinion supports every measure of any Government and, so long as he is free to express his opinions, doubtless sometimes expresses dissent. But it is the custom of our parliamentary system that a member of the Government has always to vote in its support and must never express any dissent with any of the measures of any of his colleagues. Whether or not that is a sensible arrangement, it is the arrangement and not one for which Masterman was in any way personally responsible, and no one suggests that a minister ought to resign save over a grave issue. Therefore doubtless Masterman did support some incidental measures which he disliked, as has every other statesman who has ever sat in a cabinet. Belloc accused Masterman of a total abandonment of all principle at the lure of office. But in fact there are two sorts of members who go to Parliament—both valuable. There are those who go there as critics and who have no ambition for office. Such men can preserve an independence in their votes and perhaps preserve, if they will, a total consistency. Parliament needs a few men of such a type—though indeed it would be clogged up if there were very many of them. But also there are the members—and they are a majority—whose main interest is in administration. Politics is about power and those who wish to administer must decide which of the two competing parties on the balance they prefer to see in office; and, having joined their team, they must support it. They cannot afford dissent save on matters of real moment.

Of this second sort was Masterman. His interest was in administration. As Gilbert Chesterton said, he was 'an organiser and liked governing; only his pessimism made him think that government had always been bad and was now no worse than usual.' He had a good deal of what Chesterton called 'God's scorn for all men governing,' and yet the realism which made him see that, for all that, somebody must govern. His opinion beyond doubt, if one had had the opportunity of discovering it, would have been that the Liberal Government of that day was not perfectly good but that the country had to have a government, that the only practical choice was between the Liberals and the Conservatives and that the Liberals, whatever their faults, were at any rate greatly to be preferred to the Conservatives. Therefore one must choose one's side and, having chosen it, back it. The bitterness of Belloc and Cecil Chesterton's personal attack on a former friend was found by many people very unattractive. Cecil Chesterton defended his campaign by arguing in *The New Witness*—the paper that he had started, to expose political corruption—that it was a public duty to make impossible a successful career for a man convicted of selling his principles. But the pretence that Masterman was giving a unique example of corruption was absurd. Most people were rather inclined to say that, if that was all that they had to expose, they had not very much of a case.

As for schemes of compulsory insurance, Belloc might be right or he might be wrong in his analysis. But his doctrine was no part of certainly revealed truth. Belloc made his confident assertions about the desire of the English people for property. But it was by no means certain that they preferred property to security. Masterman, who had for a time lived down among working men in the East End in a workers' flat, believed that he knew a great deal more about the wishes of the working man than did Belloc, and subsequent history with its tale of the popularity of the steady extension of the Welfare State would seem to give a good deal of indication that he was right. In any event the matter was clearly one to be debated out quietly with argument and statistics. It could not be settled by wild cries of treason. Particularly unattractive was the passage which Belloc and Cecil Chesterton inserted in their book on *The Party System* in which Masterman's acceptance of office was denounced and in which the authors wrote that 'he accepted a place with a salary of £1,200 a year—it has since risen to £1,500.' The salary at either figure was not especially princely and, accepting it, Masterman had of course to deny himself any earnings from his pen. He probably, if anything, lost in his pocket by his appointment, and at any rate he was both at that time and at all times a poor man and died in the end in very straightened circumstances. Belloc and Cecil Chesterton, since they knew him well, must have known very well that he was a poor man.

Such methods of carrying on a controversy were entirely alien to Gilbert Chesterton's temper. He was entirely on Belloc's side concerning the merits of the legislation, but he was against Belloc on the personalities, and indeed the story was notable as the one occasion on which he publicly dissociated himself from a judgement of Belloc. 'Many of my own best friends,' he wrote of Masterman, 'entirely misunderstood and underrated him. It is true that as he rose higher in politics the role of the politician began to descend a little on him also; but he became a politician from the noblest bitterness on behalf of the poor.'

Masterman's defeats all came in 1910. In 1912 there broke the Marconi case. Into the complicated story of the Marconi case on its own merits we need not here enter. Our concern again is with its important effect on the development of Chesterton's character. The essence of the complicated Marconi case was that the British Cabinet made a decision to take over the English Marconi Company which had been formed in order to promote the recently developed invention of wireless telegraphy. After the decision had been taken but before it had been announced Rufus Isaacs (afterwards Lord Reading) then Attorney General, Lloyd George, then the Chancellor of the Exchequer and Murray of Elibank, the chief Liberal whip, accepted through Rufus' brother, Godfrey, who was then chairman of the Marconi Company and a member of the board of the American Marconi Company, some shares in the American company. Gossip about what had happened got abroad and Isaacs and Lloyd George both hotly denied in the House of Commons that they had accepted shares in 'the Company'. Murray of Elibank went abroad to Bogota and it was never possible to get him to give an account of his transactions. From the national point of view his shares were in one way the most important of all since there was every reason to think that he had gambled with the Liberal party funds.

Now Isaacs and Lloyd George had not of course accepted any shares in the English Marconi company, but it was an economy of honesty to say nothing under the circumstances about their shares in the American Company. A committee of inquiry was set up. The members of it according to custom were appointed in proportion to the strength of the parties in the House of Commons and, when the committee came to report, it divided lamely along party lines. All the Liberals voted for the acquittal of the ministers, all the Conservatives for their condemnation. It may be that Isaacs and Lloyd George had not been guilty of any definite criminal offence but they had clearly behaved in a most irresponsible fashion. Asquith, the Prime Minister, partly out of loyalty, partly out of a natural desire to prevent a break-up of his Government, defended his ministers, but it was generally felt that he was carrying quixotry beyond reasonable limits when immediately afterwards he appointed Rufus Isaacs, who had been lucky to escape a criminal charge, to be Lord Chief Justice. Kipling, among the minister's strongest critics, wrote one of his bitterest poems:

> Well done, well done, Gehazi,
>   Stretch forth thy ready hand,
> Thou barely 'scaped from judgement,
>   Take oath to judge the land.
>
> Unswayed by gift of money,
>   Or privy bribe more base
> Or knowledge which is profit
>   In any market place . . .
>
> Thou mirror of uprightness,
>   What ails thee at thy vows,

What means the risen whiteness
 Of skin between thy brows?

The boils that shine and burrow,
 The sores that sough and bleed—
The leprosy of Naaman
 On thee and all thy seed?

Stand up, stand up, Gehazi,
 Draw close thy robe and go,
Gehazi, judge in Israel,
 A leper white as snow.

Our concern is with Cecil Chesterton's part in the affair. His two papers, *The Eye Witness* and *The New Witness*, had from the first denounced the whole business without qualification. All culminated when on January 9, 1913, Cecil Chesterton, who was then editor of *The New Witness*, published an article in which he listed all the twenty bankrupt companies of which Godfrey Isaacs had been promoter or director. As a result of this article Cecil Chesterton was prosecuted for criminal libel. F. E. Smith and Edward Carson were the two counsels who appeared for the prosecution. Cecil Chesterton behaved somewhat curiously in the witness box. Having filled his papers with accusations of 'abominable conduct' against the ministers, he without qualification withdrew the accusations as soon as the ministers denied them on oath. The conclusion of the case was that Cecil Chesterton was fined £100. His supporters, who had feared a prison sentence, hailed his verdict as a victory.

As has been said, Gilbert Chesterton had up till that time looked on the world somewhat like a school debating society—a place where one quarrelled and argued but remained friends with one's antagonists and did not expect the arguments to lead to any serious practical consequences. The Marconi case, where the ministers appeared ready to send his brother to prison and to ruin his career, was a profound shock to him—a lesson that, as he interpreted it, there was more malice in the world than he had guessed. All the bitter personal attacks of the rest of his life were always on people who had played a part in the Marconi prosecution. For instance he published two long and amusing satirical attacks on prominent Conservative politicians. The one was on Walter Long, the other on F. E. Smith. Walter Long was a genial Wiltshire squire who, supporting the Orange opposition to Home Rule, had been so misguided as to say that he 'was never standing by while a revolution was going on.' Chesterton submits the claim of this inheritor of an ample independent income, posturing as a friend of revolution, to some genial good-natured banter.

> Through sacked Versailles, at Valmy in the fray
> They did without him in some kind of way,

and advised Walter Long to be wary of challenging the first principles of society,

> Lest man by chance should look at me and see me
> Lest men should ask what madman made me lord
> Of English ploughshares and the English sword;
> Lest men should mark how sleepy is the nod
> That drills the dreadful images of God

and to stick to the constitution under which he enjoyed so many surprising privileges. But the attack on F. E. Smith, the prosecutor in the Marconi case, for his denunciation of the bill for disestablishment of the Welsh Church, was a great deal more bitter. He slated Smith's appeal to Christian conscience as wholly hypocritical.

> It would greatly, I must own,
>   Soothe me, Smith!
> If you left this theme alone,
>   Holy Smith!
> For your legal cause or civil
>   You fight well and get your fee;
> For your God or dream or devil
>   You will answer, not to me.

Talk about the pews and steeples
  And the cash that goes therewith,
But the souls of Christian peoples . . .
  Chuck it, Smith!

Lloyd George was never forgiven and was pursued by Chesterton throughout the rest of his career. But above all Chesterton drew his lesson from Cecil's main antagonists, the Isaacs family. The Isaacs' were of course Jews who preferred, as, according to Chesterton's contention Jews generally do, their family interest to the interest of the general good. Herbert Samuel as Postmaster General, though he had in no way been implicated in the purchases of the shares, knew of them and he, too, was of course a Jew and was to be assailed—very unfairly—throughout the rest of his life as Marconi Samuel.

8

Jerusalem and the White Horse

As we have said, Chesterton in his liberal youth had been by no means anti-semitic. Rather the reverse, and a number of his friends at Saint Paul's had been Jews. Belloc, as a French Catholic, had imbibed the common French Catholic prejudice aroused by the Dreyfus case, but Chesterton had at first taken the opposite side on that case and had indeed published a poem condeming the French action over it.

> Thou hast a right to rule thyself; to be
> The thing thou wilt; to grin, to fawn, to creep;
> To crown these clumsy liars; ay, and we
> Who knew thee once, we have a right to weep.

In Belloc's attack on the South African War much was made of the charge that many of the Uitlanders for whom we were fighting were, as Belloc alleged, German Jews, but Chesterton did not make anything of that point in his attacks. Even later when he hailed the Liberal victory in 1906 it did not at first occur to him to complain that an inordinately large number of Jews had been returned to the House and that more of them than ever before had received office. When in 1903 he was writing his *Browning* he dealt with the suggestion that Browning had Jewish blood as a matter that could not possibly be of any importance one way or the other. Belloc, in his book on the Jews, makes a capital point of Browning's Jewish blood.

It is hardly possible to deny that Cecil Chesterton was what could fairly be called an anti-semite. He was as convinced as any

fanatic that there was a Jewish conspiracy for the overthrow of
Christian civilisation and that every calamity that befell a Christian
could almost always be traced back to a Jewish origin. For instance
in his *History of the United States* he merely makes it as an assumption without any pretence of evidence that Czolgosz, the man who
murdered President McKinley, was a Jew on the general ground
that all assassins were certain to be Jewish. He and Belloc, taking
advantage of the fact that Marx was a Jew and that Trotsky and so
many other of the first Bolsheviks were Jews, confidently dismissed the Bolshevik revolution as a Jewish conspiracy. They little
foresaw the day when under Stalin and his successors the Soviet
Government would put itself at the head of the world's anti-
semitism. Belloc's book on the Jews in which, in chapter after
chapter, communism is attacked as the Judaic creed, reads somewhat comically today. Both Belloc and Gilbert Chesterton would
have vigorously denied that they were anti-semites, and it was of
course true that one of the closest friends of both of them, Maurice
Baring, was of Jewish blood, though of course of Catholic faith.
Yet, to be frank, it would be hard for anyone who listened to
Belloc's private conversation or read some of his unpublished
verses to think that he was other than an anti-semite. There was in
his conversation a wealth of casual anecdotes about the mis-
demeanours of individual Jews or speculation that such and such
an undesirable person had Jewish blood.

> It serves no purpose to protest;
> It isn't manners to halloo
> About the way the thing was messed
> Or vaguely call a man a Jew

he wrote, of the South African War.

With Gilbert Chesterton it was different. He accepted from
Belloc that there was an international money-power which was
largely Jewish and which attempted to control the policies of
European nations, and that Jews were men who owed their loyalty
to their own Jewish nation and who were incapable of feeling
patriotism to an established nation of whom they were the legal

citizens. In truth there was—it was most arguable—an international money power, in the sense of a few wealthy bankers whose main interest it was to rescue the traditional monetary system, but only a few of their members were Jewish.

It is peculiar that Belloc and Chesterton took the line that Jews should be treated as incapable of citizenship of a normal country as it was of course their great hero, Napoleon, who first abolished the Jews' traditional special status and demanded that they should be treated as ordinary citizens. Belloc in his book on *The Jews* advocated his thesis that Jews should be treated as people separate from the nation in which they found themselves. They should be given their own ghettos in which to live and to work. Within the ghettos they should be given complete religious freedom and full self-government under institutions of their own choosing, but they should not be treated as citizens of the country in which they found themselves. If the Napoleonic formula was accepted and they were encouraged to live as ordinary citizens, the inevitable antipathy between Jew and Christian was such, he argued, that explosions, pogroms and massacres were inevitable. Such massacres were, as Belloc said, abhorrent. The policies which he advocated were, he argued, the only alternative to them.

It can of course be answered that at the time Belloc wrote his book, in 1922, the worst pogroms that Europe had seen had all been in Eastern Europe—a few years before in Czarist Russia and, at the moment of writing, in Rumania and Poland—where the Jews lived under legal disabilities, lived substantially in ghettos and lived the separate life which Belloc advocated for them. Their separation had not saved them from attack by the Christians. It had on the contrary made it possible for Christians to believe absurd stories about Jewish habits and the Jewish way of life—child murders and the like. Yet most people at the time of Belloc's writing would, in spite of Eastern European pogroms or of memories of such incidents as the Dreyfus case in the West, have dismissed as absurd Belloc's suggestion of the possibility of general massacres of Jews. We were, we all thought, moving into an era of growing liberality. Such things, if they had sometimes happened in the past, could not possibly happen again in the future. Only eleven years ahead, at the time of Belloc's writing, lay Hitler. The experience of Hitler must make critics wonder, whether Belloc was indeed wholly foolish in his alleged exposure of the fragility of the Liberal formula. But at the same time it hardly gives support for Belloc's own solution. For the story of the Jews under the Nazis shows indeed that Hitler and the Nazis were alone so wicked as to wish positively to kill all Jews for being Jews, but it also shows that other governments, the American, the British and others, were not willing to put themselves even to the minor inconvenience of revising their quotas and welcoming Jews as immigrants to save their lives. Hitler alone was willing to kill, but other rulers were not prepared to

strive
Officiously to keep alive.

The essence of Belloc's plan was that the arrangements for Jews should be made by Gentile governments. The security under them of the Jews would be dependent on Gentile good will, and experience was to prove to the Jews that they could not count on Gentile good will.

Chesterton accepted on this, as on so many other topics, Belloc's interpretation. He did not abuse Jews as Jews. Few Christians wrote in more ringing admiration of the Jewish contribution to religion. In *The Everlasting Man* he was to write: 'It is true in this sense humanly speaking that the world owes God to the Jews . . . Much as we may prefer that creative liberty which the Christian culture has declared and by which it has eclipsed even the arts of antiquity, we must not underrate the determining importance at the time of the Hebrew inhibition of images . . . The God who would not have a statue remained a spirit. Nor would his statue in any case have had the disarming dignity and charm of the Greek statues then or the Christian statues afterwards. He was living in a land of monsters. We shall have occasion to consider more fully what those monsters were, Moloch and Dagon and Tanit, the terrible goddess. If the deity of Israel had ever had an image he would have had a phallic image. By merely giving him a body they would have brought in all the worst elements of mythology; all the polygamy of polytheism; the vision of the harem in heaven . . . It is often said with a sneer that the God of Israel was only a God of battles, a mere barbaric Lord of Hosts pitted in rivalry against other gods as their envious foe. Well it is for the world that he was a God of battles. Well it is for us that he was to the rest only a rival and a foe. In the ordinary way it would have been only too easy for them to have achieved the desolate disaster of conceiving him as a friend. It would have been only too easy for them to have seen him stretching out his hands in love and reconciliation, embracing Baal and kissing the painted face of Astarte, feasting on fellowship with the gods; the last god to sell his crown of stars for the Soma of the Indian pantheon or the nectar of Olympus or the mead of Valhalla. It would have been easy for his worshippers to follow the enlightened course of Syncretism and the pooling of all the pagan traditions. It is obvious indeed that his followers were always sliding down this easy slope; and it required that almost demonic energy of certain inspired demagogues who testified to the divine unity in words that are still like words of inspiration and ruin. The more we really understand of the ancient conditions that contributed to the final culture of the Faith, the more we shall have a real and even a realistic reverence for the greatness of the Prophets of Israel. As it was, the whole world melted into this mass of confused mythology; this Deity, who is called tribal and narrow, precisely because he was what is called tribal and narrow, preserved the primary religion of all mankind. He was tribal enough to be universal. He was as narrow as the universe.

'In a word, there was a popular pagan god called Jupiter-Ammon. There was never a god called Jehovah-Ammon. There was never a god called Jehovah-Jupiter. If there had been there would certainly have been another called Jehovah-Moloch. Long before the liberal and enlightened amalgamators had got so far afield as Jupiter, the image of the Lord of Hosts would have been deformed out of all suggestion of a monotheistic maker and ruler and would have become an idol far worse than any savage fetish; for he might have been as civilised as the gods of Tyre and Carthage . . . But the world's destiny would have been distorted still more fatally if monotheism had failed in the Mosaic tradition . . . That we do preserve something of that primary simplicity, that poets and philosophers can still indeed in some sense say a Universal Prayer, that we live in a large and serene world under a sky that stretches paternally over all the peoples of the earth, that philosophy and philanthropy are truisms of a religion of reasonable men, all that we most truly owe under heaven to a secretive and restless nomadic people, who bestowed on men the supreme and serene blessing of a jealous God.'

Chesterton, then, in no way failed to understand and to honour the mystery of Judaism. He merely argued that the Jew in England was not an Englishman, the Jew in France was not a Frenchman and so on. He was an alien and should be treated as such. It was a coherent argument but an exaggerated one. Both Belloc and Chesterton were apt to enunciate conclusions more clear-cut than reality warranted. The Liberal thesis that the Jew only differed from his Gentile fellow-citizen as a red-headed man differed from a black-headed man was perhaps an oversimplified thesis. The counter-thesis of Belloc and Chesterton that all Jews were absolutely different from their Gentile fellow-citizens was equally oversimplified in the opposite direction. There were perhaps Jews of such a sort—Jews who cared only for their religion or for their cousins in another country and who were quite blind to normal patriotism. There were plenty of other Jews who were, when the war came, to fight and die as gallantly in the ranks of their various countries as any Gentile, and, if it was on the whole true that Jews on account of their origin were less inclined to accept the exaggerations of extreme chauvinistic imperialism, more inclined to be a moderating influence over the policies of their nation, was that altogether a bad thing? If, as Belloc argued, all people with any Jewish blood in them were Jews and all Jews should live in ghettos then presumably Robert Browning should be put in a ghetto. Was this sane? It was curious that Catholic publicists should have been so ready to proclaim that Jews were necessarily tepid in their patriotism because of their connections with foreign co-religionists, since that was exactly the accusation which, of course, so very many non-Catholics in England and other countries levelled against the Catholics.

Before the Marconi case broke, Chesterton had already held in a restrained form the position to which he subsequently came. In 1911 he addressed the Jewish West End Literary Society. He praised the Jews most highly. They were, he said, the most civilised of races. One never met a Jew clod or yokel (I do not think that he, any more than most other people, at that date knew—or at least consciously registered—that there were Asian and African Jews or even thought very much about Jews in Eastern Europe.) When he went to Palestine after the war he noted justly enough that the Jews were unpopular among the Arabs because they threatened the traditional pattern of Palestinian life by their restless energy. It was true. But they did this not because they were Jews but because they were Europeans. Indeed Chesterton criticised the Jews because they were not Europeans, but the Arabs criticised them because they were Europeans. Now that the immigration into Palestine is predominantly of Asian or African Jews the tempo of the country is likely to change.

Chesterton proclaimed without qualification that a Jew could not by his nature share the national passion of his fellow citizens. If such was the analysis and Belloc's solution was impractical, the question remained, 'Where, then, should the Jews go?' Chesterton gave an answer to that question. He supported the solution of Zionism. The Jews should go to their natural home of Palestine, and he defended Zionism in the most lively and best of his travel books, *The New Jerusalem*. *The New Jerusalem* is a book that must always be of interest to the student of Chesterton, because it was at Jerusalem that he finally made the decision to join the Roman Catholic Church. His determination, as he wrote to Maurice Baring, 'came to an explosion in the church of the Ecce Homo in Jerusalem.' To that we shall return.

Naturally enough it was Christian Jerusalem which mainly engaged his attention.

> Do you remember one immortal
> Lost moment out of time and space,

What time we thought who passed the portal,
　Of that divine disastrous place
Where Life was slain and Truth was slandered
　On that one holier hill than Rome,
How far abroad our bodies wandered
　That evening when our souls came home?

But it is with his attitude towards Zionism that we are for the moment concerned. In one of the chapters of *The New Jerusalem* he vigorously defended Zionism. He claimed that the accusation so commonly levelled against him of anti-semitism should rather be an accusation of Zionism. He would have liked to have seen the Jews rebuild in Palestine a Third Temple—although not of course on the site of the Dome of the Rock. The Jews, necessarily aliens everywhere else, should be allowed to return, and should return, to the one place where they could be truly at home. The test, he wrote in that book, that Palestine was the true home of the Jew would have been finally vindicated if the Jews could show that they were able to turn themselves there to agriculture. If that be the test, it seems to have been abundantly justified by the kibbutzim.

Of course Chesterton wrote *The New Jerusalem* in 1920, immediately after the war, and the Zionism of which he wrote was a very different Zionism from that which we see today. As is known, the hope to create a country in which Jews and Arabs would live together in friendship has failed. The expectation of a liberal, Wilsonian world in which Jews and all others would be able to live peacefully in their homes and in which by consequence only small numbers of enthusiasts would wish to emigrate was by no means fulfilled. Renascent Poland took advantage of its independence to persecute the Jews. The Jews, expelled from Eastern Europe, seeped over into Germany and there earned an unpopularity which encouraged Hitler to make the persecution of them one of the main planks of his platform. The Jews, persecuted in Germany, were refused admission in any sufficient numbers into any other country. British policy had been to restrict Jewish immigration into Palestine to a small number so that the balance there between Arab and Jew was maintained. This was a reasonable enough policy so long as there were other places where the Jews could go. When Palestine was their only refuge it was hardly to be expected that Jews would not defy the quota in order to save the lives of their fellow Jews. It was hardly to be expected that Arabs would not resent this invasion. The conflicts which had already begun back in the middle of the 1920s, long before Hitler was heard of but well after Chesterton published his book, became violent and intolerable. The British, despairing of a solution, abandoned their mandate and an independent Israel was established. This is no place to recount the story in detail, nor to pass any judgement on it. What Chesterton would have said on all these developments had he lived to the time of the Second World War and to the years that followed it, who shall say? It is certain that, as the Rabbi Wise, the famous New York rabbi, bore witness, when Hitler's persecution of the Jews began, Chesterton was one of the first to protest against it. 'When Hitlerism came,' recorded Rabbi Wise, 'he was one of the first to speak out with all the directness and frankness of a great and unabashed spirit. Blessing to his memory.' Chesterton, we can certainly say, would never have acquiesced in a supine policy that did nothing at all to support the Jews in their agony. Yet the Zionism which he did support—a plea for a Jewish national home in Palestine as Balfour promised—was something quite different from the Zionism which under stress of circumstances has later developed. It was Belloc who condemned the Mandate Plan, by which the Jewish settlement was supported by British arms, as absurd and said that the experiment could only succeed if the Jews defended themselves.

The last of Chesterton's pre-war extravaganzas, *The Flying Inn*, appeared in the early months of 1914—just shortly before the war. It is mainly concerned with the battle and triumph of two friends of freedom, Patrick Dalroy and Humphrey Pump, in their efforts to defeat the machinations of Lord Ivywood for the destruction of the English pub. By a curious and somewhat improbable provision, the imaginary law there supposed to be enforced has been drafted to the effect that no liquor can be sold anywhere except in a building that has an inn sign outside it. The adventurers therefore have the notion of carrying the sign of *The Old Ship* in a wild and typically Chestertonian cross-country chase around the country and setting it up on a number of improbable buildings and thence dispensing the rum that they had brought with them.

It was because of this attack on the restrictions on the sale of drink that this book was mainly popular, and to Chesterton's views on what was known as temperance we shall return later. For the moment our interest is in the light that the book throws on his views on Jews and Arabs. In this book by a curious fantasy he makes Lord Ivywood, the leader of the temperance party in England, bring in a secret Turkish army to rob the people of England of their freedom.

Turkey in those years had just been defeated in two wars—by the Italians and by the Balkan states. In the Balkan war, informed opinion in Britain was mainly concerned to prevent the fighting from spreading into a general conflict. Uninformed opinion, so far as there was such opinion, was for the most part on the side of the Balkan kingdoms. Certainly it was no moment at which there was any prospect of the Turkish power extending itself. The notion of a Turkish army invading Britain was so bizarre as to be hardly worth suggesting even as a joke. But what is more important and more interesting is that any notion that there were divisions within the Turkish Empire—any suggestion of an Arab revolt against the Turks—was wholly absent from Chesterton's mind. Turk and Moslem are throughout used as entirely interchangeable terms. Nor had Chesterton at that date any notion of any sundering difference between Arab and Jew. Dr Gluck, Germany's Jewish representative, is unhesitating in his support of Lord Ivywood's plans for imposing Mahomedanism on the English.

To Chesterton, Judaism and Mahomedanism were great monotheist religions which had much more in common with one another than either had with Christianity—a thesis which he was to argue on a more serious plane in *The Everlasting Man*. He admired them both but thought their uncompromising, unqualified monotheism made them religions that were inevitably inhuman—in contrast to Christianity which believed indeed that there was one God but which, far from seeing Man as merely God's slave and creature, believed that Man was created in God's image and that God had taken on himself the form of Man. There was much to be said in theory for Chesterton's diagnosis, but, even when he wrote *The Flying Inn*, he had no suspicion at all of the antagonism in practice between Jew and Arab. Chesterton was heir to Belloc and, inheriting Belloc's high Roman traditions, thought of Christendom to an exaggerated extent as a wholly European affair. 'The Faith is Europe and Europe is the Faith,' Belloc was to write immediately after the war on the title page of his *Europe and the Faith* and it did not seem to Chesterton an absurd judgement. Europe to him was Christendom and what came from outside Europe was an attack on Christendom. Disraeli's conception of 'an intellectual colony of Arabia called Christendom' seemed to him no more than a witticism.

Another curiosity of *The Flying Inn* is that not only does the Jew in the book take the Moslem side but that that Jew—Dr Gluck—is sent to the negotiations between the Sultan of Turkey and the 'King of Ithaca' as the representative of the German Government. It is doubtful if even in the days of the Kaiser the German Government would have appointed a Jew as their ambassador, but it is a curiosity of Chesterton in view of subsequent developments that, unwilling to attack France or Poland and knowing little of Russia, he always spoke of Jews as coming most naturally from Germany. From the time of the Boer War onwards he and Belloc hardly ever mention a Jew in fact or fiction who is not described as a German Jew, and during the World War and after that war it is always spoken of as a Jewish interest to save Germany from final defeat or to put her back on her legs after her defeat.

The conflict of *The Flying Inn* ends in most typically Chestertonian fashion with a battle between the untrained citizens of London and the trained Turkish army, in which victory goes against all probability to the untrained—a duel with swords between Patrick Dalroy and the Turkish commander in which the Turk is killed and, after it all, the return of England to a tranquil, peaceful life quite unaffected by the disturbances through which it had been carried. The complications of a guerrilla warfare, the effect on character of the resort to killing and violence were matters to which Chesterton never adverted. It never seemed to have occurred to him in this book or anywhere else that a mob was an ugly thing. He always imagined it as going its good-humoured, democratic way, doing violence to no one. His picture is curiously different from reality. Nor has he in many places in this book taken the satirist's necessary precaution of making improbability accurate. He was justified enough, if he so wished, in guying the proceedings of Parliament, but he would more effectively have got things wrong if he had first put himself to the trouble of understanding how they went when they were right—informed himself a little on the machinery and ritual of Parliament. If we are to accept the basic improbability of a secret Turkish army being encamped in Southern England, we ought at least to be given some proper explanation of the further improbability that they were there apparently without any equipment or arms. Again it may be reasonable to laugh at an English professional social reformer for his insincere sentimentality about animals, but it can hardly be pretended even in satire that he was likely to have learnt that extravagance from the Moslems.

The book is not a tightly constructed book and, in spite of the jolly songs which were afterwards collected into *Wine, Water and Song*, it is a bitter book—what might be called a post-Marconi book. Chesterton was throughout all his life in protest against the class structure of English society—against the scandal that, under a pretence of democratic forms, all power was in fact in the hands of the aristocracy. The complaint was—and indeed is—a just one and never was it more just than in the England of the days before the 1914 war. Chesterton's lords were always immensely rich, able without trouble to pay for whatever might happen to suit their whims or interests. But in *Magic*, his play which was written before the Marconi case, the Duke, who owns and can pay for anything that he wishes, is an idiot but a genial idiot. He subscribes impartially to all causes—to those who want to build the new pub and to those who want to destroy it—to the vegetarians and the anti-vegetarians. He hires the conjurer and subscribes to the Society for the Suppression of Conjurers. When his secretary points out to him the inconvenience if the vegetarians and the anti-vegetarians both of whom he supports should come to a conflict, he gaily replies that there would be no inconvenience at all as he would certainly be also the magistrate who would try the case and could be relied upon to be impartial. Lord Ivywood, the aristocrat of *The Flying Inn*, the humourless reformer determined to destroy all the liberties of the poor with his designs and to impose himself on them as a superman, is a very different figure—a creature of the more bitter post-Marconi era in which Chesterton had, as he thought, learnt that cruel things do really happen.

Bitter warnings against the creeping danger of Prohibition were perhaps more necessary in those days than they are today. Today the obsession of Belloc and Chesterton with the praise of strong drink—with what Douglas Woodruff once called Cathalcoholicism —is apt to appear tiresome and to some a little adolescent. Grown-up people today admit the value of drink as a lubricant of social life. Plenty of people can use it with moderation. On the other hand there are also plenty—quite apart from the alcoholic or the dipsomaniac who drinks himself to death—who would be better in their own health and give less embarrassment to those with whom they have to live if they drank rather less. The balance between the good that it does and the harm that it does is very even, and as a consequence endless jokes about drunkenness or songs bawled in its praise become very easily tedious. An occasional essay of drunkenness in the young is only to be expected but there is no bore in all the world like a middle-aged drunk.

Yet of course the situation today is very different from that of the years in which Chesterton wrote. Today, whatever may be thought about drink, hardly anybody believes that the problem can be solved by police prohibitions. We owe that deliverance to American experience. Immediately after the First World War the Americans put into their constitution an amendment committing the nation to total Prohibition. From the first there were of course very many who broke the law but on balance in the first half of the 1920s it appeared to have more supporters than opponents. The Protestant Churches took it up as almost a holy cause and few in those years would have prophesied that the legal obstacles in the way of removing the amendment from the constitution would ever be surmounted. But it soon became apparent that the issue created by Prohibition was not merely the issue whether a man should or should not be allowed to have a drink. A consequence of an attempt to suppress by criminal prosecution a habit which to many people appeared wholly innocent and civilised was that a vast industry, operating outside the law, came into existence. Unable to appeal to the courts, the masters of this industry settled their differences with one another by violence. Great cities were devastated by disgraceful and appalling gang-wars and in the end many who did not especially mind whether they got drink or not yet reached the conclusion that for the sake of the nation's law and order it was desperately essential to get the Prohibition amendment repealed. Eventually with the financial collapse of 1931 and Franklin Roosevelt's accession to the Presidency the repeal was carried. Why the financial collapse should have caused public opinion to swing so suddenly against Prohibition, why they should have imagined that the defects of the banking system would be automatically remedied by everybody drinking more whisky, it is not altogether easy to see, but that is the way that it was.

Just as the collapse of American Prohibition has brought with it a world-wide acceptance that the problem cannot be solved that way and not even the suggestion of Prohibition is heard today in any white-inhabited country, so in the early days when it at least appeared from a distance that Prohibition was welcomed by the majority of the American people, there were plenty in England and elsewhere who demanded that others should follow the American example. A Prohibition candidate succeeded in defeating Winston Churchill at Dundee in the election of 1922. Prohibition in Britain appeared by no means an impossibility. Severe legal restrictions on drinking appeared more probable than not, and, incidentally, in those years Chesterton's *The Flying Inn* was the recipient of much popularity; the songs from *Wine, Water and Song* were freely bawled by the more exuberant opponents, at Universities and elsewhere, of what were known as Pussyfoot proposals. They even, as Bernard Shaw records in a letter to Chesterton, found their way into Fabian committee meetings.

There was a similar situation in only a slightly modified form in the years before the 1914 war. Few people, it is true, in those days before the American experiment, were prepared to go so far as to demand total Prohibition. But the very moderation of the demands made them the more dangerous because they were more likely to be conceded. The demand of those days was for local option—for a system by which each locality should be allowed to decide by its own vote whether or not it would have any public houses. A vote of local option of course in no way prevented a person within the dry area from keeping drink in his own house, and this fact was eagerly seized upon by Chesterton as an outstanding example that such laws in England were always made by the rich and imposed by them upon the poor, the rich always taking care not themselves to be incommoded by their own regulations. There is a great deal in *The Flying Inn* about the lavish flow of drink in Lord Ivywood's own house, in the House of Commons and elsewhere at the very meetings at which these drastic assaults upon liberty were being devised. The policy of local option was in those days the policy which had been accepted by the Liberal party because opposition to drink was strong among the Nonconformists who relied upon the support of god-fearing working-men who had raised themselves out of destitution by refusing to spend their scanty wages upon drink. A little oddly and ungenerously, seeing for how long he had written his column in Cadbury's *Daily News*, Chesterton concentrated his special animus upon the Cocoa press.

> Tea, although an Oriental,
>   Is a gentleman at least.
> Cocoa is a cad and coward,
>   Cocoa is a vulgar beast,
> Cocoa is a dull, disloyal
>   Lying, crawling cad and clown,
> And may very well be grateful
>   To the fool that takes him down,

Patrick Dalroy is made to sing. After this, Chesterton had to abandon his contributions to *The Daily News*.

The Liberals were of course in power and might well pass

measures to implement their promise. On the other hand, Chesterton was justified in thinking that such Liberal leaders as Asquith or Churchill did not greatly care about such restrictions and would certainly see to it that their own private habits were not incommoded by any legislation that they might find it politically convenient to pass.

Gilbert Chesterton was of course in no way involved in the details of the Marconi case. Indeed the whole controversy moved on a plane which in its ramifications would have been quite incomprehensible to him. He, who barely understood how to take a penny out of his pocket in order to buy a newspaper and asked wonderingly whether pyjamas were things that one could buy, would have been even more ignorant how to set about buying a share or borrowing the money to buy one. But during these years he was writing articles for *The Daily Herald* which were published as a volume of essays under the title of *The Utopia of Usurers*; the book appeared in America in the middle of 1917. They were written with great bitterness under the influence of the Marconi revelations. It is apparent in them that Chesterton did not indeed very well understand what bankers do. It is apparent also that he, to whom theory was so much more easily intelligible than practice, was in some ways repeating the error of the old orthodox economists whom he was attacking. Those old economists proclaimed it as a law of nature that man must always buy in cheapest markets and sell in dearest. They overlooked the fact that though this might be what the Economic Man was doing, the Economic Man—the man who looked all the time to his economic advantages and to nothing else— did not exist. In real life men are moved by economic motives but by plenty of other motives as well. Victorian England was indeed filled with men making money, but it was also filled with W. G. Grace playing cricket, and Queen Victoria not being amused, and Alice in Wonderland, and Robert Browning running away with his wife, and a hundred other things that had nothing to do with money—and if these truths were overlooked by the orthodox economists they were equally overlooked by Marx and Engels. They were to some extent also overlooked by Chesterton. The usurer, who was nothing but a usurer, was as unreal an abstraction as the Economic Man. Yet Chesterton was right in his suspicion of a system in which so little power was in the hands of those who actually produced things and so much in the hands of those who controlled the counters—of those who, as he put it, 'fight by shuffling papers.' He was right in suspecting these men and in denouncing their pretence that they were the masters of a mystery, that they held the secret of the laws by which alone the world could go round, and the more sincere they were in their belief in their own system the more dangerous they were. The years after the war were to show—what even their critics had not till then guessed at—that the one thing which was certain about bankers was that they did not understand the banking system. 'They rule men,' wrote Chesterton, 'by the smiling terror of an ancient secret. They smile and smile but they have forgotten the secret.'

There was one notable point about Chesterton. He raised his voice in protest against a system which kept secret about corruption among politicians. His own standards of sexual fidelity were high. Yet he never thought it right to speak of politicians' sexual failings. These were to him private matters. He must have known something about the private life of Lloyd George. Yet in all his attacks on him he never referred to it. The personal irregularities of H. G. Wells were never mentioned. Chesterton was by no means the Victorian who thought it his duty to pass verdicts on people's private lives. The bed was to him man's own business.

As we have often said, Chesterton did not seem capable of telling a story without bringing into it a mock battle and a duel with swords. It was a strange obsession for the least military of men. Belloc, though he was not interested in duels, wrote often about battles. But Belloc had served in the French army. He had studied military history. He prided himself—and with justice—that he knew how armies worked and his writings, whether historical or the studies of the battles of the World War that appeared in *Land and Water*, are models of exact and accurate descriptions. Chesterton knew so little about the working of armies that in *The Ballad of the White Horse* he describes the English and the Danish armies as drawn up in line opposed to each other and makes the English right wing face the Danish right wing.

A white horse had always had a fascination for Chesterton. He had seen it in early dreams. The first night of his honeymoon had been spent at 'The White Horse' at Ipswich and in *The Ballad of the White Horse* he took the white horse as the symbol of continuing English life. There are a number of White Horses scattered about on the hills of Western England. Of these the majority are modern and of no interest, but there are two of immemorial antiquity—the Wiltshire White Horse above Westbury and the Berkshire White Horse above Wantage. It is characteristic of Chesterton's carelessness about detail that he never in his *Ballad* makes up his mind which of these horses was the scene of the battle and talks indifferently of 'Berkshire hinds' and of finding the horse 'along the road to Frome'.

There is no great harm in the language of military symbolism so long as it is always recognised as symbolic. Chesterton wrote his *Ballad* in an England that had not known a major war for a hundred years but which was in a very few years to find itself engaged in such a war and in a war that seemed to many a war for total right against total wrong. It was not surprising that in such a war his *Ballad of the White Horse* should be widely adopted as a sort of Battle-credo. The wife of a sailor who had gone down on the submarine R.38 in the Humber wrote to Chesterton during the First World War to tell him how her husband had always carried the *Ballad* in his pocket and how it went down with him. At the worst moment of the Second World War a *Times*' leader quoted Our Lady's lines

> I tell you naught for your comfort,
>   Yea, naught for your desire,
> Save that the sky grows darker yet
>   And the sea rises higher.

And, when later our fortunes improved,

> 'The high tide!' King Alfred cried.
> 'The high tide and the turn!'

The Ballad of the White Horse tells the story of the battle of Alfred and his Christian army against the heathen Danish invaders and their defeat of them at the battle of Ethandune in the shadow of the White Horse, but it is far more than a mere account of battle and victory. It is the story of the eternal warfare against evil to which the Christian man is by the nature of his profession unendingly committed. But of course it is totally to misinterpret the poem to see in it some promise of security finally achieved as a result of victory. The whole lesson of the poem is that security can never be finally achieved. It is always of its nature under challenge and death is always the end.

The real battle of life is not the battle between the goodies and baddies, the battle of Roland in which *'chrétiens ont droit, paiens ont tort.'* It is only occasionally that conflict bursts out in the crude, overt form. The continual battle—the battle that never ends—is the battle of good and evil within the individual soul, and of this Chesterton was well aware. In *The Ballad of the White Horse* the concluding verses tell how after Alfred had won his victory and returned to a peaceful life the word came to him that in his old age the war had broken out again. The messenger came to him with the news:

> And even as he said it
> A post ran in amain,
> Crying 'Arm, Lord King, the hamlets arm,
> In the horror and the shade of harm,
> They have burnt Brand of Aynger's farm—
> The Danes are come again.'

Alfred went out to repel this new and never-ending attack, and the poem ends on the deliberately inconclusive note.

> . . . away on the widening river,
> In the eastern plains for crown
> Stood up in the pale purple sky
> One turret of smoke like ivory;
> And the smoke changed and the wind went by
> And the king took London Town.

Like Rossetti and the Holy Grail, it was not quite clear what he

JERUSALEM AND THE WHITE HORSE

was going to do with London town when he had taken it.

Chesterton was here almost admittedly adopting and repeating the lessons of *The Song of Roland*. In an introduction to *The Song of Roland*, written in 1919 and reprinted in *The Common Man*, he wrote, 'That high note of the forlorn hope, of a host at bay and a battle against odds without end, is the note on which the great French epic ends. I know nothing more moving in poetry than that strange and unexpected end, that splendidly inconclusive conclusion. Charlemagne, the great Christian emperor, has at last established his empire in quiet, has done justice almost in the manner of the Day of Judgement, and sleeps as it were upon his throne with a peace almost like that of Paradise. And there appears to him the angel of God crying aloud that his arms are needed in a new and distant land and that he must take up again the endless march of his days. And the great king tears his long white beard and cries out against his restless life. The poem ends, as it were, with a vision and vista of wars against the barbarians and the vision is true. For that war is never ended which defends the sanity of the world against all the stark anarchies and tending negations which rage against it for ever.'

When Chesterton finally came to write *The Ballad of the White Horse* he wrote it with enormous rapidity, throwing off sheet after sheet and casting them on the floor whence his wife had to pick them up and arrange them. The whole composition only took about a fortnight and, when the revision was done, very little indeed had to be altered. The story of the *Ballad* is, as has been said, the familiarly Chestertonian story of a battle—Christian men against Christendom's heathen assailants, the Christian men of Wessex against the heathen Danes. But it is not a simple story of good against bad or of men of one faith against men of another faith. In later years under Belloc's influence Chesterton was to accept to an exaggerated extent the thesis that England owed all her civilisation to the Normans and that the Anglo-Saxons were rude and un-lettered barbarians. When towards the end of his life he wrote his book on Chaucer he went out of his way to pour scorn on any notion that Caedmon had a claim to be accepted as a founder of English poetry. There is none of this Norman chauvinism in *The Ballad of*

the White Horse. The cause of Christendom is upheld by an indisputably Anglo-Saxon king. Eldred, his first vassal, was, we are
told, a Saxon, Alfred is a king who has brought learning to his
people. His army is a Christian army drawing its rulers impartially
from every part of Christendom:

> The king went gathering Christian men
> As wheat out of the husk—
> Eldred, the Franklin by the sea,
> And Mark, the man from Italy,
> And Colan of the Sacred Tree,
> From the old tribe on Usk.

Colan had Irish kinsfolk and

> . . . his soul stood with his mother's folk
> That were of the rain-wrapped isle,
> Where Patrick and Brendan westerly
> Looked out at last on a landless sea
> And the sun's last smile . . .
> For the great Gaels of Ireland
> Are the men that God made mad,
> For all their wars are merry
> And all their songs are sad. . . .
> He made the sign of the cross of God,
> He knew the Roman prayer,
> But he had unreason in his heart
> Because of the gods that were.

He had

> That little worm of laughter
> That eats the Irish heart,

while

> Mark's were the mixed tribes of the West
> Of many a hue and strain,
> Gurth with rank hair like yellow grass,
> And the Cornish fisher, Gorlias,

> And Halmer came from his first Mass,
> Lately baptised, a Dane.

Opposed to the Christian army are the heathen Danes, and the contrast between Christian and heathen is not so much the contrast of good and bad as the contrast between men who build and men who destroy. Western man, Chesterton had written in his book on Blake, is the product of pagan poetry, Roman order and Christian faith. It was of such that Alfred's army was built.

The Danes on the other hand, 'beautiful half-witted men' to whom 'hate alone is true', for all their loud boasting had no notion but to show their strength by destruction. Harold, King Guthrum's nephew, sings the song of destruction.

> He sang the song of the thief of the world
> And the gods that love the thief,
> And he yelled aloud at the cloister-yards
> Where men go gathering grief.

But Guthrum, the old king, is wise enough to know that violence and frantic boasting may satisfy the young man, not yet troubled by thoughts of mortality.

> A boy must needs like bellowing
> But the old ears of a careful king
> Are glad of songs less rough.

And Elf, the minstrel, reveals the sad tragedy in all such pagan promises which appear to offer felicity but always offer it with a catch that will prevent achievement.

> There is always a thing forgotten
> When all the world goes well;
> A thing forgotten, as long ago
> When the gods forgot the mistletoe,
> And soundless as an arrow of snow
> The arrow of anguish fell.

> The thing on the blind side of the heart,
> On the wrong side of the door,
> The green plant groweth, menacing
> Almighty lovers in the spring;
> There is always a forgotten thing,
> And love is not secure.

And Guthrum agrees that in the end all is vanity and all is nothing.

> Do we not know, have we not heard
> The soul is like a lost bird.
> The body a broken shell?

To all this Alfred, who is present in the Danish camp as an unknown harpist, is able to reply that it is the Christian alone who has hope and the Christian alone who is the guardian even of heathen things, of which the White Horse, which he had scoured, is the symbol.

> What have the strong gods given?
> Where have the glad gods led?
> When Guthrum sits on a hero's throne
> And asks if he is dead? . . .
> Ere the sad gods that made your gods
> Saw their sad sunrise pass
> The White Horse of the White Horse Vale,
> That you have left to darken and fail,
> Was cut out of the grass.

> Therefore your end is on you,
> Is on you and your kings.
> Not for a fire in Ely fen,
> Not that your gods are nine or ten
> But because it is only Christian men
> Guard even heathen things.

Life was a mystery. All things go out into mystery, and that equally for pagan and for Christian. But it was the Christian alone with his promise of resurrection who had the key to the mystery. It was he alone who could love this world because it was he alone who could accept it carelessly, as it was meant to be accepted, knowing that one day it was to be lost—accept it as a gift given to him to play with, and not ceaselessly pester it to reveal its secrets.

> The men of the East may spell the stars,
>   And times and triumphs mark,
> But the men signed of the Cross of Christ
>   Go gaily in the dark.

Whether or not Guthrum's acceptance of Christianity after his defeat was either wholly edifying or plausible may be argued. The Church has not been the gainer by drumhead conversions and indeed a conversion with as little evidence of reason behind it as is put into Guthrum's mouth would clearly not in reality have been accepted. It would have been well if Chesterton had made it a little less sudden and a lot more reasoned but the meaning of Guthrum's conversion is obviously to assert that the Church is the natural home for man, in every age accepted, in every age attacked, and that in it alone the heart can rest.

The theme verses of the *Ballad* are the well-known lines of Our Lady, previously quoted, when in a vision she appears to King Alfred before the battle and at a low moment in his fortunes gives to him the message,

> I tell you naught for your comfort,
>   Yea, naught for your desire,
> Save that the sky grows darker yet
>   And the sea rises higher.
>
> Night shall be thrice night over you,
>   And heaven an iron cope.
> Do you have joy without a cause,
>   Yea, faith without a hope?

What does this message mean? There have been those—the

Times' leader-writer for instance—who have sought to interpret it to mean that, though things may be going badly for the moment and will perhaps get even worse, yet, if you endure, you will conquer in the end; but it is hard to see how any such promise can be found in the words. Their meaning is rather that of all false goddesses, the 'bitch-goddess Success', is the most evil; that, although perhaps *après tout c'est un monde passable* and it may be right in gratitude to enjoy the world's pleasures, yet this life contains within itself no promise of beatitude. Indeed it cannot of its nature offer beatitude, since, even if all else goes well, there still remains at the end inevitable death. Therefore this world is of its nature an unfinished place. Chesterton had already quoted with approval from Stevenson in his *Twelve Types*, 'Whatever we are intended to do, we are not intended to succeed.' What could be more empty, vulgar and contemptible than 'the man of mere success', the man who spends his whole life in the desperate struggle to reach the top of the tree, 'god's scorner in despite of righteousness'? Either we must accept this universe as unfinished or accept that there is no hope of beatitude. As Guthrum said,

> And the heart of the locked battle
> Is the happiest place for men,
>   Where shrieking souls as shafts go by
>   And many have died and all may die;
>   Though this word be a mystery,
> Death is most distant then.

This life is but a testing ground for the ultimate reality. Whether it happens to be enjoyable or not is comparatively irrelevant. All that really matters is to acquit ourselves well in it.

Chesterton could of course have cast his tale of the essential conflict of life in any context. There was no reason in itself why the conflict should have been a conflict of physical battle. But with his strange obsession with battles and duels it was perhaps only to be expected that he should have made such a choice. Nor would it have greatly mattered had it not chanced that the *Ballad* appeared on the eve of a world war in which it was so fatally easy to use this

language of a battle between good men and bad men with a belief
that the language corresponded to reality. To Belloc the language
of Christian pacifism was merely absurd:

> Pale Ebenezer thought it wrong to fight,
> But roaring Bill who killed him thought it right.

It never occurred to Belloc that Pale Ebenezer might have thought
it a Christian duty to be killed rather than to kill. Chesterton was a
little less unsophisticated. 'If the whole world were suddenly
stricken with a sense of humour,' he wrote in *Twelve Types*, 'it
would find itself mechanically fulfilling the Sermon on the Mount.'
But unfortunately men were humourless and so must be fought.

9

Gesta Francorum

Nowhere was Chesterton more obediently the disciple of Belloc than in foreign politics. Chesterton, brought up as a Liberal of progressive views, was in his youth an admirer of the French Revolution and thought of France as to be preferred to other Continental countries in that she was democratic. On the other hand like most people in England he was shocked by the manifest miscarriage of justice of the Dreyfus case and wrote a poem—for which he afterwards unnecessarily apologised—expressive of his shock. It was from Belloc that he learnt a much fuller gospel of France. Belloc was born in Paris as the Germans were approaching the city in 1870, and was only just smuggled out to England in time to escape them, and his mind was ever afterwards dominated by the Franco-German antagonism. To his interpretation France was the central fortress both of European and of Christian civilisation. (He did not indeed much distinguish between the two. The Church was to him the continuance of the Roman Empire.) France stood as the eternal defender of Christendom. The alien unroman Prussia was its enemy, continually aggressing against it. Whether this was because he was a Frenchman at heart, or whether because he enjoyed shocking his audiences and his readers, and found the development of an unfamiliar but nevertheless coherent point of view an easy way of administering this shock; whether the line in his poem on Battersea Bridge in which he claimed that he 'had never in my rightful garden lingered' referred to his choice of England before France or whether, as Mr Sheed had claimed, it meant that he had eschewed verse for dogmatic prose—these are as may be.

He also—in his younger days at any rate—was a very strong supporter of the French Revolution. To conservatively-minded Catholics this championship might appear odd in company with the defence of Catholicism. But Belloc never admitted that there was any real conflict between the principles of Catholicism and the principles of the Revolution. The conflicts between them, he argued, were incidental. 'You made the revolution of 1789 without us and against us but for us, God wishing it so in spite of you,' he would have agreed with Bishop Dupanloup. The Revolution, he said one day in the Balliol Senior Common Room, deprived no man of anything that he had a right to possess; nor did he deign to answer a quiet little man in the corner of the room, who murmured 'Heads?' In later years it is true his enthusiasm for the Revolution abated and he came to champion monarchy. 'It needs a king,' he said. But through both periods his thesis remained that France was the true centre of civilisation and that therefore the French cause was at all times to be upheld. He championed Napoleon, 'the most splendid of human swords,' and what he called 'the cause of all the world at Waterloo.' Above all he saw as a supreme catastrophe the defeat of the French by the Prussians in 1870. He grew up in the atmosphere of the French defeat. As a result Prussia was to him always the barbarian. He wrote of the Prussian character, 'It is already half mad. Before long we shall see it run amok. And if we do not kill it, it will kill us. Prussia can no longer think widely; she cannot paint; she cannot write. And now most of what Germany had patiently learnt from the civilised West and South through centuries of industrious pillage, Prussia has got rid of and tarnished in no long interval of time.' Prussia's evil was not only that she had conquered France but also that she had established her domination over the civilised south Germans and Austrians. She was the modern Carthage to be destroyed. It was in these terms that in *Europe and the Faith* Belloc interpreted the First World War and it was fatally easy and unfortunate to see the battle of Alfred and the Danes as a similar battle of Christian defence against barbarian and heathen aggressors.

But, however it may have been with Alfred, it was clear that the view of the world which Chesterton adopted from Belloc was a grossly selective view. There was no need to have any special liking for the Hohenzollern régime or to look for excuses for its violation of Belgian neutrality. But to pretend that over the centuries the story, with Richelieu and Louis XIV and Napoleon as its protagonists, had been an unvarying story of German aggression against France was simply silly. It was the fashion among the Chesterbellocs to pretend that Austria was less guilty than Prussia, that the Catholic South Germans were to be preferred to the Protestant North Germans, and, when Hitler came to power, it was their whim to pretend that he was the puppet of the German General Staff who were the real architects of the policy of revenge. There is no reason why a person should not on balance prefer the French way of life to the German but it cannot be seriously maintained that it could be more than a preference on balance. Nor can it be seriously maintained that the German story was entirely a story of wicked North Germans bullying good Catholic South Germans into following them in wickedness. In July 1914, it was the Austrians who by their intransigence forced Serbia into war. It can be argued that at that time Berlin's policy was a ruthless and foolish policy. It cannot possibly be argued that it was more ruthless and more foolish than that of Vienna. In a confused situation it was in Vienna that the most outspoken advocates of war such as Berchtold and Conrad von Hotzendorf were found. Similarly in more recent times the notion that Hitler was a creature of the German General Staff of course proved wholly false. It was the General Staff who made their admittedly feeble and ineffectual protest and it was Hitler who drove through his reckless policies. It was in South Germany—in Bavaria—that the Nazi creed originated and South Germans of Catholic origin had more than their fair share of the executants of that creed.

Belloc attempted in his *Europe and the Faith* to describe the war as a Catholic battle fought around France. The facts gave the thesis little support. France herself at that time far from being a strongly Catholic country suffered ten years before the most savage anti-clerical legislation and it was impossible for any practising Catholic to hold any post of political importance there. It was the anti-Catholics in Italy who brought Italy over to the Allied side.

The clericals were in general pro-German. In Central Europe Bismarck had indeed conducted the anti-Catholic Kulturkampf immediately after the establishment of the Reich in 1870, but that quarrel had been composed and in all probability there were more Catholics and a larger proportion of them practising in the Central Empires than in the Allied countries.

German Catholics, bishops among them, in the First World War and even—which is somewhat stranger—in the Second World War were found commending the German cause as a cause of the defence of Christendom against Russian barbarism. As Bernard Shaw not unfairly pointed out, an Irishman was not likely to be much moved by contrasts between English freedom and Prussian domination of subject Catholics, and Chesterton who was always a champion of the Irish cause, felt the force of the point. When the war was ended and the frontiers were redrawn, Chesterton wrote how once again 'Ancient laughter walks in gold through the vineyards of Lorraine' but in fact the rights and wrongs and preferences of the people of Alsace-Lorraine—*les sujets allemands du roi français*, as they used to be called—were much more doubtful than the rhetorical verse might choose to pretend. Catholics, where they had any freedom of choice in the matter—in Spain, in Ireland, in Quebec, in South America—were determined to be as little involved in the war as possible. The attempt to make a Catholic war out of it was really absurd.

The war was to Chesterton's mind a chivalric war—only justified if it was such—and of course to be fought in a chivalric way. If the enemy indulged in atrocities, the Allies must not indulge in atrocities in reprisal—and that for deeper and more basically Christian reasons, but also because, doing so, they blunted their power of protest. If the argument was reduced to an argument of who did it first, then, even supposing—which was improbable—that the facts were crystal clear, yet critics would be certain to say, 'If it is only a question of who did it first, then it cannot be so unspeakably bad to do it at all.' Yet, if this be an argument against atrocities, is it not equally an argument against war? Is not war itself the supreme atrocity? Can there be such a thing as a chivalric war? Of course Chesterton—and many others—complained in the sordid days after the war, 'This was not what we fought for. We never intended this.' Of course they did not intend it, but had they any right not to expect it?

The attempt to make a Catholic war out of the war was not only absurd. It was more than absurd. For Belloc's theory of the war was in direct contradiction with that of the Pope of the day, Benedict XV. Benedict's attitude towards the war was one of what he himself called 'apostolic pacifism'. The war, he saw from the first, must certainly bring incomparably more evils than it could remedy. Above all, if the two groups of European powers insisted on fighting one another to a standstill, the consequence would be not the victory of one group or of the other group but the destruction of the European hegemony of the world. It never occurred to Belloc and Chesterton or indeed to many other people that, if the Allies succeeded in their object of getting rid of the Kaiser, they would do so in order to put somebody almost infinitely more evil in his place. Benedict XV had been loud in his denunciation of the monstrous tyranny of conscription. Cecil Chesterton in his *History of the United States* speaks of conscription as a beneficent invention of the French Revolution and thinks of anyone who criticises it as an irresponsible crank. Gilbert Chesterton took at that time much the same line but later in his life, when he came to collect his essays for *The Thing*, he somewhat modified his view. The politicians, he then wrote, 'conscript by violence boys of eighteen, they applaud volunteers of sixteen for saying that they are eighteen, they throw them by thousands into a huge furnace and torture chamber, of which their imaginations can have conceived nothing and from which their honour forbids them to escape; they keep them in these horrors year after year without any knowledge even of the possibility of victory; and kill them like flies by the million before they have begun to live.' What tyranny devised by the Church was to be compared to this appalling tyranny of the State?

It was horrors of this kind that were present to the minds of the great Benedict and of all too few others among his contemporaries. With such policies in mind Benedict did his best to bring the war to an end on a policy of 'no annexations and no indemnities', but he met with no success in his endeavours—indeed, as is so often the fate of mediators, he earned the ill will of both sides. However that may be, although they never attacked Benedict by name, Belloc and Chesterton throughout the war were loud in their denunciation of what they called 'a premature peace'. Their policy was the exact opposite of that of the Pope. Now Belloc's Catholicism was always a robustly unclerical Catholicism. He defended the institution of the Church, as the great bulwark of civilisation. But he judged any individual clerics, Popes or others, entirely on their merits. It was no difficulty to his faith to criticise the political wisdom of a Pope. Benedict was in fact a much wiser man than Belloc, but Belloc thought him a fool. Yet this conviction never in the least bothered him: 'However angry we may at times become with the purely human instruments of a divine dispensation . . .' he wrote of priests. Chesterton would never have written thus. He was by nature a more humble man. Father Ignatius Rice has recorded that after he became a Catholic Chesterton paid what Father Ignatius called an 'almost ridiculous attention to any opinion expressed by a priest. He would carefully weigh their opinions, however fatuous,' he recorded. Chesterton's theology and reading were such that he well knew it was no Catholic teaching that every passing judgement of a Pope was necessarily wise; yet he had grown up in the special atmosphere of the late nineteenth century when, owing to the indignities heaped upon Pius IX, a strong feeling of loyalty induced most Catholics to pay to the words of Popes an absolute attention that would not have been common in previous ages. Growing up in his own liberal family circle, he identified Catholicism with this personal devotion to the Pope—in his earlier years as a suasion against Catholicism—in his later years as a suasion in its favour. By consequence it was beyond question one of the obstacles which delayed him on his path towards the Church that in the years in which he was still hesitating to take the plunge the two Popes who reigned were not men with whom he personally sympathised. He sympathised with Pius X's theoretical condemnation of modernism. The methods enjoined for the suppression of modernism—censorship, proscription, secret vigilance committees—could not be attractive to his liberty-loving temperament. To Benedict XV's pacifism he was equally unsympathetic. It may well be that time has proved that in this respect Benedict was a wiser man than Chesterton even as he was a wiser man than Belloc, but the obstacle must be noted.

There were plenty of other obstacles to be overcome. Ever since the writing of *The Ballad of the White Horse* a reader would have imagined that Chesterton was already intellectually convinced of the Roman case, but it is said that reluctance to pain his parents held him back so long as his father was alive. Many who knew him best could not imagine that he would ever take such a step so long as his wife was not yet ready to accompany him, and she was in the years before his own reception still some way from the Church. Yet whatever the strength of these subsidiary motives it is certainly not without significance that Chesterton did not join the Church while either Pius X or Benedict XV were on the throne but waited for the accession of Pius XI.

Of course it can well be argued that subsequent history has shown that there is an essential unbalance in the German soul which makes a strong Germany inevitably dangerous to the world's peace. If Belloc and Chesterton were wrong in thinking that Hitler was the creature of the German Staff, they were only wrong, it can well be argued, because the state of Germany was incomparably worse than they had imagined. Hitler was not the creature of the General Staff but something incomparably worse, incomparably more wicked, than the General Staff—something so inconceivably wicked that even critics of the Germans like Belloc and Chesterton failed to imagine it; and even today, at the moment of writing in 1969, while the battle is by no means lost, who can be free of anxiety about the forces of violence and tyranny that seem again to be abroad in Germany? The simplistic Wilsonian faith that problems of the soul could be easily solved simply by giving everybody a vote and telling him that his country was a democracy has indeed proved itself a wry folly, and the machinery of parliamentarianism has now run into difficulties in every country—even in Britain. In pinpointing its weaknesses Belloc and Cecil Chesterton proved themselves wise prophets and the machinery has of course proved as brittle in France as in Germany. But, their friends may argue, is not the proof of France's superiority to Germany demonstrated by looking to what has happened in the two countries when democracy collapses? Whatever may be said of de Gaulle, his bitterest critics cannot assert that he is to be compared to Hitler. Comparing the two, one can fairly say that their careers show that there is an essential final sanity in the French soul and an essential final madness in the German soul. But even if it was true that there was this ultimate madness in the German soul, surely it was not a wise policy to carry the First War to its bitter conclusion and to destroy the German monarchies. Unattractive and ridiculous as in many ways they were, the monarchies did at least preserve some relic of tradition which was a certain bulwark against the sheer madness that took its place. Our war aim should have been to preserve the German monarchies—not to destroy them. The world of kings was much more nearly a world safe for democracy than was the world of dictators. The Kaiser's Government was not a very lovely government but it was a great deal better than that which the world got under Hitler.

Chesterton was born in 1874. He was therefore just over forty when the World War broke out. Many men of that age found their way into the army and Chesterton with his love of battles and his devotion to the particular cause to which Britain was then dedicated would, we may be sure, have done the same had it been possible. It is true that with his untidiness and inconsequence he would have made an almost unbelievably bad soldier, but with his humility it would never have occurred to him to allow incompetence to deter him from his duty. But, as it happened, he had not only forty years but also bad health, and military service was out of the question. Indeed in the first months of the war he had a very serious illness from which for a time it looked likely that he would die. He had of necessity throughout the war to be content to fight the Kaiser with his pen. He published in 1915 *The Crimes of England* and, in a composite book called *The Appetite of Tyranny*, essays on *The Barbarism of Berlin* and *Letters to an Old Garibaldian*. *The Crimes of England* was written in order to show that an Englishman was not blind to the faults of his own country—that he was aware that Englishmen had sinned but that the English, unlike the

Germans, had at least repented of their sins. The broad purpose was admirable but in execution the book was deprived of its value by its selectiveness. It turned out that the sins of England consisted of little other than that over so many centuries she had fought the French and in the course of fighting the French had not infrequently been allied with the Prussians. Repentance meant little more than that she had at last made alliance with the French. Frederick the Great, Chesterton said, 'hated everything German and everything good.' In contrast the petty German principalities had 'preserved the good things that go with small interests and strict boundaries, music, etiquette, a dreamy philosophy and so on.' Frederick the Great was certainly no very lovable man but one would not have guessed from such sentences that he had given hospitality to the Jesuits at a time when they had been expelled from every Catholic country in Europe. Chesterton pointed—fairly enough—to the German invasion of Belgium and contrasted it with the British refusal to invade Holland. 'Whether they say that we wished to do it in our greed or feared to do it in our cowardice the fact remains that we did not do it.' Chesterton was justified in condemning the German invasion of Belgium but it could hardly be maintained that such violence of neutral countries was unique to Germans. Shortly after his book was published the Allies landed in Salonika.

Chesterton also in these years published his *Short History of England*. It is a jolly, high-spirited book in which he prided himself that no single date was included. But again it is Bellocian and selective history. That is to say, it justly corrects the Whig and Victorian history in whose eyes nineteenth-century stability was the solid, final achievement of man and all that leads up to it automatically to be praised. He justly insists, as against the Macaulay-esque paean in praise of progress, on the price that was paid for the industrial revolution in the uprooting and degradation of the poor, and condemns the Victorians for the blind eye which they turned on this great evil. He finds Nelson his great hero, a little strangely—for there appears here no great connection with his general philosophy—and ends with a fine rhetorical panegyric about England's entry into the war: 'The day came and the ignorant fellow found he had other things to learn. And he was quicker than his educated countrymen for he had nothing to unlearn. He in whose honour all had been said and sung, stirred and stepped across the border of Belgium. Then were spread out before men's eyes all the beauties of his culture and all the benefits of his organisation; then we beheld under a lifting daybreak what light we had followed and after what image we had laboured to refashion ourselves. Nor in any story of mankind has the irony of God chosen the foolish things so catastrophically to confound the wise. For the common crowd of poor and ignorant Englishmen because they only knew that they were Englishmen, burst through the filthy cobwebs of four hundred years and stood where their fathers stood when they knew that they were Christian men. The English poor, broken in every revolt, bullied by every fashion, long despoiled of property and now being despoiled of liberty, entered history with a noise of trumpets and turned themselves in two years into one of the iron armies of the world. And when the critic of politics and literature, feeling that this war is after all heroic, looks around him to find the hero, he can point to nothing but a mob.'

Things may not have worked out quite like that but this is splendid writing. On the other hand Chesterton derives Christian society from the conversion of Constantine and betrays no doubt that it was a good thing that the Church unhesitatingly requested the support of the State, but there is no saying of Christ that even indicates that such a relation is conceivable. The Christians are always in the Gospel bidden to take it for granted that they will be a minority and to be concerned if they do not find themselves a persecuted minority. He criticises Britain for fighting against the French Revolutionary armies and Napoleon and for enlisting German allies to help her to do so. He puts his point in the curious terms, 'We purposely fed and pampered the power which was destined in the future to devour Belgium as France would never have devoured it.' As if the armies of the French Revolutionaries and Napoleon had so religiously respected the frontiers of Belgium! In a manner strange for one who had so recently been praising Alfred, he assigns the credit for the building of England almost

167

exclusively to the Normans. He links closely together the destruction of the monasteries and the overthrow of Catholicism with the rise of capitalism, but his identification there suggested is much closer than any that the facts justify. When we come to modern times the familiar story of Prussia as the devil is repeated.

10

The Irish Question and
Father Brown

Though Gilbert Chesterton was not able to join the army in World War I, his brother, Cecil, six years his junior, could become a soldier and died in hospital a few days after the Armistice. This loss, a tragedy in itself, had its very great influence on Gilbert Chesterton's life. Gilbert Chesterton was essentially a man of ideas. Cecil Chesterton was a political journalist. Cecil Chesterton had produced his weekly journal, *The Eye Witness*, and after his death Gilbert felt it a point of honour to continue the paper, which he did under various names such as *The New Witness* and finally *G.K.'s Weekly*. It was dedicated to the tasks to which Cecil had given himself—to the exposure of the political corruption and the sham of the party system and to the preaching of the doctines of distributism. The complaint was made that the issue of distributism and the issue of parliamentary government were distinct from one another and that it was a mistake to run them together in the same paper. There was some force in this complaint, but our concern here is with Gilbert Chesterton. Chesterton was of course well qualified to write on the principles of distributism, though he had little conception how to draw up a detailed programme or to set about doing things. As for parliamentary corruption, there remained with him the great memory of the Marconi case. But since then he had gone to live quietly in Beaconsfield. He did not mix with politicians or in political circles. He simply did not know what was going on, nor, since the paper had no financial standing, was it in any position to employ people in London to find out facts for it. Its pages came to be increasingly a repetition of stale old

jokes about the Marconi case, which, to a generation that had
grown up since the war, seemed all a very long time ago. In any
event Gilbert Chesterton had none of the gifts of an editor. The
effect of his assumption of this debt of honour was that for the
remainder of his life he had to live under strain. Many people—
and above all his wife—regretted that he could not let the paper
die, and it cannot be denied that he expended energy which he
could ill spare on tasks for which he was not especially suited.

One incidental consequence of his obsession with the paper and
his weekly article for it was that he wrote very few private letters.
All letters of business were answered by his wife or his secretary,
Miss Collins. He made no attempt to deal with them. Nor, as he
once told me, did he attempt to deal with private letters about
matters of general opinion. He said so completely everything that
he had to say on such topics in his many articles that he saw no
point in writing it all over again in answer to a private correspon-
dent. There are as a result a few letters of intimate concerns of the
soul to Maurice Baring and Ronald Knox, written at the time of his
conversion, but very little else in the way of private correspondence.

Coincidentally with his history of England Chesterton wrote a
book about Ireland—*Irish Impressions*. It is now out of print and,
since it is entirely concerned with the ephemeral problems of that
time, it would today be of little interest. Yet it has its importance
in the story of Chesterton's mind. Chesterton, as has been said, was
always the champion of the small unit against the great—of the
Boers against Chamberlain's imperialism, of Notting Hill against
gigantic London. The first small nation whom he was able to
champion were the Boers; but it was clear enough that, while the
Boers perhaps deserved to be free, they were not a people with
whom, except in their desire for freedom, Chesterton had any
special sympathy, as his opinions subsequently developed. Quite
apart from their treatment of the blacks—an aspect of their life
that he never seemed especially to grasp—they were Calvinists,
standing quite without traditions and outside the general stream of
European culture. No Boer would ever have been at home in
Alfred's armies. They would not have understood what the battle

was about. Among small nations, on the other hand, it was the Irish who especially appealed to him. They in every way engaged his sympathies. They were a small nation, rightly struggling to be free, and one which had bravely defied the monster of mere bigness which was the imperialistic fashion of the age. They alone understood the absurdity of Cecil Rhodes. Beyond that, they were Catholics. They had revolted against an evil landlord system and Chesterton's greatest friend among politicians, George Wyndham, had established among them a distributist land system of peasant proprietors. Hard-headed practical men—as they fancied themselves—were impatient with what seemed to them the extravagances of Irish nationalism, such as that of writing up the street names in Gaelic. Chesterton strongly approved of this. It was natural enough that Michael Collins, the great Irish leader, when looking for a book that could be the inspiration of his philosophy, should find it not in any Irish patriot's purple passages but in Chesterton's *The Napoleon of Notting Hill*. I was surprised a few years ago, when invited to lecture in Cork, Michael Collins' own home town, to be told, when I offered Chesterton as my subject, that there was little interest there in Chesterton because he was so English an author.

He had never visited Ireland before 1914. In those pre-war years, though English politics were so greatly dominated by Irish issues, many of the Englishmen who most interested themselves in the Irish question very rarely visited Ireland. Gladstone never went there, and Asquith but once. With the communications of those days, the visit was a difficult one, and the Irish politicians could be met at Westminster. Chesterton himself was keenly interested, indeed almost obsessed, by Irish issues—as long ago as *Orthodoxy* he had hailed the Irish as the most essentially Christian nation in the world and in *The Flying Inn* the Fenian Patrick Dalroy was his hero—and yet there was nothing odd in his delaying his visit to the country. It was not until after the war, and when he was still not yet a Catholic, that he went there, anxious to see for himself what he could see about the post-war Sinn Fein troubles.

In all the years before the 1914 War, when Irish Home Rule was the main issue of British politics, Chesterton as a loyal Liberal, and a supporter of Gladstone like the rest of his family, was of course an unquestioning Home Ruler. It was a paradox of the politics of those years that while in Ireland itself opinion was divided broadly —though not absolutely—along denominational lines, the Catholics being Nationalists and the Protestants Unionists, in Britain the Nonconformist vote went to the Liberals and to Home Rule, and among the Old English Catholics—such as there were—many were Unionists and opposed to the Irish. At the great Orange gathering at Blenheim the Duke of Norfolk presented Sir Edward Carson with a golden sword. The English Catholics felt that they had but recently obtained their political emancipation and that the Irish were wantonly endangering this freedom by preaching treason to the Crown. In such an atmosphere it was, by an odd accident, the very fact that Chesterton's upbringing was not a Catholic upbringing which made it easier for him to champion the Catholic cause.

So in these years before becoming a Catholic, he was a Home Ruler. The hero of *The Flying Inn*, Dalroy, was a Fenian who had been dismissed from the navy for his Irish nationalism. Chesterton's only complaint against the Redmondite Irish Nationalist members of those years was that their two representatives on the Marconi commission had sided with the Liberals in white-washing Lloyd George and Rufus Isaacs. They did this not because they were convinced by the evidence but because they had a political pact with the Liberals by which they would support the Liberals on other matters in return for the Liberal introduction of a Home Rule bill. Chesterton, in post-Marconi mood of bitterness against the Liberal politicians, prophesied that no good would come to the Nationalists out of this trafficking and that the Liberal politicians would find a way to break their word. He interpreted—probably not justly—the threats of Carson and his army as a piece of manufactured play-acting to give the Liberals an excuse to get out of their promise. The fears of the Orangemen about what would happen to them under Rome and Dublin rule seemed to him too absurd to warrant belief.

The folk that live in black Belfast, their heart is in their mouth;
They see us making murders in the meadows of the south.

They think a plough's a rack, they do, and cattle calls are creeds,
And they think we're burning witches when we're only burning
    weeds.

sang Patrick Dalroy in, *Wine, Water and Song*. The fears were
doubtless absurd. Indeed experience has shown them to be so. But
that did not necessarily mean that they were not sincere, and he
doubtless underestimated the strength of the genuine anti-
Catholic passion of many Ulster Protestants.

In any event Chesterton without, I think, anywhere exactly
defining what should be done about the indisputably Unionist
areas of Northern Ireland, was, and remained to the end, a fervent
supporter of Irish Home Rule. When the war came and Redmond
gave it his support, and Sir Edward Grey said that Ireland was 'the
one bright spot on the horizon', he rejoiced. He praised in an essay
afterwards reprinted in *The Uses of Diversity* 'the brilliant instinct
by which the Irish leader cast into the scale of a free Europe
the ancient sword of Ireland'. As a result, he was very rightly
bitterly critical of the follies of War Office policy by which Lord
Kitchener refused to allow the Nationalist volunteers to serve
under their own colours while granting such a privilege to the
Orangemen.

In this and in so many other ways Redmond's task of raising re-
cruits was made impossibly difficult. Chesterton's view was that
there was no reason at all why Irishmen should fight in England's
war but that Ireland had been the friend of France and the enemy
of Prussia long before England was either and that a war for the
freedom of small nations was essentially an Irish war. It was as such
that Ireland should join in it and as a result of their intervention
England should accept the obligation in honour to grant Ireland
her freedom. But the trouble about this argument was that it was
again based on a very selective view of history. It was not true that
historically Ireland was the enemy of Prussia. They moved in
different worlds and their paths had not crossed. It was not true
that Ireland was in any particular sense the friend of France. If at
various times in her history she had appealed—usually without
much success—for French assistance, that was merely because

France was at that time the enemy of England, who was her enemy. If it was possible to take the line—which of course Chesterton did take—that Prussia was the devil, then it was reasonable to ask the Irish for the time being to forget their local grievance and to join in the great war for the defence of Christian civilisation; but if, as the more realistic and less romantic Irishmen believed, all imperialisms were much of a muchness and all evil, then it was reasonable, without any illusions about Germans, to say nevertheless that Ireland must concentrate on the imperialism by which she was menaced and act on the old maxim that 'England's necessity was Ireland's opportunity.'

It was indeed certainly true that at the time of 1916 Easter Week only a small minority of the Irish people favoured the Sinn Fein rebellion. But it was equally untrue that a majority still supported Redmond's recruiting campaign. The majority probably agreed with the Pope that the policies of all the great Powers were so far from being Christian policies, that the immediate evil of the war was so great, and the benefits promised as its outcome so uncertain, that the wisest policy was to bring it to an end; or, if one was not in a position to do that, to remain neutral. After 1916, Ireland would in any event have relapsed into neutrality. The folly of British policy, which first minimised the dimensions of the rebellion and then shocked the world by the executions which it imposed after its suppression, almost compelled Irish opinion to rally to the Republican cause.

At the outbreak of the war the English had put the Home Rule bill on to the statute book but postponed its application until the war was over. English opinion seemed to think that this was the most that they could do and that the Irish should be satisfied with it; and indeed, granted the need to avoid party quarrels in face of the war, and granted that the Conservatives were opposed to Home Rule, it is not very easy to see how the Liberal Government could have done more without destroying national unity. Nor did many people at that time think that the war would go on for years and that postponement would therefore be so serious a matter. Yet the Irish had from the first some reason to be sceptical of English promises. Even supposing for the sake of argument that they had reason to trust the Liberals—a fairly large assumption in view of the record—what reason was there to think that the Liberals would be in power when the war ended? There would then certainly be an election and it was all too probable—as indeed happened—that Ireland's enemies, the Conservatives, would gain a majority at that election. The British talked a good deal about breaking up the German and the Austrian Empires and the formula of self-determination was to be liberally employed in order to justify their destruction; but the British had as yet given little sign of applying that formula anywhere against themselves or in any way envisaging the break-up of their own Empire.

They that draw the sword perish by the sword, and the consequence of Sinn Fein attacks on British soldiers and policemen after the war was not so much that a few supporters of the failing British Government were immediately killed as that, once the Treaty was signed, Ireland could only return to peace after a bitter and hateful civil war in which Irishmen recklessly shed the blood of Irishmen. Over the whole business Irishmen shed incomparably more Irish than English blood.

The consequences of the successful Irish guerrilla resistance to the British have been enormous and world-wide. Again and again—with Grattan and the Irish Parliament, with O'Connell and Catholic Emancipation, with Parnell and the Land League, with Carson and the Ulster Volunteers—it had been proved that England would make no concession to any Irish demands when they were advanced by reason, but conceded them at once when they were advanced by force; and, that being so, there was plausibility in the Republican contention that the English would cheat Redmond once again at Westminster and that Ireland would be able to win her freedom only by demanding it with violence. They indeed were proved correct, at any rate in their second contention. Bitter experience over the years had proved that for an untrained peasant rabble to challenge a regular army in pitch battle was to invite defeat and suicide; but a guerrilla force of men who had the support of the population and who, when their exploits were accomplished, could fade back again into the civilian background, was almost impossible to defeat so long as it was fanatical in its devotion to its cause and so long as the imperialist power was not prepared to employ methods of utterly ruthless extermination, as the British for all the horrors of their reprisals were not prepared to do. A public opinion in Britain and the world was aroused which left the British Government with no alternative but to make a treaty. Those on the Irish side who accepted the treaty were in faith as Republican as their opponents. Their argument was that once an Irish Government was established its precise powers were comparatively immaterial. In the course of time it would certainly be able to annex to itself additional powers. It was perhaps folly on the British part to insist on the verbal formulae of oaths of allegiance to the King. It was even greater folly on the part of the Irish Republicans to plunge their country into civil war on account of these formulae. In fact experience was to prove that the Fianna Fail had no chance of winning so long as they continued fighting but were able to gain a majority as soon as they ceased to fight for it. But the effects of the Irish action were of importance far beyond the boundaries of Ireland.

The Irish through their guerrilla tactics had discovered a method by which a small nation could effectively defy an imperial power and in the crumbling revolt against imperialism those tactics were employed all over the world in country after country—in Israel, in Vietnam, in Indonesia, in Algeria—and were to an enormous extent responsible for the destruction all over the world of the whole imperialist system. Whether this fragmentation of the world was on balance a good thing or a bad, or whether it is not perhaps rather the truth that it was merely inevitable, who shall say? But certainly the Irish part in bringing it about was enormous. Chesterton's responsibility for it—with which alone we are here concerned —was obviously not direct. His friendships were with the Irish parliamentary Nationalists—in particular with the member for Donegal, Hugh Law, an old Rugbeian, a convert to Catholicism from the Church of England, a wise and cultured man but a man very unlike the prophets of the Gaelic revival who were clamouring at that time to speak for Ireland. Nevertheless his irresponsible talk about the glamour of war and the blaring of the barricades had, as we have seen with Michael Collins, its effect in blinding young men to the horrors that they were unleashing when once they made their first appeal to violence. Yeats was troubled in his conscience at the thought that his writings might have had their effect in causing young men to have gone out to battle. 'A terrible beauty was born' he said of Easter Week, but at the same time wondered

> What if words of mine sent out
> Certain men the English shot?

Similarly Chesterton, when he read of Michael Collins, could not but wonder whether words of his had not to some extent sent out certain Irishmen whom other Irishmen shot. At least the verdict of my friends of Cork that Chesterton was too English a writer for Irishmen to hear about was a very curious one.

The years of the Irish civil war were naturally sad years for Chesterton and, when at last the shooting ceased, he reasonably felt himself under no obligation to take a side between one Irish party and another. It was enough that Ireland was now ruled by Irishmen. He wrote from time to time in his passing articles about Ireland and always lovingly. The only other book that he wrote about it was at the time of the Eucharistic Congress in Dublin in 1932 which he visited, and of which he wrote that he 'felt something disproportionate in finding one's own trivial trade amid the far-reaching revelation of such a trysting place of all the tribes of men.' (Whatever other gallicisms they might adopt, neither Belloc nor Chesterton ever had anything but contempt for the French habit of exaggerated worship of the literary maître. It seemed to both of them absurd.) In that book he was not concerned with specially Irish affairs and still less with Irish party politics. He saw Dublin as the capital of the world, to which men from all nations had flocked. 'This,' he wrote, 'is the real League of Nations.' He argued that there could be no real unity which was not based on dogma. Absolutely he might be right. It may be that it would be better for all the world if all men could be united in their accept-ance of Catholic authority—although even then history gives us little reason to think that Catholics would not still continue to fight with one another. But the trouble with such a judgement is that it

avoids the real difficulty. The fact is that men are not united in
dogma, whether they should be or not. The problem is how to bring
peace to a disunited world. Recent Popes—John XXIII and Paul VI
—have both bidden Catholics accept the fact of disunion as a
political fact and to work with vigour within a United Nations that
contains men of all faiths. In comparison they have surely shown
themselves wiser than Chesterton with his mere acceptance of the
fact of conflict.

The truth is that both Chesterton and the more extreme Irish
Nationalists were too narrow in their conception of Irish nationalism. The Irish were of course right to demand Home Rule for
Ireland. They were perhaps right to demand their own language—
or at least to demand to choose for themselves whether they kept
their own language. But the Irish did not live only in Ireland.
Compare the population of Ireland with the population of England
and England was clearly the predominant partner. But look out
over the new countries of the world and there was much more
nearly an equality between the two races. The Irish were one of the
great world races, like the Jews in Diaspora throughout the Catholic
world. It was odd that Belloc should complain that the loyalty of
Jews was to their Jewish nation and that they could not truly have
a double loyalty, being loyal also to the country of their residence,
for the Irish and the English were the two races who, in their exiles
over the world, most notoriously preserved for themselves this
double loyalty. If it was true that the Dublin Eucharistic Congress
was the real League of Nations, it was because Catholics from every
nation could feel at home in Dublin in a way that they would not
have been able to feel in any other city—even in Rome. The facts
are, whether we like them or not, that the twentieth century has
seen in religious and secular affairs an increase of the relative
importance of the New World as against Europe, and that the
predominant force in the New World's Catholicism has been Irish.
There are perhaps advantages and disadvantages in that. It can be
argued that there is a twist of Jansenism in Irish Catholicism—that
it is often neither aesthetic nor intellectual—but at least it is true
that, whereas the nineteenth-century Continental tradition demanded a close connection of Church and State through Con-

cordats and an alliance of Throne and Altar and was not favourable to dissent, Ireland, alone of European countries, had through the obvious fact that the Established Church there was not the Catholic Church but the strongly anti-Catholic Protestant Church, no tradition of looking to the State for support. The pluralistic countries of the New World were willing to tolerate equality but would never have tolerated a Catholicism which demanded privileges. It was the great fortune of the Church that it was there represented predominantly by Irish Catholics who had no tradition of privilege. But it was a strange blindness in Chesterton that he never found anything to admire in Australia, which was of all countries that in which his principles were most attended to.

Of all Chesterton's books those that have had the widest circulation have been his Father Brown stories, and some would say that by an odd paradox his most popular have also been his least important books. In so far as we are seeking to discover Chesterton's opinions that is obviously in a manner true. There is no pretence to any detailed lesson in the Father Brown stories. They were confessedly thrown off as an amusement. The criticism of basic improbability that can be made against all stories about private detectives can be made against them. In real life we never run across these extraordinary crimes or at the most once in a lifetime. Yet every time that Lord Peter Wimsey motors into a quiet English village he finds that a murder has just been committed there, and in the same way every time that he happens to drop in at a party Father Brown finds there a murder or a robbery. Nor is it in the least clear as a general rule why Father Brown is frequenting all these exotic parties. For a quiet Essex priest—as he is sometimes described— his parochial duties seem to sit very lightly on him. Nor is Chesterton at all careful here any more than elsewhere to collate his details. Father Brown is sometimes a priest in Clerkenwell and sometimes in Essex. His church is, it seems, dedicated to Saint Dominic, but he is not a Dominican. The detective story, to hold the reader's attention, has to have a surprising solution. In real life crimes are more often than not committed by the person who from the first looked the most probable perpetrator. Not so in the detective story, and in Chesterton's stories both the crime and the solution are almost always of a bizarre complexity that quite challenges probability. In the more conventional story the writer is only concerned to set and to solve a problem. It is essential that he surprise the reader. Therefore the criminal must always be one who at the beginning of the story appears least likely to have committed the crime. To achieve this purpose many detective writers defy psychological probability. They fix the crime on a person whom in real life we would know to be incapable of crime. Chesterton never allows Father Brown to do that. Father Brown always eliminates suspects by the psychological impossibility that a man of such a sort would do such a deed.

Still, it would be quite beyond the terms of reference of this book to analyse the plots of the Father Brown stories. But there is one point about them that it is pertinent to notice. The first of these stories, *The Innocence of Father Brown*, appeared in 1911—long before Chesterton had come to any personal crisis in his relations with the Church of Rome. *The Wisdom of Father Brown* appeared in 1914—just before the war. Then the war brought a long gap until *The Incredulity of Father Brown* and *The Secret of Father Brown* which appeared in 1926 and 1927, long after his reception into the Church. The last of these books, *The Scandal of Father Brown*, which appeared not long before his death, is quite frankly little more than potboiling. The character of Father Brown develops with the development of Chesterton's own spiritual nature. The first Father Brown of *The Innocence* is little more than a priest who happens to be able to resolve problems. As we have recorded, the notion of creating a priest-detective was suggested to Chesterton by his discovery that Monsignor O'Connor knew through the confessional so very much more about the secrets of the soul than the simple young Cambridge undergraduates who thought of him as a man innocent of the world. From that Chesterton derived the notion of creating a man apparently innocent of the world, in fact far more astute in it than the children of this world. But that is really all that there is in *The Innocence of Father Brown*. Father Brown is simply a man who solves problems. But he is not yet a man who not only absolves sins by the mechanical action of hearing Confessions and pronouncing the words of absolution but who enters into communion with the sinner by sharing his sin and his suffering.

In the later books Father Brown is much more than a mere detective. In such stories as *The Strange Crime of John Boulnois* in *The Wisdom of Father Brown* or *The Oracle of the Dog* in *The Incredulity* he solves the problem entirely by his psychological interpretation of the characters. (Whether either the psychology or the characters are wholly credible is a matter of opinion.) It is a weakness, I think, of the Father Brown stories that Chesterton gives us a good deal of description of the scene and furniture but he does not of himself very clearly describe his characters. Their peculiarities are left to Father Brown's description and, on account of these peculiarities, are either dismissed from or condemned of the crime. This makes things perhaps a little too easy for Father Brown. He is judge as well as prosecutor. One cannot help sometimes wishing that he might for once be wrong. In *The Arrow of Heaven* Father Brown turns himself in the last paragraphs from detective into prophet and denounces the American family which had been anxious to expose the criminal when they thought that he was a man of no consequence and then became much more anxious to conceal him when they found that he was a rich man and a member of their own family. In *The Dagger with Wings* in *The Incredulity of Father Brown*, Father Brown is made to denounce persons who dabble in a language of bogus spirituality and to say that all murderers who make any pretence of intellectual capacity are always of that kind. One wonders how many murderers of whom Chesterton had heard were really of that kind or how far he was merely taking an opportunity to tilt at people against whom he had a prejudice, or how far perhaps he wantonly imputed this prejudice to Father Brown in order that he might have more interesting subjects on which to work. Writers of detective stories have to make their murderers more interesting than the murderer of reality, to save their stories from intolerable boredom.

There is another lesson to be learnt from the Father Brown stories. Chesterton so often told us that he became a Catholic in order to be absolved of his sins. We take his word for it, but, as

Evelyn Waugh said of him in his *Life of Ronald Knox*, we cannot quite guess what were the sins of which this man 'so plainly innocent' can have been guilty. We have his own word for it that he was never guilty in his youth of any of the common sins of the flesh. But it seems with his vivid imagination he did during his time at the Slade School give himself to an imagination of pictures so horrible that to his sensitive conscience at any rate the entertainment of them seemed a sin. Some of the crimes described in *The Innocence of Father Brown*—for instance, Valentine's attachment of a wrong head to the body of the man whom he had murdered in *The Secret Garden*—are so horrible and obscene that if we forget for the moment that this is a mere conundrum set for our solution and think of it as a picture of real life, it is impossible not to shudder a little at the mind that can have composed such a picture. In that story Valentine, the atheist French detective, kills at a party in his own garden an American philanthropist who is suspected of an intention of becoming a Catholic. Valentine cuts off his victim's head but hides it outside his garden. He substitutes by the side of the American's body a head of a murderer who had been guillotined that morning. One might question the probability of the story—the probability that a man generally thought sane, and who indeed in the previous story had hailed Father Brown as his master, should have been so filled with hatred that he would murder a man simply because of his intention to become a Catholic. And why did he do it in the middle of a large party, and why was Father Brown at that party? But such improbabilities are in the inevitable nature of the detective story. The technique of the story requires that the murder be always committed by the person whom one would not naturally suspect. But the problem that the story really raises is not so much: 'What sort of guilty man would have committed so revolting a crime?' as: 'What sort of innocent man would have imagined it?'

Only a streak of strange morbidity could ever have invented such an atrocity, and I do not think that the post-war, converted Chesterton of the later Father Brown stories would ever have allowed his imagination even to dwell on things so horrible. But *The Secret Garden* shows the horrors to which he was tempted.

The psychologists have brought in a new vocabulary in which to discuss the perversions of the soul and there are some moderns who imagine that the men of earlier generations, because they did not know the vocabulary, therefore did not know the perversions. I cannot think that a reader of *Barnaby Rudge* can doubt that Dickens knew all about them when he created Dennis, the hangman, in that book, or that the reader of *Porphyria's Lover* can think that there was much that Browning did not know about them. So Chesterton, innocent doubtless in act, was not at all innocent in the sense of ignorant in mind. He only appears to the modern reader to be so because he belonged to a generation before the jargon. Were temptations of this sort the temptations to which Chesterton was prone in youth, to which he was not quite impervious even at the time that he began his Father Brown stories, and from which he required the strong authority of the Church to protect him in later years?

11

The Raising of Lazarus

The first journey that Chesterton made when the war was over
was to Palestine and the book that he wrote as a result of it was
The New Jerusalem. We have already spoken about it in our discus-
sion of Chesterton's opinions about the Jews, quoting what he said
about Zionism. The Zionist experiment was of interest to him but
it was naturally only of secondary interest. He understood and
respected the Jews' belief that Palestine is to a Jew the Promised
Land and that he cannot be fully at home until he can celebrate
Seder 'next year in Jerusalem'. But naturally to him the land was a
Holy Land not primarily because it was the Land of the Promise
but because it was the land of fulfilment—the land of Christ—and
the great battle of history there had not been a battle in which the
Jews played any part on the one side or the other, but the battle
between Christian and Moslem. Towards the Holy Places his attitude was essentially that of a Crusader. It is a sad irony to those
who read today the culminating argument in his view, written after
the First World War: Palestine was a land of divine destiny because
it had at last—and, as he thought, finally—after all its troubles
returned to Christian rule. He did not advert much to Belloc's
point that the Zionist experiment could only succeed if Jews had
the duty of defending themselves. Palestine was indeed in a way a
land sacred to all three religions—the Christian, the Jewish and the
Moslem—but that very phrase concealed as much truth as it
revealed. To the Jew and the Christian the essential events of their
religion took place in Palestine. To the Moslem Jerusalem was
indeed the third Holy City. It was from Jerusalem that Mahomet
ascended up to heaven. Yet the central events of the Moslem

religion did not take place in Palestine. Indeed it was arguable that Jerusalem was only elevated to the rank of Islam's third Holy City because the Abassid Caliphs wanted for economic reasons to divert the pilgrim traffic from Mecca, which was outside their dominions, to Jerusalem, which was within them. Yet in fact Jerusalem had been under Moslem rule a great deal longer than it had been under the rule of either Jew or Christian.

There was in Chesterton's belief an inevitable warfare between Christian and Moslem. It was thus that he saw the wars of the Crusades—neglecting subsidiary modifications, such as quarrels among Christians, acts of friendship between Christians and Moslems, or economic motives. It was thus that he saw the battle of Lepanto:

> Don John pounding from the slaughter–painted poop,
> Purpling all the ocean like a bloody pirate's sloop.

He condemned Victorian statesmen such as Palmerston, and after him the Conservatives, who bolstered up the Turkish Empire through their greater fear of Russia. He spoke with a sneer of those Armenian lands where

> the Tory name is blessed
> Since they hailed the cross of Dizzy
> On the banners of the West.

When the Balkan wars came immediately before the Great War, he saluted the Montenegrins who had begun it by their defiance of the Turks.

> What will there be to remember
> Of us in the days to be,
> Whose faith was a trodden ember
> And even our doubts not free?
> Though the crooked swords overcome it
> And the Crooked Moon ride free
> When the mountain comes to Mahomet
> It has more life than he—

and, to take a more ridiculous example, it was as we have said a Turkish army which was supposed to be invading England in *The Flying Inn*.

In typical Chestertonian fashion he paid to the Turks the salute that was due to an honourable opponent:

> Warrior by warriors smitten,
> Gambler whose luck has turned,

he wrote of the Turks in the day of their defeat, and contrasted their fidelity to a false faith with the infidelity to a true faith, with which so much of Christendom was filled.

> Because our sorrow has sufficed
> And what he knew we know;
> And because you were great, Lord Antichrist,
> In the name of Christ you go.
> But you shall not turn your turban
> For the little dogs that yell
> When a man rides out of a city;
> In the name of God farewell.

Among the complexities of the situation I do not know that Chesterton in the years before the war took it in that, though Palestine was inhabited by Moslems and ruled by Moslems, yet its Arab inhabitants were in bitter rebellion against its Turkish rulers. He always speaks of Turks and Moslems as if they were almost interchangeable terms. In any event the important story of the war was not to him, as to T. E. Lawrence, that the Arabs were promised their freedom from the Turks, nor, as to Balfour and the Zionists, that the Jews were offered their national home in Palestine. It was that the Christian General Allenby, at the head of a Christian army, entered Jerusalem on foot and established there once more after so many years a Christian government. Chesterton was without ill will either to Jew or Arab but the Palestine which he visited was a Palestine whose mandate had been given to Britain. His only regret was that the British Government should have appointed as High

Commissioner the Jewish Herbert Samuel. Chesterton had a personal bias against Samuel because of his involvement in the Marconi case. This was unjust. Whatever might be said about the Isaacs', there was no dishonour in Samuel's conduct in that case, nor did Samuel in Palestine act in any way other than one of complete justice as between Arab and Jew. He was impartiality itself. But in Chesterton's mind it was a Christian ruler who should rule in Jerusalem, and indeed, quite apart from Samuel's personal character, it was most arguable that there were at least two logical absurdities in his appointment. If the British Government had committed itself to Zionism—to the proposition that Palestine was the proper home of the Jew—it was somewhat absurd to put in charge of the policy a Jew who quite clearly preferred to live in England. If the difficult duty of the British mandate was to hold the balance between Jew and Arab then clearly at the head of it should have been a man who was neither a Jew nor an Arab.

It was not for its passing political problems that Jerusalem was mainly of interest to Chesterton or of importance in his life. What mattered to him was to feel that he stood on the sites where Christ had stood two thousand years before. He was not especially interested in the nice problems of archaeology—in deciding whether precise identifications were correct, whether the historical Via Dolorosa ran exactly along the present lines. It was moving to him to find, as he did happen to find, that snow was actually falling in Bethlehem on Christmas night.

> We have grown wiser and lost not wonder
> And we have seen Jerusalem

he wrote in his poem of dedication to his wife.

The things that he found in Palestine were not only pleasant and exciting things. Palestine was not only the land where Christ had lived and taught. It was also the land where He had wrestled with the devil. He found evil there. It was at Sodom, it seems, that Chesterton was finally converted. 'It is here,' he wrote, 'that tradition has laid the tragedy of the mighty perversion of the imagination of man; the monstrous birth and death of abominable things.

I say such things in no mood of spiritual pride; such things are hideous not because they are distant but because they are near to us; in all our brains, certainly in mine, were buried things as bad as any buried under the bitter sea, and if he did not come to do battle with them, even in the darkness of the brain of man, I know not why he came.'

Reading the Gospels, Chesterton saw that, more than anything else, they were the story of Christ wrestling with evil spirits. He appeared in them as an exorcist much more often than He appeared as a poet or prophet. The Moslems and the Jews—so much more like to one another than either were to the Christians—had indeed understood the great truth that there was one God who made the world, but they had not understood that the world which God had made good had in some mysterious way gone evil—or at the least was now impregnated with evil—that Man in it had to wrestle with evil but that God had come down again into it to help him in his struggles. The Moslems with their stern monotheism had 'one idea—a very great idea—but they had no second idea.' They had not 'one idea to rub against another.' What man needed, what Chesterton himself needed in this world was an authority which could give him absolution. The Jews and the Moslems had no such authority and now, he had come to think, even among Christians there was no voice that dared to speak to him the words of absolution except only that of the Catholic priest.

The contact with reality removed Chesterton's last hesitations, and on his return to England he got in touch with Monsignor O'Connor and was received by him into the Catholic Church at Beaconsfield in July 1922. To Chesterton it was an overturning of the world, a new birth. He wrote in his sonnet on it,

> The sages have a hundred maps to give
>   That trace their crawling cosmos like a tree.
> They rattle reason out through many a sieve
>   That stores the sand and lets the gold go free,
>   And all these things are less than dust to me
> Because my name is Lazarus and I live.

But to the student the difficulty is rather to understand why he delayed the step so long. One of course understands the personal reasons: the reluctance to pain his parents; the still greater reluctance to go forth on a journey upon which his wife was not yet able to accompany him; the feeling that, on what seemed to him the Holy War against Prussia, neither the Pope nor the general body of Catholic opinion throughout the world was with him. He was held back by the reluctance of the Irish support to the war. Could a cause towards which the Irish were so reluctant be so certainly a Catholic cause? Why was it that in Italy it seemed to be the anti-clericals who supported the allied cause, the clericals who were neutral, if not positively opposed? The death of Benedict XV and the accession of Pius XI made his path easier, but the Italian developments were not wholly fortunate. For Chesterton's reception nearly coincided both with Pius XI's accession and with Mussolini's seizure of power, and Chesterton, critical of all parliamentarians and critical of anti-clerical parliamentarians in particular, hailed Mussolini's accession both as a good thing in itself and as on the whole a Catholic triumph, with what proved afterwards to be an unfortunate enthusiasm.

Yet from some points of view Chesterton's step does not appear to be as sundering a step to us as it did to him. He never lost himself either before or after his conversion in detailed controversies about such matters as the apostolic succession, the validity of Anglican orders or the exact nature of the Papal headship. As a consequence there is no very striking difference between the sort of arguments with which he defended the Church before his reception and after it—between the approach of *Orthodoxy* and that of *The Everlasting Man*. By the time that he wrote *The Ballad of the White Horse* he had to the ordinary reader moved totally to a Catholic position and that reader, had he not known it otherwise, would have been surprised to have learnt that the author of the ballad was not a Roman Catholic. As we said earlier, in neither communion was he an enormously frequent church-goer. He was brought up in a liberal circle, which knew nothing of sacraments, where one only went to church if there was a good preacher to be heard. There was no question of any obligation to go regularly. He first became interested in Catholic things before Pius X had recommended the faithful to more frequent Communions, and Belloc, who was in those days the Catholic whom he knew most intimately, did not care for Pius' reform when it came nor think that his exhortations would be effective. Chesterton never quite adjusted himself to the changed habit of Catholic life.

When he actually came to his conversion the world at large still thought of Belloc as the Catholic to whom he was most closely bound. On these matters this was probably not so. There is on record one letter only which Belloc wrote to Chesterton on such a matter, and that as far back as 1907, recommending to Chesterton that he follow the will of Our Lady. It was not natural to Belloc to write private letters on such matters. He only sent it, as he records, with hesitation and reluctance and never wrote to him again on such a matter until he wrote to congratulate him on his conversion. He has left it on record that he never expected that Chesterton would become a Catholic. He did not think that Chesterton had sufficient strength of character to take such a step in defiance of the sympathy of his wife. (Belloc's over-combative nature always grossly exaggerated the alleged courage required to become a Catholic in modern England.) He thought Chesterton's attraction to Catholicism was purely 'aesthetic', that he liked taking the unfamiliar side in argument for the fun of the argument and was irritated by what he called his 'paganism'. To Belloc the world by itself was a hideous, senseless place from which a man might be rescued by salvation, if the promise of salvation were true. The choice lay between the Church and nihilism. Outside the Church were what he called in an open letter to Dean Inge 'the puerilities and the despairs'. 'We Catholics may doubtfully admit some sceptics to be our equals but none others.'

Chesterton, on his part, has recorded that, as with most converts, he was in his period of indecision somewhat put off by Catholic acquaintances who offered to help him on his way and, though Chesterton was too courteous ever to say as much even in a private mood, Professor Willis has conjectured that Belloc might have been among those who were on the whole an obstacle. In any event it is certain from his correspondence that the Catholic layman to whom at this time he was closest was Maurice Baring. Among priests he turned to Monsignor Knox and of course to Monsignor O'Connor, who received him. Father Ignatius Rice of Douai was also present at his reception. Of other priests—for instance of the priests at High Wycombe and Beaconsfield—he knew strangely little. He never cared to know many priests. All roads—or at the least many roads—lead to Rome. Of the many converts who were brought by Chesterton's influence into the Catholic Church a large number doubtless were the disciples of his social and political policies. But, as we have seen, his two most intimate friends among English converts were Maurice Baring and Ronald Knox. Yet their Catholicism was a very different Catholicism from his. Baring, member of a wealthy aristocratic banking family, a Jew, came from an origin very different from that of Chesterton. Though a Liberal who in a vague way shared Chesterton's political opinions, he was not deeply interested in politics. A linguist of almost phenomenal facility, he could learn any new language in a few weeks; an ex-diplomat who had lived in many capitals and was familiar with all, he was essentially a cosmopolitan. He left the Church of England and joined the Church of Rome because a purely national religion seemed to him an absurdity. Ronald Knox was of a clerical family, the son of a Low-Church Anglican bishop, who never since his Eton schooldays had seriously thought that he would be anything but a clergyman nor had ever passed through any agnostic phase. For him the great problem was the problem of authority. Where was the voice that could speak to him with authority? Unlike Chesterton, he was deeply troubled neither by the personal problems of solipsism nor by the need for absolution. Evelyn Waugh, who had of course little sympathy with Chesterton's egalitarian social beliefs, was greatly attracted by his more fundamental opinions but, perfectionist as he was, reacted against his disorganised and unclassical literary style. 'What wonderful things,' he once said to me, 'Chesterton would have had to say if only he had been an educated man!' There was something of affinity between Mr Graham Greene's obsession with the menace of evil and that of Chesterton, though Chesterton of course derived from Mr Greene's kinsman, Robert Louis Stevenson, a more robust technique for routing the attacks of the devil. Of all the literary converts of that time perhaps the one who would be most unqualified in his recognition of a discipleship to Chesterton would be Sir Compton Mackenzie, though as Sir Compton would be the first to confess, he brings to life also an actor's liking for self-display which Chesterton wholly lacked.

An immediate consequence of Chesterton's conversion was a slightly peculiar one. He wrote his sonnet on conversion, likening himself to Lazarus who had risen from the dead, but the experience was, it seems, too tremendous for him to be at once ready to write about it in any detail. It was not until some years later—in 1927—that he was prepared to give a straightforward account of his conversion in *The Catholic Church and Conversion*, and even then the work was not one of his major works. Chesterton was not a man to offer the world a public confession of intimate private details. The influence and the rights of his wife were too strong for that.

Yet honour demanded that he strike a blow for his faith and he therefore threw himself with more vigour than hitherto into the battle for what may be called the peripheries of the faith. His next two books were on divorce and eugenics—*The Superstition of Divorce* and *Eugenics and Other Evils*. In them he defended the traditional view of marriage and sexual relations against the progressives who were undermining them. The books contain some characteristic Chestertonian paradoxes of expression, but they do not contain or pretend to contain any novelty of thought. He was defending ancient ways, not new ways. Therefore the argument is not of sufficient interest to give the books any very enduring importance. The comment that can reasonably be made of them is that in both of them Chesterton to some extent sets up a man of straw and knocks him down again rather than meeting a real antagonist.

Thus, with eugenics. In so far as Chesterton made fun of faddists who wanted to sterilise the unfit and to breed according to supposedly eugenic laws a race of perfect children, he was fighting an important battle for the freedom of the normal man and woman. The experiments of Hitler a few years later were to prove that it was a more necessary battle than many at that time imagined, though

Chesterton would have made his jokes more effective if he had himself taken a little more trouble to read the books which he was proposing to satirise. He disliked the psychoanalysts because he thought—not altogether fairly—that by providing reasons for every action they were undermining human freedom just as he thought that Blatchford had been undermining it twenty years before. His main attack was on birth control to which of course he was strongly opposed. At that date it would not have been possible to find a Catholic whose opposition to it would not have been taken for granted. But again, is the issue quite fairly posed? Chesterton contrasts Our Lady who offered the world 'love without lust' with the birth-controllers who offer it 'lust without love'. Is this fair? No doubt a wise tradition, secular as well as Christian, unites to condemn those who seek to divorce sex entirely from fecundity and demand its pleasures without wishing at any time to have children. But what of those who wish to have, or who have, a reasonable family but who are concerned about what they should do during the interstices when for medical or economic reasons another child is for the moment not possible? The teaching of the Vatican Council would hardly justify Chesterton's charge that intercourse which does not intend to be fecund is necessarily 'lust without love'.

In discussing topics of this nature Chesterton never quite clearly defined his position. Up to this century it could be said that general public opinion was agreed in asserting the indissolubility of marriage and the sinfulness of contraceptives. There was no difference on those points between Catholics and Protestants and both joined in their attacks on the pioneers of birth control such as Bradlaugh. Today we live in an admittedly pluralist society, where the Catholic cannot reasonably ask for more than that he himself be not attacked in his adherence to his traditional practices. He cannot claim to impose them by law on others who do not accept them. But in the earlier years of this century it was still the custom of all religious denominations not only to claim freedom for their own beliefs but to think that they should impose their practices on all society. The Nonconformists not only thought it wrong to drink or to play games on Sunday. They would, if they could, impose on the nation prohibition, local option or sabbatarian laws. Similarly both

Catholic and Anglicans not only accepted for themselves an obligation of indissoluble marriage but fought every proposal for any extention of the secular divorce law. Chesterton, when he fought against divorce, was never quite clear whether he was seeking to persuade his readers that marriage ought to be indissoluble or to impose indissoluble marriage by law on those who were not persuaded by his argument.

Thus his *Eugenics and Other Evils* is also in some ways oddly dated, in some ways an oddly prescient book. As he explains in the book's preface, the eugenic proposition had been first presented to the world in the years before 1914 and Chesterton, characteristically repelled and moved to ridicule by it, had at that time got together some notes to write about it. Before his book was written the war came. The war turned men's minds to more urgent policies. In particular, since these eugenic speculations had come largely from Germany and were recommended as a part of the German scientific Kultur, he thought that they had been rendered irrelevant by terrible events—by the awful example which had been offered of the consequence of such eccentricity. He laid his notes aside. It was only after the war, when in spite of German defeat he saw such speculations cropping up again, that he took up his notes and wrote his book.

The eugenic idea was, in brief, that, instead of leaving couples to arrange their own marriages as in the haphazard romantic fashion had been the custom, breeding should be arranged between human beings on scientific principles as among animals. The most suitable father should be selected and paired off with the most suitable mother to produce the ideal child. It is easy to see that such crude folly was ready meat for Chesterton's mockery. He asked, as one would have expected him to ask, who was to select, and what the selectors were to consider the ideal qualities to look for in the child. If we breed pigeons or horses, it is a man who breeds the animal or the bird and he knows for what purpose he wishes to breed it. But who is the all-wise man who is to say what other men are to be like? 'There are as many separate types of excellence as there are separate individual souls.' Men were not created to be merely of a pattern. But the theory in the world of 1922 broke down, as was admitted by sensible people who by no means shared Chesterton's full philosophy, simply because, whatever the theoretical possibilities of such selective breeding, men clearly did not at that time as yet know enough about the principles of heredity to justify such experiments. Chesterton would clearly have rejected such experiments as an interference with essential liberty whatever the degree of scientific certainty that had been attained.

This was generally agreed, and the crudity of such principles of eugenics that had had a little fashion just before the 1914 war were generally laughed out of court in the years after it and indeed have not seriously reappeared in that form. But it was argued by such men as Dean Inge that, although admittedly we did not know enough to be able to breed a second Shakespeare or a second Michelangelo, we did know to some extent, if not what to breed, at least what not to breed. There were some diseased and feeble-minded people of whom it was obviously to the public interest that they should not have children. Chesterton had a healthy democratic dislike of such a line of argument. There were, he of necessity admitted, certain people who were not merely eccentric but so violently dangerous in their conduct towards others that society with infinite reluctance had no alternative but to call them mad and to shut them away from normal contacts. He denounced very rightly the Feeble-Minded Bill which was then before Parliament by which restrictions which had hitherto been placed only on the mad were to be widely extended. Madness from that point of view, he argued, was a definite, objective and fortunately a comparatively rare affliction. He who was adjudged mad was a man who had shown by his actions that he was mad and was so adjudged because he acted with causeless violence towards other people. But anyone could be called feeble-minded. Everybody was at times accused of being feeble-minded by somebody else. If it be objected that the feeble-minded are a nuisance to their neighbours, Chesterton justly replied that the nuisance of the too feeble-minded was as nothing to the nuisance of the too strong-minded. By far the greater part of the suffering of mankind on any plane down from the national and political to the personal and family had been caused by people who are too strong-minded, who are possessed by the passion for power, by the desire for success, by the need to compel other people to notice them and to obey them.

Chesterton's just complaint against the Feeble-Minded Bill was that it turned the exception into the rule, that it threatened to impose on anybody exceptional restraints that had previously only been imposed on the exceptional. Of course Chesterton's critics replied to him both on eugenics and on lunacy that he was making a mountain out of a molehill. Whatever detailed redefinitions there might be, they argued, there was no intention of interfering with the liberty of the ordinary man or woman. The eugenists intended to study and to publish the conditions of mating that were likely to produce good children. They had no intention of asking for compulsory powers—of dictating who should mate with whom—of forbidding normal parents from having children. Who could suggest such a thing? Chesterton's reply that the principle of freedom should be asserted the moment that the denial of it was asserted, that there was no limit to the practical lengths to which such a challenge could be carried, seemed at the time exaggerated. Yet twenty years after he wrote his books we saw the experiments of Hitler and learnt what men who had broken with traditional morals might not only advocate but actually do.

In the same way with birth control. Chesterton, as indeed all Catholics at that date, opposed birth control. Today even among Catholics the morals of contraception are much more widely debated and many Catholics would hotly denounce his general stigmatisation of contraception as 'lust without love' as greatly unfair. But there again, whether or not he was right in his basic standpoint, he at least showed a basic prescience. The issue today is still generally debated as one of whether couples should be allowed to use contraceptive devices. The issue up to the present is an issue of freedon. But in recent years we have seen the beginnings of a counter-charge that the demographic problem is so grave that those who have more than a few children are bad citizens, guilty of 'a form of social delinquency', as a Labour politician the other day put it. It could not, the argument ran, in the age of the welfare state be considered merely a couple's private business how many children they had. And one can hardly doubt that before long legislation will be proposed to limit by law the number of children permitted and to impose compulsory birth control. Chesterton, characteristically to his mood at the time, ascribed all these plans for interference with freedom to capitalists who were anxious to keep down wages. They could pay lower wages if their wage slaves had fewer children to keep. That argument is now somewhat dated. On this and on other aspects of what Belloc and Chesterton called 'the servile State' experience has proved that the masters of society are indeed possessed of an offensive ambition to interfere with the lives of ordinary people but that this ambition is found as commonly among Socialist reformers as among capitalists. Also typical of Chesterton was that he contrasted the dingy life of English industrial towns with the alleged free life of the Continental peasant society. There again his writings are dated. Anyone who drives through the red slums of Paris or the dock districts of Marseilles can hardly believe that dreary slums are exclusive to Britain, nor one who drives through the country districts of Alsace on a Sunday morning, that sodden, hopeless drunkenness is only found in this island.

By a curiosity which shows how fashions have changed, when Chesterton wrote his *Superstitions of Divorce* he found that one of the arguments of the advocates of divorce which he had to meet was that, if marriages were not dissoluble, there would necessarily be a smaller birth rate. When a man found his wife incapable of giving him a child, he could with free divorce get rid of her and acquire instead a fertile partner. Chesterton denied that there would in fact be a higher birth rate, but what is interesting is that both parties to the argument agreed that an increase of population was desirable. Chesterton found himself in the strange company of Zola, who had used such arguments in his *Fertilité*.

Chesterton of course continually called for a reform to what he thought of as a simpler and saner England of the past. He championed rural life against industrialism. He denounced the impersonality of large units and the state-control or capitalist-control of welfare schemes. He replied to those who said that you cannot put back the clock by asking 'Why not?' But neither did he recognise, nor did his critics in any place ever put to him, the obvious point that 'you cannot put back the clock because you cannot put back the population.' The England to which he looked back may or may not have been a happier England, but it was certainly a less populous England. The main reason why we must have industrialism and larger units and by consequence more impersonal relations is that we have a much larger population to support; and it was a reasonable criticism of Catholic conservatives that, while asking for the preservation of old patterns of society, they were at the same time by their clamour for large birth rates the main advocates of an increase of population, which was the most potent cause of the destruction of the old patterns.

The weakness of Chesterton's book on divorce is that it evades the real challenge. Chesterton has no difficulty in making fun of the advocates of free love—of Higgins' aunts who were not married, yet demanded to be divorced. He showed that so-called free love is not really love at all, that the essence of love is that the lover has what he called an 'ambition of fixity' and wishes to tie himself to a permanent arrangement, and that the casual liaison which each side feels free to abandon as the mood takes him or her is not love, nor likely to be productive of happiness. One fire is certain to go out when the other is still aflame, and such liaisons inevitably end in tears. For happiness people need the power to bind themselves. All this is doubtless true enough, but responsible advocates of freer divorce in no way denied it. They said, 'We are not advocating free love. We fully proclaim the importance of marriage. Certainly it is very much best for children to be the offspring of happy marriages. Certainly it is necessary both for their own sakes and for their children's sake for married people to behave with restraint and with fidelity. All that we freely grant. We are not attacking marriage. All that we are saying is that, when every precaution is taken, unfortunately some marriages do break down, and, when they break down, it is the lesser evil frankly to confess as much, to call the marriage at an end and to allow the partners to contract new marriages.'

Obviously, the principle once accepted, there is large need for argument, as experience has shown, how exactly the law should define the breakdown of marriage. The machinery for reconciliation should be fully used. But into those detailed arguments it was not to Chesterton's purpose to enter. He argued that divorce should be refused altogether. He did not indeed deny the existence of sad, hard cases and was prepared in face of them to allow judicial separation but no divorce—and not remarriage. 'Nobody,' he wrote, 'does deny that a person should be allowed some sort of release from a homicidal maniac. The most extreme school of orthodoxy only remains that anybody who has had that experience should be content with that release. In other words it says that he should be content with that experience and not seek another.' The divorce-law reformer naturally asked what was the logic and what was the humanity in that denial. The Catholic Church proclaims that some few people have a gift of continence and pays them honour. It does not pretend that the average man or woman has it, and there is less than no reason why those whose marriage has irrevocably broken down should be expected to have it. What cruelty to condemn them for no purpose to a lifetime of celibacy! What an invitation to incontinence! It is patently unfair to argue in generalisations that he or she who has made a mess of one marriage has proved himself or herself unfit for a second. There are some people who are constitutionally unfit for marriage. There are plenty who fail in a first marriage and make a brilliant success of a second.

Obviously if a pious Catholic argues, 'The Church has laid down these rules. My duty is to obey them,' there is no further argument. God has in his view seen fit in this life of trial to impose on him such a cross. He obediently accepts it, and that is the end of the matter. Chesterton, as he in several places explains, was not concerned with an exposition of Catholic doctrine for Catholics but with a defence of what in his opinion should be the secular law to be imposed on everybody in a pluralist society.

His argument is not easy. There are two different sorts of liberty —the liberty from the policeman and the liberty of the moral code. It is reasonable that in a pluralist society the criminal law should be invoked as little as possible—only those actions forbidden which self-evidently interfere with the freedom of others. But arguments as to what shall be prevented by the policeman can clearly only establish a negative freedom. The more important problem is the positive problem—by what code should a man regulate his life? And there, the merely preventive answers are insufficient. For it is not in the nature of the mind to live without a code. The sceptic rejects the traditional codes but, as Chesterton truly commented, he does not therefore fall into a mere repudiation of authority. He simply substitutes a code without reason for a code based on reason. 'The modern world,' Chesterton wrote, 'will accept no dogmas upon any authority but it will accept any dogmas upon no authority. Say that a thing is so according to the Pope or the Bible and it will be described as a superstition without examination. But preface your remark with "they say" or "don't you know that"— and try (and fail) to remember the name of some professor mentioned in some newspaper, and the keen rationalism of the modern mind will accept every word you say.' The answer to the plea that it is the affront to freedom to expect men and women to bind themselves by marriage vows is that the strongest right that the lover demands is the right to bind himself. The freedom that he demands is the freedom to bind. So Chesterton appeals to experience and to tradition. In so far as that appeal is against the advocates of free love it is cogent. He has no difficulty in showing that man everywhere has had an institution of marriage—has never been content to leave sexual relations and the birth of children to casual whims. But in so far as he appeals to traditions against the advocates of some modern divorce law his task is more difficult. For it is certain that, though Christian societies have indeed for better or for worse demanded absolutely indissoluble marriage, they have in that been not the rule but the unique exception. Non-Christian societies without, I fancy, exception have had indeed an institution of marriage, have desired the stability of marriage as a general rule but have admitted exceptional conditions under which a marriage can be dissolved.

Chesterton based his argument very largely on the importance of the vow. At marriage the man and the woman vow fidelity to one another. Societies are in anarchy if they do not respect vows. The argument was not very compulsive, for the divorce-law reformer of course replied, 'If the vows in that form are so very uncompromising, why should we not change their form? Certainly the husband should promise to be faithful to his wife and *vice versa*. He should accept the obligation to be patient and kind and forgiving, to pardon her faults and so on. But, if the wife utterly deserts the husband and thus breaks her vow and brings the marriage to an end (or again *vice versa*) can the husband still be held unilaterally to his vow?' Nor indeed is Chesterton's argument that all free civilisation is built upon irrevocable vows altogether convincing. He compares the marriage vow to the monk's vow of obedience. Now it is indeed true that when an Abbot accepts a monk's postulant vow, he expects and intends that the postulant shall keep that vow and persist in his vocation. But, if for some reason or other the monk fails to remain in his vocation, there is a machinery by which he can be dispensed of his vows. It would seem to be in the logic of Chesterton's argument that on this principle spouses should indeed be expected to keep their marriage vow but there should be for exceptional cases some machinery in the Church for dissolving— and not merely for annulling—irrevocably unfortunate marriages.

Certainly by the 1920s the day had passed when Christians could hope to impose by penal law their code on the general society and there was no possibility but that there should be some divorce laws, whatever the exact form that they might take. There is little reason to think that Chesterton imagined otherwise. He could not refute in argument those who responsibly argued for some moderate facilities for divorce. But he could warn that, if the door was once opened a little way, it would not be possible in such an atmosphere as that of the post-war world to prevent it from being forced right open. Responsible people might argue for divorce in very exceptional circumstances, but once divorce became the fashion and socially acceptable, breaches of the obligations of matrimony were certain to become more and more widespread, marriage more frequently to fail and a reform which was in all good faith introduced in order to remedy misery would in fact prove to be a very potent cause of misery. And no one can deny that this has substantially happened. Whatever the logic of indissoluble marriage, it is possible that, if there were no divorce laws, much unhappiness would indeed be imposed on some respectable people but that on the balance more unhappiness would be prevented than would be caused. Chesterton wrote his book for the citizens of a secularist society and from a secularist point of view. But it was of course his real belief that marriage was of its nature an institution that required the grace of God for its success and that men and women would continue to be unhappy so long as they attempted to exclude the request for grace from their lives. It is a condition of success in marriage that those who contract it shall recognise in some form that it needs a blessing from beyond this world. It is a road upon which no man or woman dare set out unassisted.

12

The World After the War

To Chesterton, as has been said, Prussia was the evil power and the war of 1914 a Holy War. He had indeed no admiration for Lloyd George or for those who managed the coupon election of 1918, but the proposition that Germany had made the war and should therefore be compelled to pay for it seemed to him the plainest common sense. The problem how international transfers on anything like this gigantic scale could be possible was a technical problem wholly beyond his competence. As he saw it, the arguments of economists like Maynard Keynes that such transfers were not possible were exercises in dishonesty, designed to further the sinister purpose of international finance, and Jewish New York finance in particular, to put Germany back again on her feet and to enable her to escape from the penalty of her sins. Why exactly Jewish finance should have been so keen to rehabilitate Germany he never clearly explained. Sir Oswald Mosley in the next decade was to accuse international finance of plotting war *against* Germany. So far as a reason was given it was that finance was opposed to France because the French were peasants and self-supporting and less interested in the interchanges of commerce than the men of other nations, and there was in his opinion an intrinsic baseness in commerce. As Goldsmith said, 'Honour sinks where commerce long prevails.' The reason for the financiers' alleged preference was never very clearly explained. Yet the consequence of his conviction —not to say, his obsession—was that he saw the post-war years as years of a bitter betrayal, France alone standing firm and demanding the security to which she was entitled, the British and the Americans welshing on their word. This note of bitterness runs through the book of poems, *The Ballad of Saint Barbara*, which he published in those years.

Whatever we may think of the complaint, the bitterness cannot be denied. Captain Fryatt, the captain of *The Great Eastern*, had been captured and executed by the Germans during the war. His body lay in Flanders. Chesterton wrote:

> Trampled yet red is the last of the embers,
>   Red the last cloud of a sun that has set;
> What of your sleeping though Flanders remembers?
>   What of your waking if England forget? . . .
> Sleep and forget us, as we have forgotten;
>   For Flanders remembers and England forgets.

In resurrected Poland he found a place

> Where war is holier than peace.
> Where hate is holier than love.

and where

> Shone terrible as the Holy Ghost
> An eagle whiter than a dove.

Of the English who had fallen he wrote:

And what is theirs though banners blow on Warsaw risen again
Or ancient laughter walks in gold through the vineyards of
    Lorraine?
Their dead are marked on English stones, their loves on English
    trees,
How little is the prize they win, how mean a coin for these—
How small a shrivelled laurel-leaf lies crumpled here and curled,
They died to save their country and they only saved the world.

For their War Memorial he suggested

> The hucksters haggle in the mart,
>   The cars and carts go by;
> Senates and schools go droning on,
>   For dead things cannot die. . . .

Still to the last of crumbling time
Upon this stone be read.
How many men of England died
To prove they were not dead.

The theme poem of the book is *The Ballad of Saint Barbara*. Saint Barbara was the patron saint of artillery. We have already spoken a number of times about Chesterton's strange passion to portray all his conflicts as physical and violent conflicts. Without here debating that issue again we can say of his two great martial ballads—*Lepanto* and *The White Horse*—that, whether or not they recounted correct history, they did at any rate tell a clear story, a story in both cases of Christendom standing in defiance against the barbarian who was seeking to break into its domain. *The Ballad of Saint Barbara*, which is concerned with the German attack on Paris in the early days of the war, carries the same lesson but it carries it much less clearly.

The touch and the tornado; all our guns give tongue together,
    Saint Barbara for the gunnery and God defend the right;
They are stopped and gapped and battered as we blast away the
        weather,
    Building window upon window to our lady of the light.
For the light is come on Liberty, her foes are falling, falling
    They are reeling, they are running, as the shameful years have
        run;
She is risen for all the humble, she has heard the conquered
        calling,
    Saint Barbara of the Gunners, with her hand upon the gun.

One need not be an absolute pacifist, or deny that there may be wars that are on balance justified, to be yet doubtful of the taste of canonising the weapons of them. 'Barbara the beautiful', is an uncomfortable phrase for a woman saint who is a patron saint of gunnery, seeing what guns are and how great is the difficulty in remaining obedient to the Church's teaching on the conditions of a just war.

Chesterton's literary life divided itself into two almost equal periods—that before the First World War and that after it. Of these two periods most people would say that it was the earlier which was the more creative. To some extent that was doubtless because in his earlier pre-Catholic years his conclusions were less predictable. 'Chesterton, in the days when he still used to think . . .' I once heard an Anglican clergyman saying in the train. He meant of course 'In the days when he was still an Anglican.' Yet it would not be fair to say that that was all that he meant. It was not merely a change of religion which slowed up the exuberance of Chesterton's output in his second period. His health was by no means what it had been in the earlier years. Catholic societies in every part of the country—indeed one might say in every part of the world—were ruthless in their demands on him, and, although his wife did all that she could to protect him, he gave an inordinate amount of his time and energy to peripatetic lecturing. Above all this was the constant demand of the paper which Mrs Chesterton so bitterly regretted and which was so heavy and so continuing a drain on him.

Thus, if we set out the balance sheet of his opinions in international politics, it is with the advantage of hindsight today fairly easy to distribute the pluses and the minuses. He clearly showed himself a great deal more prescient than simple-minded Liberals who immediately after the war imagined that the Germans had overnight changed their whole nature because they had been given votes and a parliamentary constitution. On the other hand he showed himself equally gullible in thinking that the Germans could be simply divided into good and bad according to whether they were southern and Catholic or northern and Protestant, and, as has been already argued, was greatly in error in thinking that Hitler was a mere puppet of the General Staff. He did not of course live to see the Second World War but he did see what he called in the title of his last and posthumous book *The End of the Armistice*. He saw the imminence of the Second World War but he was in error in seeing it as a mere repetition of the First. He had started off with a strong prejudice in favour of Mussolini. He died while the Abyssinian campaign was still on. Some of the writers on his paper had been shockingly outspoken in entire support of

Mussolini. Chesterton was too ill to take an active part in that argument, but, as his letters to Maurice Reckitt showed, he died profoundly disturbed on the issue. The Spanish War was still raging at the time of his death. On that war he naturally supported Franco. What he would have made of some of the subsequent achievements of Franco's policy and in particular of his hostility to Catalan and Basque nationalism is as may be, but whether by accident or wisdom he showed himself more prescient than other critics in being very doubtful of the extent to which Franco would prove an obedient puppet of Hitler and Mussolini.

Chesterton died three years before the Second World War came but ever since Hitler came to power in Germany and indeed even before that he had clearly forseen war as inevitable. In that respect, in so far as he foretold what did in fact happen at a time when very many others were not foretelling it, he can justly be labelled a prophet; and in the early days of the war Mr Sheed collected his essays on this subject, labelling him as such, and published them under the title, *The End of the Armistice*. Chesterton did indeed prove himself a true prophet in so far as he not only foretold the war but foretold that it would come over Poland and as a result of a Nazi-Soviet Pact. 'The Prussian patriot may plaster himself all over with eagles and crosses,' he wrote, 'but he will be found in practice side by side with the Red flag. The Prussian and the Russian will agree about everything—especially about Poland.' This, written at a time when Hitler was still pouring out his rhetoric about the Bolshevik bogey and when statesmen of the West were talking about the necessity for an alliance with Russia, was indeed remarkable prophesying. Yet there was the characteristic selectiveness in Chesterton's analysis. He prophesied the Nazi-Soviet Pact because of the essential enmity of the two régimes to Christianity and Western civilisation. He forgot to tell us that the French had already made an alliance with the Russians. Writing at the time of the Dolfuss murder, he pardonably exaggerated the hostility of the Austrians to the Nazis. Some of the most obedient and most vile of the Nazis like Seyss Inquart were Austrians. He counted on Mussolini as unhesitatingly on the Christian side. He had no suspicion of the rottenness of France under the Third

Republic nor guessed that such a man as Maurras would be found on the side of collaboration. Above all throughout he spoke of Nazism as a Prussian disease. But Hitler himself and an inconveniently large proportion of the Nazi leaders were from the South —particularly from Bavaria—and were of Catholic origins. When the war came, the Catholic German bishops urged their flock to do their patriotic duty of fighting against Poland. Poland, worthy though she was of support, was at that time under a singularly unlovely régime and, far from having any natural hostility to Hitler, she was willing to share with him in the spoils of Munich annexed from Czechoslovakia; only in the end did she defend herself because Hitler gave her no alternative.

As for the power of international finance, Chesterton had of course a general feeling that the man who made or grew something should be honoured above the mere trafficker in credit and that it is an evil in society if the supreme power over policy is in the hands of those who fight by 'shuffling papers.' Here he was the inheritor of a long and honourable tradition and from Carthage to Venice history has rightly been suspicious of societies where the commercial element has been predominent. Chesterton in his *History of England* imagines Bolingbroke as saying in echo of the words of Strafford 'Put not your trust in princes—and least of all in merchant princes.' But, though Belloc had made a detailed study of the workings of the financial system, Chesterton knew little about them. He was not capable of making the smallest purchase and would have had no notion how the banking system worked, whether for better or for worse. But by a curious accident, it could be said of those years between the wars that in this aspect of ignorance, he was in no very different condition from the international bankers themselves; but, though they were indeed mismanaging the banking system, they were mismanaging it in quite a different way from that of which Belloc and Chesterton accused them. Belloc believed strongly that a currency must have a metallic basis. That in fact meant in the early years of this century that he believed in the gold standard. In theory he admitted that money was but a ticket for the exchange of goods against goods and that the ticket could be made of anything, but gold had the great advantages that it was indestructible and the supply of it was limited. If the quantity of money in circulation was not limited by physical supply, then it would be settled by the decision of politicians and from his experience of politicians he did not think it probable that their decisions would be either honest or wise; and certainly in favour of this thesis he could convincingly point to the fact that the essential business of a monetary system was to provide a stability of prices and that prices had in fact been kept remarkably stable for the ninety-nine years from 1815 to 1914. With the coming of the war we had—inevitably—suspended cash payments but, the war ended, the first necessity was, in his argument, to return to them—to return to what he thought of as the old and tried system.

The bankers thought the same. But what neither Belloc nor the bankers took in was that in fact the circumstances after 1918 were entirely different from the circumstances before 1914; consequently a return to the gold standard under those new circumstances was a return to a gold standard when, on its own terms of reference, it could not possibly work. In the years before the war, though the nations based their monetary supplies on gold holdings, the overwhelming majority of transactions were not in fact paid for in gold. They were paid for by book entries which cancelled one another out. Gold was only required to redress the occasional and exceptional balance and, since in those years London was the financial capital of the world and Britain was a free-trade country, willing to accept the payments of dividends due to it in any goods that its debtors saw fit to send her, the volume of gold holdings required to keep the system working was minimal. But the United States, which before the war was still a debtor country, emerged from it the world's major creditor country. Both Britain and all the other Allied countries owed it debts, and America as a creditor country was quite a different proposition from Britain as a creditor country. For America, far from being a free-trade country, was a high-tariff country. Far from lowering her tariffs in order to fit her new circumstances as a creditor, she greatly raised them by the Fordney tariff. As a result it was impossible for any foreigner to import goods into the United States on any considerable scale, and those who had to pay debts to America could only pay them in gold.

Under such conditions, for another country—for Britain—to accept an obligation to base its monetary supply on gold was to submit itself to a steady deflation with its inevitable consequences of poverty and unemployment.

Belloc and Chesterton, like everybody else, were well aware of the poverty and unemployment in Britain between the wars. They were slow in understanding the responsibility of banking policy for these sufferings. So, too, with Europe. It was the Bellocian thesis that international finance had a special love for the Germans—it was not, as I say, very clear why—and that its main purpose was to set the Germans on their feet again. The truth was that the financiers did indeed wish to set the Germans on their feet again, not out of any special love for Germans but because the world's economy was interlocked and, if one important section of it was not working, then its failure damaged the prosperity of everybody else. The collapse of the German and Austrian economies in the early days of the 1930s was not the result of any Machiavellian machinations of the financiers but directly the reverse. It was a result of the fact that the masters of the monetary machine did not know how to manage their own machinery. They imposed on Germany and Austria, as on Britain, a gold standard under conditions under which it was mathematically impossible for it to work. The result was deflation and, as in Britain, unemployment by the millions. The result of that was that German opinion turned against the Weimar politicians, who were held responsible for these calamities, and it put Hitler into power. But whatever Hitler's enormities it was even more absurd to see him as the creature of international finance than it was to see him as the creature of the General Staff. International finance did not make the Second World War. It was simply too stupid to know how to prevent it.

There was a similar unreality of detail about Chesterton's domestic policies of distributism and his opposition to the schemes of compulsory insurance. The broad conception that in opposition to the capitalists, who concentrated all effective property in the hands of a few rich men and the Socialists who would concentrate it all in the hands of the state, property should be as widely distributed as possible so that as nearly as possible every father of a family should have his limited share of it—such a conception was attractive. Property gives the common man an assurance of freedom against both state and capitalists which nothing else can give him and, advocating a wide distribution of property, Belloc and Chesterton were once more accepting the gospel of a long and important tradition. It is true that they tended to identify that tradition more closely with Catholicism than reality justified. One can hardly call the mediaeval feudal landed system a distributist system. The pretence that capitalism and usury arose as a result of the destruction of the monasteries which Belloc adopted from Cobbett and Max Weber, and Chesterton from Belloc, was much too crude. Tawney in his *Religion and the Rise of Capitalism* has shown that there were plenty of examples of usurious practices to be found among Catholics before the Reformation and plenty of Protestant denunciation of them after the Reformation. The abdication of organised religion from any attempt to control man's economic activities, if it is to be given a definite date, can be much more nearly ascribed to the second half of the seventeenth century, when the *politiques* obtained control of the state as against both sincere Protestants and sincere Catholics, than to the sixteenth century, with the Protestant revolt against Catholicism. As Tawney says, the only man of the sixteenth century who seems to have preached a gospel that was at all recognisably like the distributism of Belloc and Chesterton was Luther—the earlier Luther, before his surrender to the princes.

If we pass on to modern times it cannot be pretended that the earlier nineteenth-century Popes, obsessed with the alliance of Throne and Altar and with the absolute rights of property, were in any way distributists. It is not until Leo XIII and *Rerum Novarum* in 1891 that we get any papal teaching on the desirability of a wide distribution of property. Even then Leo so combined his advocacy of wide distribution with a reassertion of the wrongfulness of any attack on the present owners of property that it was not very easy to see how his teaching was likely to have any practical effect. The truth is that it was very particularly applicable to new countries where there was still plenty of unoccupied land and where therefore the newcomers could be given more without anything being taken from the old possessors; and almost all the practical experiments in distributism have been in new countries—in Australia, in Canada with the Antigonish experiment and in the Middle West of the United States. It is a curiosity that, though of all countries Australia was the one where Chesterton's distributist principles were most widely practised, he and Belloc both had an almost insensate prejudice against Australians, whom Chesterton was to accuse of being suburban, though why that should be either a term of abuse or true was not easy to understand. On the European continent the country that lived most nearly according to distributist principles was Denmark where the Catholic population was of course negligibly small; and Chesterton, though he spoke at large about peasants, usually drew his detailed examples of small property from the small shopkeeper, with whom he was much more familiar than he was with peasants. 'The Faith is Europe and Europe is the Faith,' thought Belloc, but it is a little comical that the disciples who followed his teaching were almost all of them either non-Europeans or non-Catholics.

Pius XI, the Pope of Chesterton's day, in his *Quadragesimo Anno* repeated Leo's assertion of the absolute right to private property. It was not until Pius XII's broadcast message of Whitsun, 1941, that papal approval was given to the teaching that there could be occasions when, for the greater general good, private property might be confiscated. 'The right of every man to use these [material goods] for his own sustenance,' said Pius, 'is prior to every other economic right, even that of private property.'

It was Pope John XXIII who frankly threw overboard his predecessors' assertions of the absolute rights of private property. He wrote in *Mater et Magistra*: 'Concerning the use of material goods our predecessor declared that the right of every man to use these for his own sustenance is prior to every other economic right, even that of private property. The right to the private possession of material goods is admittedly a natural one; nevertheless in the objective order established by God the right to property cannot stand in the way of the axiomatic principles that the goods which were created by God for all men should flow to all alike according to the principles of justice and charity.'

The distributists professed to derive their principles from Leo XIII and his encyclical *Rerum Novarum*. In a way their claim was justified. Leo did advocate a wide distribution of property. But there was a difference between his teaching and theirs. The principles of distributism are much more easily applicable to an agricultural than to an industrial society. In an agricultural society it is possible, whether or not it be desirable, to break up the large estates and so to distribute land that each peasant has his little plot. It is not easily possible to see how the industrial worker can own the little bit of machinery on which he works. The distributists were naturally well aware of this difficulty. They would apply to industry a co-operative system of guild ownership, but no one was more alive than Belloc to the misrepresentations of a system of election by votes if applied to large units and, if it was so largely untrue that elected representatives to Parliament really represented the voters who had voted for them, there was no great reason why those who were elected to represent the miners or the railwaymen should be any more faithful to their pretensions. The distributists were well aware of the strength of such an objection. Therefore, while the great majority of them, with only a few exceptions such as Penty, were realistic enough to recognise that industrialism in the modern society was inevitable, they did not want to have any more of it than they could help. The larger the number in a society that could be persuaded to go back to the land, the more nearly a society could become self-supporting in food, the better in their eyes.

Now Leo XIII's approach was the direct opposite of this, and in this he showed himself to be more realistic than the distributists. The labour that was required to produce a given quantity of food was, owing to mechanisation, so much less than it had been in previous ages that it was inevitable that the proportion of labour employed on the land should decrease. Belloc pointed to France and Ireland as the two ideal peasant communities to be held up for admiration. A Frenchman, he said, was 'a natural peasant'. 'He has created a host of songs and he has turned all France into a kind of walled garden.' The Frenchman in industry was 'like good wine turned sour'. But the passage of the years ever since he wrote has shown a steady increase in the industrial development of both those countries. Alike in industry and in agriculture their modern development has been towards large units and mass production. Chesterton would of course have told us that this was an evil development and rebuked us as fatalists for accepting it. But it is certain that Chesterton did not at all understand the technical reasons why larger units were favoured. 'Ownership of shares in small amounts,' wrote Belloc, 'a very wide distribution of the interest upon national and municipal debt, free men owning and farming their own land or holding it in low customary leases, artisans working with their own tools in their own shops—these were to be found in all the civilised countries of the West from Ireland to Italy, the proportion of families economically free in some countries so large as to determine the whole character of society.' There has been a steady decline in such proportions even since he wrote.

Now in Leo's mind industrialism had happened to grow up in the first place in England and the United States—in countries where the total Catholic population was small and where the Catholics among the owners of industry had been almost non-existent. Therefore during the early years of industrialism that Church had had nothing to say to the industrial workers and this had proved a great disaster, being largely the cause of the Church's loss of the urban proletariat. The prime purpose of his encyclical was to bring home to the industrial worker the principles of Catholic teaching. Cardinal Manning, Leo's great English adviser, had preached his gospel not to the peasants but to the dockers.

As for compulsory insurance, although it is true that this was a principle first invented in Prussia and consequently suspect in Belloc's eyes, his confident pronouncement that such a principle was and would always be contemptuously rejected by the free workers of France has proved singularly false. To the contrary, the principle of what it is now the fashion to call social benefits has been universally accepted in every country and, so far from being opposed by modern Catholicism, has been explicitly approved of by John XXIII in his *Mater et Magistra*. Pope John there wrote, 'The modern trend is for people to aim at proficiency in their trade or profession rather than at the acquisition of private property. They think more highly of an income which derives from work and the rights consequent upon work than of an income which derives from capital and the rights of capital. And this is as it should be.' Security, taught the Pope in opposition to Belloc, was more important than property.

Chesterton wrote his distributist article every week in *G.K.'s Weekly* and afterwards collected them into a volume which he published under the title of *The Outline of Sanity*. This book may be accepted as the definitive statement of his beliefs about the wide distribution of property. It is not one of the most successful of his books. There is too much repetition—too much of wordy piling up of comical and extreme analogies and *reductiones ad absurdum*. This was perhaps inevitable if we remember that these books consisted of reprints of articles that had to be written every week on a thesis on which there were only a limited number of arguments. I cannot think that the articles were specially effective as propaganda. They had about them the nature of a sermon to the converted and an entertainment to the lover of words. They were full of verbal jokes and he was satisfying the yearnings of those who were already looking for his truth. But when he wrote on the wide distribution of property he was writing not for disciples, but for a public which for better or worse did not in any way see this as the need of the age. Shop assistants, factory workers, agricultural workers wanted more wages and more security far more than they wanted more property. Most of them were not much at ease with the written word or literary illusions. They could not follow Chesterton's jokes. For all his boasts to be a common man he was far from common or plain in his methods of expression. Chesterton continually complained that he could never understand why people would not take arguments seriously if they were expressed amusingly. He was right in saying, like Shaw, that such a refusal was illogical but he should have recognised that it was the fact. Yet although puzzling experience had taught him that it was so, he never attempted to change his style to suit his readers. Doubtless he could not have done so. The style was the man—the way in which his mind worked. It was not a fad that he had taken up *pour épater le bourgeois*.

Again, he was in these essays explaining how practical things should be done and his greatest weakness was that for all his grasp of principles he had no knowledge of the practical details of methods. He praised peasants but he would have had no clear idea how to set about the practical business of farming—how to sow, how to reap, how to milk, how to feed—whether such business was done by a peasant or by a large farmer. The names of flowers occur fairly frequently in his writings but they appear there, I fancy, rather for the euphony of their names than for their intrinsic beauty. I remember being told by his gardener that 'Mr Chesterton always goes to look at the daffodils because they are the only flowers that he can recognise.' He had no idea how a factory worked—whoever owned it. I doubt if he had ever been in a factory in his life. As has been said, though his basic argument was concerned with peasants, his examples of the virtue of ownership are usually taken from small shopkeepers. He attacked the large multiple shops and championed the small men, and this was doubtless because he had at least been in a shop. But even there, though he had been in shops, numerous anecdotes bear witness to his total incompetence as a shopper and it is certain that he had but the vaguest notions how a shop was managed. Some of the absurdities, as he saw them, of a multiple shop will not seem at all absurd to many housewives. To many—particularly in our English weather—the notion that every sort of article can be brought under a single roof will appear as a great advantage and not at all as an absurdity. Nor does he consider a point that, whether valid or not, is at least commonly made, that even the small shopkeeper has usually an assistant or two and that shop assistants in small shops often get worse wages and worse conditions than the organised assistants in large shops. He argues that the dependence on a centralised water supply is a badge of slavery and that the free peasant would wish to fetch his water from his own well. It is not likely that many peasants would agree with him and *Top Meadow* was certainly on the central supply for water and electricity, though very likely Chesterton was not aware of it.

Yet, whatever the defects of the book, it sets out very clearly in its first paragraph Chesterton's basic position on these matters. He

speaks of 'the institution of private property now so completely
forgotten and the journalistic jubilations of private enterprise. The
pickpocket is obviously a champion of private enterprise. But it
would be perhaps an exaggeration to say the pickpocket is a
champion of private property. The point about capitalism and
commercialism as conducted of late, is that they have really
preached the extension of business rather than the preservation of
belonging, and have at last tried to disguise the pickpocket with
some of the virtues of the pirate. The point about communism is
that it only reforms the pickpocket by forbidding pockets.' He
wrote later of capitalism and communism, 'They are both powers
that believe only in combination and have never even heard that
there is any dignity in division. They have never had the imagination to understand the idea in *Genesis* and the great myths, that
creation itself was division.' To Calvin the Church should be
omnipotent over the State. To Luther the State should be omnipotent over the Church. The Catholic Church alone held that both
Church and State had their authority in their own spheres and that
freedom was preserved through their tension.

Chesterton's contention was that one should accept, and should
attempt to love, Man as he is here and now—that it was for Man
here and now that Christ died. 'These are they for whom their
Omnipotent Creator did not disdain to die.' In the same way, with
The Outline of Sanity he pokes characteristic fun at progressive
prophets like Shaw and Wells who, finding that Man will not fit
into their formula, advocated not the abolition of the formula but
the abolition of Man. 'That is why,' he wrote, 'Mr Bernard Shaw
wants to evolve a new animal that shall live longer and grow wiser
than Man. That is why Mr Sidney Webb wants to herd the men
that exist like sheep, or animals much more foolish than Man.
They are not rebelling against the abnormal tyranny; they are
rebelling against what they think is a normal tyranny—the tyranny
of the normal. They are not in revolt against the King. They are in
revolt against the citizen.' And in reply to H. G. Wells' *Men Like
Gods* Chesterton asked, 'Will men be like Gods?' He preferred men
to be like men, and died too soon to see Wells reacting from pre-
sumption to despair and proclaiming *Man At The End Of His*

Tether. In his day all such speculations of Chesterton seemed plain common sense to all his fellow Catholics. But what would he have made of Teilhard de Chardin's evolutionary dreams, of the consummation of a new man at Omega Point and even of hints that there might be one day what Teilhard calls in one place 'a super-Christ'?

Beside *The Outline of Sanity* Chesterton wrote two works of fiction which can fairly be described as distributist: *The Tales of the Long Bow*, in which the heroes unite in a symbolic battle for English land and English eccentricity, and *The Return of Don Quixote*, in which the Tory Murrel and the Socialist Braintree, under the direction of the librarian scholar, Michael Herne, stage a pageant of mediaeval chivalry in the Seawood Boarding House, and when they are expelled from it on the discovery that they take their masquerading seriously, go out into the world to crusade for liberty. But both books are confined too closely to their thesis to be very much successful either as propaganda or as fiction.

There was something mechanical about these later stories of Chesterton. These books work out to an inevitable and foreseeable end of a triumph for distributism and the Faith. It was not that Chesterton was so simple as to believe that the gift of faith automatically turned all those who had received it into wise men or into saints. He was under no illusions in his mind. I once heard him comment in private talk on what seemed to him the mystery of the many Catholics whom he had come across who firmly believed their Faith and yet, in forming their own opinions, seemed entirely unaffected by its message. But, conscious as he was of this defect, he still did not think it right to comment on it in public print. Charity and humility combined to deter him from criticism of what he thought of as a city under siege. Such reticence may have been a virtue in his character. It was a defect in his writing.

He set out his political creed in one book—*The Outline of Sanity*—and proclaimed the hero of it in another—his life of Cobbett. Beside this biography there were in these years other biographies—of Saint Francis and Saint Thomas, the biography of his great mediaeval hero, Chaucer, and of his great Victorian hero, Stevenson, and the great apologetic work of his closing years, *The Ever-*

lasting Man. But these years were largely the years of travel and of travel books—Palestine and *The New Jerusalem*, America and *What I Saw in America* and some time later Rome and *The Resurrection of Rome*. He did not think very highly of his travel books and indeed they certainly suffer from a great lack of concentration. There are so many incidental anecdotes irrelevant or barely relevant to the place or the journey before we ever get there. Of *The New Jerusalem* we have already spoken.

His American book is perhaps mainly of value today for its reminder of how changed is modern America from that of forty-five years ago. To some extent the book was already out of date even when it was written. He contrasted America as a country founded on a proposition with the countries of the old world which were the product of their history. America was, he argued, a land which had proclaimed its creed of equality and welcomed any who came to it irrespective of their origin provided only that they accepted the creed. There had of course throughout all American history been one paradox about American pretensions—the position of the Negro. Chesterton was naturally enough aware of this and contented himself with saying that he would not discuss that topic because he had nothing valuable to say about it. His brother, Cecil, had written a history of the United States during the war and had championed the Southern side. Since nobody else had at that time any solution to offer of the Negro problem, it would be hypercritical to complain that the Chestertons had not got one; but it is evidence of how when they spoke of the rights of man, they were thinking so exclusively of the rights of Europeans that they were not much bothered by the paradox. Secondly, for all their professions of equality, the industrialists were of course busy building up in America a capitalist society as unequal as any that the world has seen. Of that Chesterton was well aware, and prepared to criticise it unsparingly. But what was more peculiar was how little he realized, when he preached transcendence of race, that though this was largely true of the America that had built the Statue of Liberty— of the America up till the war, which had received the immigrants from every race and after a generation turned them into American citizens—the policy was being changed at the very moment of his writing by the new strict post-war immigration quotas. Today it seems a strange paradox indeed to find America signalled out as the country that knows nothing of racialism.

America at the time of the war had saddled herself with the experiment of Prohibition and after the war had inserted that prohibition by way of an amendment into the Constitution. Naturally enough Chesterton, like all other visitors to America of the period, was invited to give, and gave, his opinion on the experiment. Naturally enough from his point of view he was strongly opposed to it. He was opposed to it because he was in favour of drink and he was opposed to it because he was in favour of liberty. He objected that restrictions which had been imposed to meet the abnormal circumstances of war should be extended into the supposedly normal circumstances of peace. He objected that the Prohibition law, in form a general law, was in fact a law imposed by the rich on the poor. The rich could, and did, go on drinking as they wished. It was only the poor who were prevented from it. There was a degree of truth in this. It was not as simply true as Chesterton imagined. There were plenty of rich Americans who drank but there were also rich Americans who did not drink. I happened to be at that time travelling through the United States debating about Prohibition. Votes were taken at the end of the debates and there was no doubt that in almost every part of the country a majority of the people of every income was in favour of Prohibition. One might like Prohibition or one might dislike it, but, considering the difficulties of altering the Constitution, one could not think it very probable at that time that the amendment would ever be repealed. Chesterton's prophecy that the experiment would be but a transient one, which was in fact so completely fulfilled, seemed then like wishful thinking. But what is more interesting about his chapters on Prohibition is that, piling up the arguments against it, he did not at all foresee—and indeed could hardly have foreseen—what was to prove its most gigantic evil and perhaps the evil that more potently than any other was to cause the turnover of public opinion against Prohibition in 1932: the appalling gang warfare and murder between the bootleggers which Prohibition was to produce.

The third of Chesterton's travel books, *The Resurrection of Rome*,

was written somewhat later and published in 1930. It is generally—
and, I think, justly—thought to be the least satisfactory of these
books. His voyage to Jerusalem was a voyage of discovery from
which he brought back his faith. About America he had no *parti
pris* and was willing to distribute praise and blame without fear or
favour. But he went to Rome as a committed man. It was not only
that by then he was committed to be a Catholic but he was committed to being a particular sort of Catholic. The dogmatic teaching
of the Catholic Church tells us nothing about Rome. The keys of
heaven were, we are told, entrusted to Peter, but there was no
promise that he would be Bishop of Rome. It was no more than
political accident which caused him to establish himself at Rome
and his successors to have remained there, and the time may very
well come in the future when it is convenient to the Pope to move
elsewhere. If so, there will be no violation of the divine promises.
But to Chesterton, in this the heir of Belloc, Rome had a much more
important role than this. The Church was the heir of the Roman
Empire and Christian things and Roman things were identified to
what in the modern world, in which Europe is no longer the master,
may appear a dangerous extent. It may do no great harm that the
simple, unthinking Catholic should sing his curious hymn about
'Full in the panting heart of Rome' but the serious Catholic writer,
if he writes of Rome, must be prepared to write of it impartially—
to praise the glorious things that have been done there and to
condemn its crimes. To do him justice Chesterton does in a passage
on Pius XI's support of missions meditate on the extension of the
Church beyond Europe but this, though a fine passage, is an
uncharacteristic one. For the most part to him 'The Faith is
Europe and Europe is the Faith.'

In Chesterton there was, during his Catholic days, a curious,
childlike loyalty—in some ways humble and attractive—which
forced him to abjure impartiality. He felt himself under obligation
always to see to it that 'the Whig dogs did not get the best of it'—
that every passing trivial contest ended in Catholic victory, and this
robbed his writing of that power of surprise which was in itself one
of its main attractions. Of the early Chesterton one never knew
what he was going to say. Of the later Chesterton one always knew

what he was going to say. The most interesting Christian architecture in Rome is that of the Renaissance, but this was by no means its most Christian period nor the period of greatest interest to Chesterton, who was much more at home in the Middle Ages. Yet he felt under obligation to praise the Renaissance Popes not only for their patronage of the arts but for the purity and piety of their faith. He contrasts them rightly enough to their advantage with the puritans, with their hostility to art. He who loves God should wish to create beauty in His honour. But such a sentence as 'The Popes fasted and made the city beautiful; the puritans feasted and made their city hideous' is to strain antithesis beyond the tolerable.

The reader of today with the advantage of hindsight will inevitably fasten on two apparent errors in *The Resurrection of Rome*. He will complain that in that book Mussolini and fascism, if not accepted with total approval, at the least receive far more laudatory treatment than they deserve. And he will point out with wry amusement that, while Chesterton praised the Papal Guards and their uniforms as a part of the pageantry that was needed to remind people that the Papacy transcended particular ages, John XXIII has since that day called the Church to an *aggiornamento* and Paul VI has abolished the Papal Guards and their uniforms as unnecessarily ostentatious. Both these charges against Chesterton's book are certainly just.

In reply it might indeed be pleaded that it was in 1930 that Chesterton spoke in admiration of Mussolini and that such language of admiration was by no means unique upon English tongues at the time. Chesterton's admiration at that date was a great deal less fulsome than that of Churchill. Nor, when Chesterton praised Mussolini, did he praise him for the reasons common enough among English Conservatives and English tourists. He did not praise him simply because the trains ran on time and strikes had been smashed. He praised him because the movement was, as he thought, a movement of reaction against the false parliamentary liberalism under which corruption was rife and under which the machinery of the state was used in order to impose slavery upon the poor. Under parliamentary liberalism the machinery of the state was simply a tool for the use of the rich. Under fascism a third

truly independent force was brought into play—a truly independent state which would impose discipline alike on masters and
men and suppress corruption. Whether fascism did in fact ever do
this or whether it did perhaps to some extent do it for a time in its
first years of enthusiasm but afterwards, as is the way of human
nature, become corrupt itself is as it may be. It is power that
corrupts—not one particular organisation of society or another. It
is easy enough in all discontented societies to raise up a rhetoric
against the wielders of power and to promise freedom and justice
if only they are swept out of the way. But in fact the new masters
depose the old masters, only to establish not a régime of justice but
merely themselves as the new masters of a new tyranny. Thus in
the days of the French Revolution the capitalists overthrew the
feudal lords and established themselves as the new governing class
in its place. In the days of the Russian Revolution the commissars
overthrew the capitalists and established themselves as a new
governing class in their place. The case against revolutions of
violence is that they do not in fact change anything. They merely
depose Tweedledum to put Tweedledee in his place. So the
Italian revolution may have to some extent been justified in what
it was against; it may have been directed against a corrupt, false
and incompetent régime; it may have been in its beginning a new
broom which, with all its violence, was at least intending to sweep
clean. But—except possibly for a very short time—it did not do so.
No one was more aware than Chesterton of the great difficulty
about a system of the 'career open to talents'; under modern
conditions, the means that were required to attain success—
whether of wealth or of power—were such that whoever attained
success would almost inevitably be slightly mad by the time he had
attained it. The talents to which a career was open were all too
often talents that were singularly unattractive. Strangely he overlooked the likelihood that this law would apply with Mussolini as
much as it did with all other successful men.

Chesterton called his book *The Resurrection of Rome*. He proclaimed with confidence that, whatever else came out of the First
World War, it was certain that one of its consequences was the
resurrection of Rome as the central city of civilisation against the

barbarians of the East. He spoke as it turned out far too soon. *Non Abbiamo Bisogno* and the protests of the Pope against fascist enormities were at that time still in the future. He greatly exaggerated the extent to which the Concordat and the Vatican Treaty had satisfactorily settled all the problems in Italy of Church and State. He did not foresee the day when 'a Cross that is not the Cross of Christ' would be seen in the streets of Rome. It is curious that in all his discussions of fascism Chesterton had no word to say about fascism's foreign policy—despite the fact that fascist Italy had already, even before Chesterton wrote, given evidence of its reckless readiness for foreign aggression in the Corfu incident with Greece in 1923. Still in the unforeseeable future was of course Italy's aggression against Abyssinia. Still further in the future was what would have been to Chesterton the gravest blow of disaster—almost the full refutation of all his hopes about Mussolini—the Italian alliance with Nazi Germany and her involvement in singularly ungallant fashion in the Second World War on the German side.

The abolition of the uniforms of the Papal Guards is a matter of lesser moment. Many would think that on it Chesterton was in the right and Paul VI in the wrong. When Pope John called for *aggiornamento* he demanded that the machinery of the Church should be brought up to date on essentials. But Chesterton's argument that the papal life should be surrounded by a reasonable pageantry to remind the spectator of its traditions would seem sensible. In so far as Pope Paul has taken action to keep down the deadening power of an overcentralised machinery at Rome and to circumvent its intolerable delays he is to be commended, but the only valid argument against the uniforms of Papal Guards could have been their expense and it is hard to think that the expense was sufficient to make of that a serious argument.

A good deal of the book—as was always the case in Chesterton's travel books—could just as well have been written had he never travelled at all. There are chapters that tell us how Constantine moved the capital of the Empire to the East, how this transfer and the danger of anarchy in the West forced on the Popes temporal responsibilities which they would not otherwise perhaps have claimed, how on the great controversy of iconoclasm it was the West which stood for the sane solution, the East which was fanatical. Or again there are chapters towards the end of the book about the modern decline of parliamentary liberalism. All these could as well have been written had he never gone to Rome at all—and indeed, as far as the chapters on iconoclasm go, would perhaps have been a little more difficult to write had he chanced to see the growth of some habits of austerity in the Western Catholic world—strictly functional architecture and, as we have said, even the abolition of the uniforms of the Papal Guards. But in general, whether we consider Chesterton's opinions on fascism or on the Papal Guards, one can but say that, while he has been proved wrong—wrong in the details, that is, as so often happens with him—he has none the less given expression to a deep fundamental instinct that is all too commonly overlooked. It is true that fascism did not prove itself the power to liberate Italy from the insincerities of party politics for which he had hoped. It proved itself to be no more than another and a worse party and another and a worse insincerity. Power corrupted there even more absolutely than in the English compromises. It is true that, far from the world moving back to the wide distribution of small property for which Chesterton had hoped, the development has been all in the direction of larger and larger units of production. The pundits have explained that this development is demanded by modern technical necessities. Far from a flight back to the land the world is becoming more and more industrialised, the production of the world's food is requiring less and less labour on the land, agricultural units are becoming larger and larger.

Yet at the same time, while that is the way that the world is going, the world, while travelling in this direction, is becoming—most people cannot exactly say why—increasingly discontented. The young call for education, are offered it on a far more ample scale than it was to their parents, and riot and go on strike against it. People say that the only thing that they want is a higher material standard of living. They are given it and they are discontented. The battle between capitalism and communism is rapidly becoming as unreal a sham battle as the old battle between Liberals and Conservatives at which Chesterton jeered. Communists and capitalists stand together in alliance against the dangers of anarchy. The pundits tell the young that the nation's great need is technical progress and efficiency, but the young stage against them a revolution by deserting the sciences for the arts. The young are by no means as yet clear what they want—by no means as yet ready to face the fact that less science and less organisation may mean fewer gadgets and what might be called a lower standard of living—but they all are in their bewilderment and with their quotations from Marcuse in revolt against the excessive organisation of life. Too high a price can be paid for the rat-race—ruthless competition and endless examinations. They no longer believe, as Belloc in satire imagined his contemporaries to believe, that

> When science has discovered something more
> We shall be happier than we were before.

They rather ask with W. H. Davies

> What is this life if, full of care,
> We have no time to stand and stare?

Of this new and very old faith Chesterton, if only they knew it, is most properly the prophet.

The central argument of the book is concluded with a defence of the Renaissance Popes for having made Rome splendid with architecture and sculpture. He defends them against the iconoclasts of the East who, whether Christian, Jew or Moslem, forbade the graven image. He defends them against the puritans of the North. He admits the tribute that the Renaissance paid to pre-Christian paganism but defends it. Christianity, in his argument, was not a contradiction of paganism. It was a reasonable conclusion of it. 'Greece,' as he was to say in *The Everlasting Man*, 'had thought all that Man could think and found that it was not enough. Rome had done all that Man could do and found that it was not enough.' The greatest of the pre-Christians had ended with a confession of their own insufficiency.

All this was sound enough sense, but, as so often, Chesterton's history was selective. The Renaissance did indeed bring with Thomas More and Pico della Mirandola a Christian humanism which used the discovery of Greek to deepen the Christian's own understanding of his Christian faith. It produced also the irreligious humanists, like Lorenzo Valla, who sought to erect Hellenism as an alternative to Christian faith. Even on the papal throne itself there were some—the Medici Popes for instance—who did not make it quite clear which was the interpretation that they gave, and because of it there were in the later days some Christian architects like Pugin, who thought of Gothic architecture as the essentially Christian architecture and the Renaissance and the baroque as pagan corruptions from it. As so often, Chesterton somewhat oversimplified his case.

13

The Secular Biographer

The first of the secular biographies of the post-war period was that of Cobbett, which appeared in 1925. Chesterton adopted Cobbett as the patron saint of distributism—almost as a mythical figure. In his *Old Song, Written on the Embankment in Stormy Weather* he wrote

I saw great Cobbett riding,
  The horseman of the shires;
And his face was red with judgement
  And a light of Luddite fires;
And south to Sussex and the sea the lights leapt up for liberty,
  The trumpet of the yeomanry, the hammer of the squires . . .
A trailing meteor on the Downs he rides above the rotting towns,
  The Horseman of Apocalypse, the Rider of the Shires.

It is curious that while Cobbett bulked so large in Chesterton's writing in the years after the war he never, I think, mentioned his name before the war. The reason is clear. Cobbett was to denounce the destruction of the rural, yeoman England which he saw around him in his time of the 1830s. The cause of that destruction was the enclosures, which had robbed the common man of his rights. He found property concentrated into the hands of a few large land-owners. Properties had doubtless changed hands from time to time over the previous four hundred years, but the root cause, as he interpreted it, of this maldistribution of property and its concentration of power into the hands of a few men was the Reformation and the dissolution of the monasteries. Cobbett was a self-educated man with no pretence at deep historical learning and indeed—to be frank—with no great interest in striking any delicate balance of historical truth. His desire was simply to expose, and history was to him little more than a weapon. He had come across the work of the first and greatest of scientific historians, John Lingard, which had appeared a few years before, and he used it as a quarry, extracting from it without much apology such damaging facts as suited his purpose. In the England of his day the clergy of the Church of England enjoyed incomes enormously greater than those of any other clergymen in the world and in return for them were content to oppose every demand for reform of any secular injustice. Therefore he wished to attack the clergy of his day as frauds and hypocrites and the lickspittle upholders of tyranny. In order to pile on the case against them he was anxious to show that they only held their possessions because they had inherited them from the pre-Reformation Catholic Church, and therefore was anxious to argue that their claims to be in any way the true descendants of the Catholic Church were wholly fraudulent. To support this case the arguments of Lingard were very useful to him, but, though he adopted Lingard's arguments, he used them for a wholly different purpose.

What were Cobbett's own religious opinions he never specifically told us, but it was Chesterton's belief, as he once confided to me in a private conversation, that in the final analysis Cobbett did not think the Christian claims in any form to be true, and it is likely enough that Chesterton was right. Such final rejection was most common in the world of the 1830s. Cobbett's main interest was in the denunciation of tyranny and therefore his main enemy in England, the Anglican clergy. In order to beat the Anglican clergy it was convenient to contrast them greatly to their disadvantage with the Catholics; and Cobbett wrote his *History of the Reformation* and dedicated it to the reigning Pope, Gregory XVI. But one can hardly doubt that, had he lived in a Catholic country where the Catholic clergy were economically powerful, had he lived in Rome under Gregory XVI, he would have been as vigorous in his denunciation of the Catholic clergy as he was of the Anglican clergy in England.

Now Chesterton, of course, in the years before the war was still an Anglo-Catholic. His position did not prevent him from deploring the Reformation or the dissolution of the monasteries, but it did require his arguing that, since the Anglican Church was still the branch of the Catholic Church in England, the changes of the Reformation, though regrettable, were not absolutely sundering. His position was inevitably different from that of Cobbett, to whom the Anglican clergy were simply a gaggle of unmitigated scoundrels enjoying stolen property to which they had no shadow of title and of which they should be despoiled without qualification by the first act of any decent reforming government. It was not until he had himself become a Catholic that it was possible for Chesterton wholly to accept Cobbett as his master unqualified.

As for Cobbett himself, we can indeed be grateful to Chesterton if he has introduced him to us. Cobbett was, like Johnson whom he had so much disliked and whom he in so many ways resembled, a man whom it is perhaps more pleasant to read about than to have met. For he was beyond question quarrelsome and rude, as Johnson so often was, and, unlike Johnson, he had not the gift for keeping devoted friends. Yet he was a good husband and father and, for all the curious vituperation with which his great prose was larded, he was a man of fearless courage who fought a battle against tyranny in an England where liberty was most dreadfully threatened. He had the courage to go to prison for his protest against the flogging of English labourers by German mercenaries at Ely. The England that he loved was dying and he did right to do battle for it. A few exaggerations were small faults to set against his great virtues. His great book, *Rural Rides*, is mainly of interest to us today not so much because of its contentions as because of its descriptions. We read in it descriptions of places that we happen to know and are fascinated by the account of what they looked like a hundred and fifty years ago before industrialism had wholly poured over them.

Yet the greatness, as opposed to the mere attractiveness, of Cobbett does not depend on the correctness of his interpretation of history or even on that of his judgement of the characters of his contemporaries. As so often Chesterton, perhaps in error on details, yet perceived, as others missed, a fundamental truth. One of the greatest obstacles to the Christian religion in England has been the use of the word 'gentleman'—a word of dubious and ill-defined meaning, which is designed to spread the impression, without frankly asserting it in exact language, that a rich man is likely to be the moral superior of the poor. The clear teaching of the Christian religion that it is very dangerous to be rich and very blessed to be poor is in direct contradiction to this, and it was the greatness of Cobbett that, whatever his historical or whatever his theological opinions, he quite certainly was not a gentleman and was fearless in his contempt for and his denunciation of the rich. Belloc, wishing to annoy the Duke of Norfolk, said that it was not possible for a Catholic to be a gentleman. Chesterton, himself no gentleman, shared this distaste and admired it across the generations. He almost out-Cobbetted Cobbett in his exaggerated detestation of Sir Robert Peel for creating a police force. 'If we want to seize the very soul of Peel and his parliamentary type,' wrote Chesterton, 'we can fix it in the fact that he organised a tremendously powerful and privileged gendarmerie, for control or coercion of the people, and thought they could be distinguished from the guards of continental despots by the fact that they wore top hats. That was the definition of Peelite citizenship, bribery in a top hat, tyranny in a top hat, anything so long as it was in a top hat.' Few, I fancy, will find this fair either to Peel or to the police.

In any event, these being the positions, Chesterton could not very well be unqualified in his championship of Cobbett so long as he himself was an Anglo-Catholic and committed to the theory that Catholicism remained in the Church of England even after the Reformation changes. Even after he had become a Catholic, Chesterton's championship was not quite simple. It might be that in England the Anglican clergy were the clergy of the Establishment, careful to guard their loaves and fishes, and the Catholics, such as they were, the clergy of the poor and the dispossessed. But it is hard, as one looks round the world of the nineteenth century, to persuade oneself that it was by any choice of the Catholics that they were fulfilling this role. Entirely obedient as he was to the Church's teaching on sexual conduct, he yet felt that obsessive insistence on this teaching was a subconscious psychological compensation for too little insistence on the graver evils of worldliness. 'The puritans,' he wrote in his essay on *The Fallacy of Success* in *All Things Considered*, 'are always denouncing books that inflame lust; what shall we say of the books that inflame the viler passions of avarice and pride?' Both the Church and the world of the nineteenth century, which talked more than any of their predecessors about the evils of incontinence, talked less than any of their predecessors in denunciation of the evils of riches. The general policy of the Church, wherever it was allowed to follow it, was the policy of the alliance of Throne and Altar. Catholic hierarchies threw themselves into the defence of the Establishment and of the sacredness of rich men's property as vigorously as did the Anglicans and, though he was too loyal ever to say it in so many words, it must have been clear to Chesterton that the Catholicism of the early nineteenth century was on social and political matters a very different Catholicism from his own. Had Chesterton been a contemporary of Cobbett he might, like Newman, have become a Catholic in spite of the Vatican. He could hardly have become a Catholic because of the Vatican. It was not until Leo XIII that he found much to admire in papal teaching on this point; nor until Pius XI, with his vigorous attack on the masters of credit who had imposed upon men so great a tyranny that 'none dare breathe against their will' and a yoke that was 'little better than slavery itself', that he found a Papacy that had resumed its traditional role of the champion of the poor.

Cobbett was most essentially a destructive writer. To him everything was going wrong and he was eager to denounce the landowners and the established clergy both of the sixteenth century and of his own time who were responsible for the corruption. It may be that his attacks were justified, but certainly he neither gave nor indicated that he was able to give, any picture of the mediaeval society from which the corruption came. Chesterton shared with Cobbett the belief that he lived in a period of decline and that it was necessary to expose corruption; but Chesterton was a man to whom religion was a positive faith, not a mere weapon with which to beat his enemies, and therefore was anxious to set against the portrait of Cobbett the portrait of a man who stood, as fully as any whom he could have found, positively for the good life. He found this man in Geoffrey Chaucer. Whatever else was just or unjust about the men of the sixteenth century or the men of the early nineteenth century it could at least not be denied that they were worldly men; and Chesterton as a Christian might of course have fairly argued that Christianity was a religion of unworldliness— that it was a religion of sanctity where, as Léon Bloy put it, nothing was really of importance except being a saint. He could have contented himself with setting the saints against the worldlings and saying 'Look on this picture and on this.' In fact he did in his closing years write two of his greatest books on two of the greatest saints—Francis of Assisi and Thomas Aquinas. Yet to his honesty that would not have been a total answer. Chesterton was indeed a very sincere lover of sanctity. He understood and respected ascetical practices. As we have quoted from Father Ignatius Rice, he paid what Father Ignatius thought of as 'a ludicrous degree of attention to any remark of a priest, however fatuous'. But this to some extent was a matter of *omne ignotum pro magnifico*. He came from this point of view too late to the Church. He often had to meet priests as he went on his lecturing tours. But he met them, as it were, on parade; with the exception of Monsignor O'Connor, Monsignor Knox and Father Ignatius Rice there do not seem to have been any priests with whom he was on terms of any personal intimacy. It was with Catholicism among the laymen that he was most at home and therefore, looking back to the Middle Ages, it was natural that he looked back to its greatest layman—or at least to its greatest English layman.

His *Chaucer*, almost the last of his books of importance to be published in his lifetime, appeared only in 1932 a few years before his death. It is in many ways one of the most attractive of his books, brimful of his enormous love for Chaucer. 'For a great voice was given by God and a great volume of singing,' Chesterton wrote in the closing sentence of the book, 'not to his saints who deserved it much better; not to any of those heroes who had made that clearing in the ancient forest; but only suddenly and for a season to the most human of human beings.'

There is one curiosity about the book, and that is the inordinate amount of space that is given to the refutation of the charge that Chaucer to the modern man was thought of as a joke. Chesterton once noted in Joseph Chamberlain, for whom he had no great liking, a talent for talking as if he stood utterly alone and was defying the world, when he had in fact limitless money and the whole city of Birmingham at his back. Chesterton—who was able to write

> For we are for all men under the sun
> And they are against us every one

—had always a great deal more popularity and many more followers than one would have guessed from his writings. So, while obviously the vast majority of the modern English electorate, if asked what they thought of Chaucer, could hardly reply other than that they did not think of him at all, yet in modern times—whether of the nineteenth or of the twentieth century—those who did speak of him, I would have thought, spoke of him always with respect and admiration. One could not have accused Tennyson or William Morris of talking of Chaucer as a joke. Indeed I do not know who ever has talked of Chaucer as a joke and whom Chesterton was refuting. But, though they estimated Chaucer highly, that does not of course mean that they estimated him rightly.

Chesterton was not fanatical in his admiration of the Middle Ages, frequently though an accusation of such a sort was levelled against him. On the contrary, as he interpreted it—and surely correctly—Chaucer did not live in the high noon of the Middle Ages as he would had he lived in the thirteenth century, or, in the case of England, in the reign of Edward I. He lived in the reigns of Edward III and of Richard II and it was Richard II's reign which saw the beginnings of the decline which was a century and a half later to lead to the plutocracy and the Reformation. Richard at the beginning of his reign had to put himself at the head of the revolting peasants, saying, 'I will be your leader.' At the end he was to fall before the rebellion of the new rich men under Henry IV. The struggle of York and Lancaster in Chesterton's interpretation was to some extent a struggle of the old traditional balance and the new plutocracy. But even if this was the correct interpretation of the political development, Chesterton does not pretend that Chaucer played any part in it. There is no evidence that he in any way took the side of Richard II against Henry IV. Rather the contrary. In so far as there is any evidence that he played a part at all in the affairs of the kings in his day, the evidence is rather that in his poem *Steadfastness* he thought it desirable to give Richard a warning to follow stabler courses. He died too soon to pass any verdict on Henry IV's reign. His death only followed that of Richard by a few months, but he was the servant of John of Gaunt, Henry's father, and his conscience in no way required him to refuse to receive from Henry the pension which Richard had been paying him. The fact seems rather to be that Chaucer, in so far as he was a man of affairs, was a civil servant and a diplomat rather than a politican and was not a man who felt called upon to take a side in contemporary political controversies. He was a describer and an observer of society—not its reformer.

It is customary to say—and indeed I have very often said it myself—that Chaucer was one of the most delightful men who ever lived. This was certainly Chesterton's own opinion. We cannot, for sure, be quite certain of the truth of the verdict. For the very few anecdotes that we possess about Chaucer's life are not sufficient to enable us to form any certain picture of his character. We can only judge him from his writings and, as is well known, some writers express themselves in their writings, but others put into their writings just that part of themselves which is suppressed in their active life and are in reality the opposite of that which they make themselves appear on the page. So it is possible that Chaucer, who always shows himself so even-tempered and full of kindliness, was in the flesh a crotchety curmudgeon. However one feels fairly confident that it was not so. Such sophistical contradictions are for a more twisted era than his. Yet, however that may be, we must deal with the only Chaucer that we have—with Chaucer the writer. Chesterton's book is largely concerned—more largely than are any of his other biographies—with literary criticism. He had read deeply in Chaucer and had no real need, other than the satisfaction of his own humility, to reiterate his expressions of little learning to contrast with the real scholars. There were gaps in his historical reading, but in English literature he was very deeply read. Chaucer, he argues, was, to begin with, a poet with a mastery of words and unrivalled power to pick out the colourful detail in face or landscape. Apart from that, he was the real creator of the English language. Up till nearly his time there had been no real English language. The laws until Edward II's reign had been promulgated in French. The Norman kings had imposed French upon the land and it looked probable enough that there might be a single Anglo-French state, using French as its language with English reduced to a peasant's patois. Chaucer was the great writer of the first years in which it was beginning to become apparent that that expectation was not to be fulfilled and that an English language would establish itself. Chaucer made it, wrote in it and, doing so, enriched it by incorporating into it phrases and manners of speech from other languages.

Chaucer's second achievement according to Chesterton was that he was the first novelist. I cannot feel quite certain that Chesterton is here using language exactly. What he means is that Chaucer collected his variety of characters and gave us the colour of the scene. That is all most certainly true. But the story of the pilgrims is not primarily the story of the adventures with which they met on their way to Canterbury, as would be required were the book to be named in the normal sense a novel. The story of *The Canterbury Tales* is of course the story of the stories, and Chesterton has a just point to make when he tells us that these stories are not merely tagged on to any author that may prove convenient but are each suited to the character that tells it and each therefore gives to us a further insight into that character. In this, Chaucer was a pioneer, showing himself the master of a technique which Boccaccio, his precursor, had never mastered.

The England of Chaucer's day was, as has been said, an England that was already in decline. That very fact so freely admitted is an evidence of the vigour of the mediaeval way of life. What sort of society, it may well be asked, must the society have been of which this was a picture of its decline? Popular talk thinks of mediaeval society as a stratified society in which each man had his place in the feudal hierarchy and was compelled to keep to it. Chaucer in his poem *Gentilesse* had opposed to the feudal idea the Christian idea which saw all men as equal. In his day feudalism was beginning to verge into plutocracy and, although the total collapse of the feudal order when the nobility were to destroy themselves in the slaughter of the Wars of the Roses was still ahead, Chaucer very clearly saw the changes that threatened and was not greatly excited or greatly disturbed by them. His attitude seems rather to have been that of the politically conservative cynic who saw that for the preservation of society there must be some ordered system, but since under any system power must be in someone's hands and since power always to some extent corrupts, it does not greatly matter who is up or who is down. His attitude seems rather to have been that of Dr Johnson, 'I would not give half a guinea to live under one form of government rather than another,' or

> How small of all that human hearts endure
> That part which kings or laws can cause or cure.

He might have said with La Fontaine

> *Le sage dit selon les temps,*
> *Vive le roi, vive la ligue.*

It does not greatly matter if some people have privileges. It only matters if they take their privileges seriously. Let each man hold his appropriate rank and perform the duties that appertain to it, but do not allow them to let their lives be dominated by the thought of those privileges.

So the first mark that is noteworthy in *The Canterbury Tales* is the extraordinary variety of social origins of the pilgrims and the freedom with which, in spite of it, they talk to one another. We only need to contrast the way in which Chaucer writes of the poor with the way in which Shakespeare writes of them, with his habitual and almost brutal contempt, to see how great a decline in this respect there has been in two hundred years. Chaucer's is a company that one might find today in Australia but which in spite of all our boasted changes one could hardly expect to find in twentieth-century England.

The second mark is Chaucer's attitude towards his pilgrims. The pilgrims are no company of saints. Some of them, both secular and ecclesiastical—the Miller, the Pardoner—are thorough-paced rascals. Chaucer makes no attempt to disguise or excuse their rascality. He passes judgement from an unflinching moral code that has no hesitation in saying what is right and what is wrong, and yet at the same time there is a kindliness even in his censure. The Shipman did not draw the line at murder when a man crossed his path on the high seas.

> If that he fought and had the higher hand
> By water he sent them home to every land—

that is to say, he made them walk the plank. Yet

> Certainly he was a good fellow.

The Summoner

> would suffer for a quart of wine
> A good fellow to have a concubine
> A twelve month and excuse him at the full.

Yet

> He was a gentle harlot and a kind,
> A better fellow could men nowhere find.

Men were not very good, but there was usually some good and kindness to be found mixed in with their badness. It was the censor's business to condemn sin, but was it his business to weigh good against evil and to pronounce a verdict on the sinner? After all, 'these are they for whom their omnipotent Creator did not disdain to die.' Chesterton shows us—truly enough—how Chaucer gives evidence in several passages of high and delicate understanding of the nature of romantic love. Had he turned to *The Paston Letters* he would have seen how marriages in the fourteenth century were very frequently no more than a brutal matter of buying and selling—how Chaucer in his treatment of the relations of the sexes almost always writes above the common level of his age.

Chesterton makes a very just point when he shows that Chaucer was not, like the modern reformer, a man obsessed with a plan for rebuilding society. It was not his concern when he passed judgement or propounded moral principles to say something that no one had ever said before. He was a man born in original sin, the companion of men who were also born in original sin. He was a sane man living in a sane world. Chesterton justly points out that in all Chaucer's work there is no mention of a character who is in the least touched by insanity—in which he is in great contrast to the Elizabethan and Jacobean dramatists, to say nothing of most modern writers. Compare him with the other great pilgrim of English literature. Chaucer travels in company with other men and women who share his faith, travelling with them to join them in giving thanks. Bunyan travels alone, concerned only to save his own soul and indeed, if we may judge from the total absence of any indication in Bunyan what heaven was like, salvation to him meant little more than the escape from damnation.

Chaucer's task was to make his small contribution to keeping society in existence. He had no expectation that he would be able to rebuild it and to create a new society. So, too, in his theorising he did not look on himself as an original thinker with a duty to say to his readers something that had never been said before. He looked on himself as the inheritor of a tradition, and his duty to apply to the circumstances of his day the principles which he had inherited. '*Securus iudicat orbis terrarum,*' he might, like Wiseman and Newman, have quoted from Saint Augustine. Men's minds resembled one another and if something had never been said before it was unlikely to be true. There have been some critics who, seeing that Chaucer did not hesitate to point his satire against unworthy ecclesiastics—the Monk, the Friar, the Summoner, the Pardoner—have thought to see in him a forerunner of Protestantism. Chesterton is unsparing and just in his exposure of this misunderstanding. It was precisely because his Christian principles were so unassailable that he did not hesitate to criticise those who had shown themselves unworthy of it. No one who reads Chaucer's apostrophe to

Our Lady, the great 'Almighty and almerciable Queen', can doubt the unquestioning frankness of his Catholic faith, nor anyone who studies the character of the poor Parson, how much he honoured Christian practice when he came across it.

When Chesterton died, Monsignor Knox wrote on him a sonnet in which he recounted how Chesterton must have won the love of the great figures from the past with whom he had found his companionship. 'He drank with me, said Chaucer, and high feast kept,' is the line on Chaucer. It is perhaps the sonnet's least satisfactory line for in spite of the Tabard Inn, in spite of the fact that his description of the Franklin and others shows that he was no puritan, Chaucer was not a Rabelaisian character as one might guess from this line. He was essentially a man of proportion, a man who understood that truth was always to be found in a balance of the whole. Unashamed in his love for colour, he was filled with the sense of a duty of gratitude, which to Chesterton was always the most potent of all reasons for a belief in God. Chaucer was indeed what, to take a phrase now made so famous, might be called 'a man for all seasons'. Matthew Arnold, in a rather silly phrase, lumped Chaucer and Robert Burns together, condemning them both for a lack of 'seriousness'. Chesterton truly shows that Chaucer and Burns were in exact opposition in their attitudes to the dominant ideologies of their day. Burns objected to the Calvinist ministers of his Scotland precisely because they were Calvinists—because they faithfully followed a creed which was to his mind a cruel and false creed. Chaucer objected, where he did object, to the Catholic ecclesiastics of his England not because they were good Catholics but because they were bad Catholics—because they were unworthy of a fine and good creed.

Dryden, as Chesterton tells us, thought that the mantle of Chaucer had fallen on him and indeed Dryden did inherit much of the spirit of Chaucer and rendered a great service by giving to the world the stories of Chaucer in the easily intelligible English of his day. Yet Dryden differed from Chaucer in that Dryden was overtly and consistently fighting a battle—fighting for a particular sort of society which he thought good and saw to be threatened. Chaucer was not a man to whom life was a battle. It is arguable that he should have been more keenly alive to the menace of the times, but in any event so it was. He was rather a man who accepted life with gratitude, who said with Browning's David

How good is man's life, the mere living, how fit to employ
All the heart and the soul and the senses for ever in joy.

Chesterton's position in life was nearer to that of Dryden than to that of Chaucer. He too lived, as he saw it, in an age in which good things were desperately threatened and in which he was called upon to defend them. His religion was the religion of a small minority in England. He—perhaps under Belloc's influence—somewhat exaggerated their unpopularity and the hostility of the society around them. At any rate he thought of himself as the defender of a cause under desperate attack and accepted it as an obligation of loyalty never to admit in public any incidental defect in his co-religionists of his own day, fully alive as he often showed himself to be in private conversation to many of their defects. For that reason among others he felt himself at home with Chaucer—with the carefree man living in a Catholic society who could afford, or thought that he could afford, to deal out blows to left and right and not to trouble on whom they fell. Chesterton would like to have been at home in such a society—or at least thought that he would like to have been at home in such a society. Whether he would really have liked it is another question—perhaps a question without meaning. For what do these large hypothetical questions mean? But in fact Chaucer was one who found life enjoyable, who accepted men as they were, not much surprised at their failings and with no wish to substitute for them the Superman. It was the essence of his opinions that they were the opinions of all sensible people around him: as he would have said, they were the opinions of all reasonable men.

Chesterton of course also claimed that his opinions were the opinions of the ordinary man and the reasonable man. He rested his case on an appeal to the past and to the traditions, and argued that he was only saying what sensible people had said throughout the ages. But he was not saying what the ordinary man said in his own day. He was convinced—probably to an exaggerated degree— that his day was an abnormal day in which men to their disadvantage had come to take up with new-fangled fads which were leading them to destruction, and he made his reputation of course mostly by saying not what everybody expected but what nobody expected —by the exploitation of the ingenious paradox. Indeed it is hardly possible to win a reputation in journalism except by saying unexpected things. No newspaper wants to fill its headlines with 'Nothing Particular Happened Yesterday' and, far from expressing the general opinion of everyone about him, Chesterton, as many thought, spent too much time—at least in his casual articles—in interminable sparring with his *bêtes noires* such as Dean Inge and Bishop Barnes. Whether in an age of ordinary men Chesterton would have been content to have been an ordinary man, who shall say? But, if he had, he would certainly not have been Chesterton as we know him.

During the fourteen years between his reception into the Catholic Church and his death Chesterton's mind was wholly occupied with problems of religion. It was not therefore surprising that of the five biographies that he wrote during that period four were of evidently direct religious import. There were his two great hagiographical works—his *Saint Francis of Assisi* and his *Saint Thomas Aquinas*. Chaucer was very deliberately the picture of an English Catholic in the days when England was still a Catholic country. Cobbett, was not, as we have argued, himself a directly religious man but his interest to Chesterton was that it was he who had exposed the destruction of England's Catholicism. All these four books were certainly books which Chesterton would never have undertaken in the pre-war days. On the other hand his fifth subject, Robert Louis Stevenson, was of quite a different kind. He had been an admirer of Stevenson ever since his boyhood. He had already written of him, if only *en passant*, in *Twelve Types* and *The Victorian Age in Literature* at a date when the name of Cobbett was still unmentioned in his works. On the other hand not only was Stevenson not a Catholic or even a near-Catholic; he would have thought of himself as a man quite devoid of Catholic sympathies. He wrote only one notable passage in praise of a Catholic—his championship of Father Damien against the Nonconformist Mr Hyde, who had attacked Damien—a eulogy to which curiously enough Chesterton in his book does not refer. When Stevenson wrote of Villon he oddly misunderstood his Catholic nature. He was brutal and stupid in the *Dynamiters* towards the Irish whom Chesterton so deeply admired. He thought of the Irish as little more than a nation of murdering blackguards. Why then did Chesterton choose to write about him?

The question is an interesting one and the answer, I think, clear. Chesterton always disclaimed any talents for pure literary criticism. In this, as in so much else, he was unduly modest. There is some admirable literary criticism in his *Stevenson*. He illustrates and praises Stevenson's mastery of the exact phrase. He defends him against critics who had too insistently brought up the accusation against him that he was 'a sedulous ape'. With great acumen he complains at Stevenson's economy in words: the result of this economy is, he says, that we are not introduced at leisure to his characters, in the way in which we get to know people in real life—or, say, in Thackeray. Stevenson is so keen on 'externality'—on making his characters do things—that they are often already on the stage and acting before we have come clearly to understand who they are. Very much the same criticism might be made about the incidental characters in the Father Brown stories and indeed it is an evidence of Chesterton's humility and sincerity that very often he comes to understand defects in other writers precisely because he was very conscious that these were defects in himself.

However, these points of literary criticism, valuable and valid as they are, are not really here our concern. Our concern is with Stevenson's ideas in so far as they throw light on Chesterton's ideas. Stevenson, thought Chesterton, was a man who had a happy childhood and an unhappy youth. He was brought up in a strict and unlovely Calvinistic discipline. When he was a child he was too young to understand, and therefore to be oppressed by, this discipline and he was therefore happy. As he grew up the shades of the prison house soon began to close around him. He revolted. He escaped from his prison by a flat rejection of the Calvinist faith in which he had been brought up. He fled from Edinburgh to Paris and from puritanism to aestheticism. But aestheticism in the closing years of the last century had its peculiar meaning. The aesthete demanded the right to defy the conventional moral standards. In particular he claimed his sexual freedom and Chesterton, though with his natural delicacy he had no wish to recount 'the detail of the sinning and denial of the sin,' yet does not attempt to conceal that Stevenson indulged in such explorations. Reacting against a too rigid Calvinism, he embraced a too unbridled licence. But the curious feature of this revolt against traditional morality was that the immoralists, throwing away the conventional restraints, did not enjoy, and indeed did not even pretend to enjoy, a greater happiness as a result of it. On the contrary they almost gloried, as disciples of Schopenhauer, in proclaiming the pointlessness of life, the insatiability of will, when a man surrendered himself to its unbridled satisfaction, and the inevitability of boredom. Not to be bored was almost a sign of philistine inferiority. So Stevenson in Chesterton's interpretation soon got bored of that pose—got bored with boredom—and reacted against it even as he had reacted against Calvinism a few years before. But he did not react into any recognised form of Christianity. The territory of Christianity was, as it were, to him so wholly pre-empted by Calvinism that he never really considered that there were other interpretations of Christianity quite different from those of Calvin and that he might be a Christian without being a Calvinist.

In any event he did not react from aestheticism into Christianity. He reacted from it into what he considered a version of paganism but a paganism of his own, a very different paganism from that either of Schopenhauer or of his contemporaries of the nineteenth century. He had an unhappy youth owing to Calvinism and an unhappy adolescence owing to aestheticism. But he had had a happy childhood and he determined to go back to childhood—to *A Child's Garden of Verses*, to the old stories of *A Penny Plain and Twopence Coloured*, or Mr Skelt of *The Juvenile Drama*. He went back and, to the derision of his aesthetic contemporaries, wrote a book for boys. He wrote *Treasure Island*. Now it is of course true that Stevenson did loudly assert and continue to assert in defiance of the *fin de siècle* aesthetes that life was enjoyable and that a condi-

tion of the enjoyment of it was a willingness to accept its simplici-
ties. In that sense indeed he believed that we should become as
little children. But, when he asserted that we should all be happy
because the world was 'full of a number of things' he was not of
course so naïve as to think that all these things were good things.
To the contrary, by a paradox, the very condition of our happiness
was that there was evil and hardship in the world. For happiness
did not come, as Kipling would have put it, by 'saying oh, how
beautiful, and sitting in the sun.' Life was of its nature a quest. It
was achieved only through the display of courage and through the
overcoming of obstacles, and there can hardly be occasion for
courage unless there are real evils. 'And,' to move from Kipling to
Browning, 'that's what blessed evil's for.' Like Chesterton,
Stevenson rejected with total contempt the vile gospel of success.
'Whatever else we are intended to do,' he wrote, 'we are not intended to succeed.'

Now it is true that Stevenson had a great love for 'externality'.
He preferred action to introspective meditation and, partly because
of his fondness for children and partly because of his own tastes,
the action which he preferred to talk was often violent action,
killing and the clash of weapons. Children like to read stories of
violence and killing because of course they have in the general way
never had personal experience of it—never seen blood in action.
To a large extent it was the same with Stevenson, and indeed the
same with Chesterton. Stevenson was throughout life an invalid,
destined to die young, Chesterton the least athletic of men. They
indulged, in their writings, in that violence with which they were
in real life least familiar. According to any normal code of morals
violence is, indeed, in itself hateful but there are occasions when
its use is necessary—in defence against another's violence. But
there is always a danger that the praise of violence will degenerate
into a mere defence of brutality. Chesterton does not really wholly
acquit Stevenson of sometimes falling into that fault. He finds in
him almost an admiration for the absolute brutality of the Master
of Ballantrae or for the Weir of Hermiston's revelling in his role of
a hanging judge, or for the loathsome Mr Attwater in *The Ebb
Tide*.

It can of course be objected against Stevenson, as indeed it has
been objected against Chesterton in this book, that, while insisting
that the world was a place of conflict, he all too often spoke naïvely
as if that conflict were necessarily and always a conflict between
people and to be fought with physical weapons. Indeed this accusation could be more fairly brought against Stevenson than against
Chesterton, for in Chesterton the contestants, like Turnbull and
MacIan in *The Ball and the Cross*, ready as they were to fight one
another in duel with their swords, are yet always as ready to explain
in so many words just why it is that they are fighting. Stevenson
to the contrary, it may be said, in the excitement of fighting sometimes seems to forget the cause or sometimes even, as with the
Jacobites, writes as if a cause with which he does not really sympathise was almost consecrated by being fought about. Yet, if the
accusation should seriously be levelled against Stevenson that he
was not aware that the true battle of life was not the battle between
man and man but the battle within the individual soul, one has only
to turn in total refutation to *Dr Jekyll and Mr Hyde*. Just as the
world was not a wholly good place but only served as man's testing
ground because it contained both good and bad, so man's internal
nature was a double nature. He was not wholly depraved, as
Stevenson's Calvinist forbears had taught him. He was indeed
created in the image of God, but the image was of a *Deus absconditus*—of a God from whose presence he was in a measure shut out
—of a God from whom he was separated by an 'aboriginal calamity'.
Thus he had within him two sorts of impulses—a double nature.

Stevenson, in *Dr Jekyll and Mr Hyde*, imagines a man who by the
use of a certain potion can transform his personality and turn himself into another person, so that those temptations which, in his
proper person, he had struggled against even if he had at times
succumbed to them, could now reign in unbridled domination.
The actual chemical possibilities are—let us at least hope—a
fantasy, but the psychology is exact. Chesterton very justly points
out that the critics all too often talked as if Dr Jekyll had discovered
how to split himself entirely into two wholly distinct personalities—
the one wholly good, the other wholly evil. This was, Chesterton
had already argued convincingly in *The Victorian Age in Literature*,

almost the exact opposite of the story. To begin with, Dr Jekyll before the transformation, so far from being a man wholly virtuous, was a man who had succumbed to temptation and who liked succumbing to it. So far from wishing to be virtuous he wished to be vicious and only to have the reputation of virtue, and the advantage of the plan of turning into Hyde was, as he at first saw it, that thus he would be able to commit the crimes which even as Jekyll he really wished to commit, and yet to escape the consequences of them. In any event, so far from Hyde being wholly divorced from Jekyll, Hyde comes more and more to make himself the master of Jekyll. He comes to commit sins so atrocious that they are hateful to Jekyll. He comes to obtain complete physical control until Jekyll turns into Hyde without even taking the dose and in the end Jekyll is unable to obtain the potion to turn himself back into his proper person. But Hyde could not live alone. He could only survive so long as he could from time to time take refuge in Jekyll. For evil is the divider. It cannot subsist of itself. 'Man cannot escape from God because good is God in man and insists on omniscience'. When Hyde can no longer turn himself back into Jekyll, he can only take refuge in suicide.

If we turn the story from parabolic form into a psychological treatise, its lesson is not that man is two people but that he is most definitely one person. We are indeed the children of original sin. We have within us these evil influences. We are tempted at times to succumb to these impulses but all too easily think that we can do so without a surrender of our character—that we can do an evil thing without becoming the sort of man who does an evil thing—that we can commit our sin and yet reject it as an excrescence. It is not true. There is evil and good within us, but they cannot live side by side in peaceful co-existence. Either the good must firmly control the evil, or the evil must control the good. In Stevenson's story Hyde, who had been at the beginning the plaything, the son, as he was called, of Jekyll, has come by the end to be his master.

It was Chesterton's interest in Stevenson that, though Stevenson in no way came to be a professing Christian or to understand that he was in any way a Christian—still less a Catholic—yet these psychological conclusions to which he was led by his own experiences were so largely Christian conclusions. It is the fashion to say of some people that they are Christians without knowing it. Stevenson, said Chesterton, was more than that. He was a Christian theologian without knowing it. Of course his theology was imperfect. Rejecting alike the optimist who said life was wholly good and the pessimist who said that life was wholly bad, Stevenson saw life as an adventure and a quest in which happiness could be won but could only be won by the man who had the courage to confront its obstacles; and, taking such a view of life, he had of course inevitably to reject the Calvinist doctrine of determinism in which he was brought up. That battle of life was won by the will. It was essential that he should assert uncompromisingly the freedom of the will. So far therefore had he moved from a Calvinist to a Catholic version of Christianity, little though he knew as much. On the other hand his faith was entirely concerned with this world. He was, as he himself confessed, entirely agnostic about survival after death. There did not seem to him convincing evidence that we did survive or, even supposing that we survived in some sense, what survival could mean. In any event the evidence was not sufficient to make it reasonable to base conduct on beliefs of what might happen beyond the grave. And yet there remained the obstinate inevitability of death, and without such a faith it is difficult to see how the final end is not defeat. Chesterton's friend, Belloc, did not share Chesterton's admiration for Stevenson and he tells us in *The Cruise of the Nona* how Stevenson's notion of 'a great task of happiness' seemed to his Gallic, Catholic intellect sentimental and meaningless. He could well understand the man who could not accept the evidence of survival as sufficient. But, if there was nothing, then there was nihilism—'the puerilities and the despairs' and no comfort. Life was about salvation or it was about nothing. Tasks were owed to God or they were not tasks. There could not be 'a task of happiness' owed to nobody in particular. And indeed it was certainly this absence of ultimate beliefs which was Stevenson's main weakness.

> Glad did I live and gladly die
> And I laid me down with a will.

He cannot have it both ways. If living was so good and living was everything, why should death also be welcome? Stoic dignity might have accepted the end as inevitable and without complaint. But by what alchemy of Pangloss can he lay himself down with a will?

14

The Saints and Everlasting Man

Chesterton's first major work as a Catholic was his life of Saint Francis of Assisi. The especial quality in Francis which he notes is his quality of gratitude. He quotes in the book the comment of Rossetti on the misery of the artist who wants to say 'Thank you' and has no one to thank, and Francis' life in Chesterton's interpretation was a life of unceasing gratitude to God for his gift of being. As Newman was the author of *A Grammar of Assent*, Francis, according to Chesterton, was the author of a grammar of gratitude. In the same way Chesterton was also anxious to make an offering of gratitude, for Chesterton in his early sceptical days had, as have many non-Catholics, a love of Saint Francis. Christian faith had brought him to the love of other saints. But the love of Saint Francis had brought him to Christian faith.

Francis of Assisi is certainly the first among those saints whose sanctity has transcended denominational boundaries. Men and women of every belief have found his universal love irresistibly attractive. Some even, as Chesterton reminds us, of those who professed to be his disciples—some among the Fraticelli— even claimed to find a greater power of attractive love in Francis than in Christ Himself. Chesterton deals with this extravagance in characteristically sensible fashion: he reminds us how appalling a blasphemy Francis would have thought such a claim—how, if we are tempted to find Francis' love more easily attractive than that of Christ, we must remember the contrast between the environments in which they lived. Christ lived in a pagan world but Francis in a Christian world—in a world whose accidents were much more similar to our own than those of Christ. Yet as he confessed,

Chesterton in his sceptical days, like so many others, loved Francis without clearly understanding why he loved him. In maturity he came back to pay in gratitude the debt which he owed to one who had played so large a part in leading him to Christ— and the part was indeed a very large one, for this Franciscan side of Chesterton was a side quite divorced from the semi-political Catholicism in which he was by that time so largely involved. If Francis was, as Chesterton claimed, a great democrat, he was a democrat of the mystical type which recognises with unquestioning faith a unique value in every created soul—not the political type that bothers about one man one vote and is concerned to praise the virtues of the alternative vote.

The simple lesson that Saint Francis had to teach was that pride was the enemy of happiness—that men were unhappy because they made claims for themselves which of their nature were usually not fulfilled. Let a man only be content to want nothing and there could be no obstacle to his universal high spirits. Saint Francis was in Chesterton's contention a great liberator of Christianity. The common contention of the sceptic, then as now, was that the pagan world lived in happy obedience to nature and that Christianity with its unattractive asceticism had attempted to suppress the natural pleasures and impose great unhappiness on mankind by doing so. Chesterton truly commented on that that Christianity had not invented asceticism so much as controlled it. He was of course right. The priests of Attis, as Catullus has told us, in revulsion from the excesses of debauch, attempted to liberate themselves by castration. Catullus prays to be delivered from such mad excesses:

> Dea magna, dea Cybele, dea domina Dindymi,
> Procul a mea tuus sit furor omnis, era, domo;
> Alios age incitatos, alios age rabidos.

(Great goddess Cybele, lady of Dindymus, banish your fury from my home, visit your madness and panic upon others.)

Christianity would have offered to him such a relief. So far from having found happiness in obedience to nature—if by nature was meant surrender to unbridled impulses—the pagan world into which Christ came was a world that had driven itself into misery and despair by excess of indulgence. Its pursuit of what it called nature had led it to the unnatural, and society needed a long purgation of repression before it could safely again give itself to the love of nature. By Saint Francis' time, in Chesterton's argument, this purgation was at last achieved and the Church could bid its children to throw overboard the excesses and once more to become natural. Saint Francis was the voice through which the need to love nature was proclaimed.

One may perhaps doubt whether even by Saint Francis' time the victory was finally won—whether indeed it can in its nature ever be finally won. If Saint Francis was to praise the life of nature in one form, Rabelais three hundred years later was to praise it in another. *Ama et fac quod vis*, said Saint Augustine. *Fais que voudras*, said Rabelais. The phrases are almost identical, their meanings very different; and for all the excesses of puritanism and Jansenism, Christianity has, in every age, before Saint Francis and after him, had to fight its battle against the temptations of unbridled indulgence. It is perhaps more nearly the truth that the praise of nature was very rarely found in Christian mouths before Saint Francis than that it was invariably so found after him. Still, it is true that those who think the world a place to be loved rather than a place to be hated can find in Saint Francis more than in any other the consecration of their wishes. Chesterton was a man who thought, as King Alfred is made to say in *The Ballad of the White Horse*,

> Our God hath blessed creation,
> Calling it good.

I wonder if the King Alfred of history would have said it. For King Alfred lived before Saint Francis. It was from Saint Francis that Chesterton learnt to use such words.

The last of Chesterton's great biographies—composed only three years before his death—was of Saint Thomas Aquinas. It is generally admitted to be one of his most masterly works. Professor Gilson, the great Thomist scholar who had devoted his whole life to the study of Saint Thomas, hailed it 'with despair', saying that he himself had given his whole life to Saint Thomas and Chesterton, writing in the midst of half a hundred other businesses, had left him and all his fellow professionals outdistanced. Our concern here is not so much with the work's literary merits as with the exposition of Chesterton's thesis and of the part which Saint Thomas played in forming his mind. To Chesterton the *Saint Francis* and the *Saint Thomas* were in many ways companion volumes. The Christian religion, born into an evil age, had as its first duty to purge mankind. It found a society obsessed with sex and had therefore as first task, by stern methods of repression, to free society from this tyranny. It was only with Saint Francis that Christianity was at last allowed to give itself to the love of nature, confident that now nature could be seen as a window to God and not a perversion to conceal him. So, too, he argued with Saint Thomas. For a thousand years men had to distrust reason. With Saint Thomas they could at least appeal to reason as a gateway to truth.

So runs his thesis. It is perhaps overneat. It is true enough that one could find in the early years of Christian history many Christians who were suspicious of learning as an obstacle to religious truths. But there were from the first also Christians who saw in Greek learning a *preparatio evangelica* and appealed back to the philosophers as guides on the road to truth. From the time of Saint John's Gospel onwards it had been a Christian fashion to appeal to the Greeks, and who was more filled with the love of the ancient learning than Saint Augustine? It was not so much that Saint Thomas appealed to philosophers where Christians before him had been content with unlearning. It was rather that he appealed to one particular philosopher—Aristotle—who had up till then been comparatively neglected in Christian circles and studied, where he had been studied, rather among the Moslems than among the Christians. The more general appeal among the early Christian philosophers had been to Plato, and the weakness of Plato as a Christian support was that he was an idealist. Matter had not in his mind an ultimate reality. What he called an object only existed in so far as it was the copy of a pattern laid up in heaven, and such a philosophy must necessarily be unsatisfactory to a Christian thinker. For Christianity is not merely the religion of a God who rules in heaven but of a God who came down to earth, who was incarnate among men and who suffered. If bread and wine and the wood of a Cross were not ultimately real, the Christian revelation hardly made sense.

It is true that as Plato had said before him and as Descartes was to say after him, every philosophy must be in a sense personalist. All are agreed that there is other existence than their own, but when they come to ask what is the nature of other existence, differences at once appear. Are there just Newman's two 'luminous beings', himself and God, and does all that exists outside my mind exist, as Berkeley would have us believe, only in the mind of God? Of course all objects that exist must necessarily exist in the mind of God and therefore, when we look at the grass and the tree, though they are real, they have only a certain contingent reality, and every object in the world is inevitably in a continual state of change. In the past it was other than it is now and in the future it will be other again. Saint Thomas admitted the force of those from the beginning of time who had played with such metaphysical fancies and told us alternatively that *Panta Hen* (All is one) and *Panta Rei* (All is in motion). Yet in his view they did not alter the facts whereby common sense told us that what we called a tree was really a tree, and what we called a table was really a table. He was a realist and in his realism he found, unpopular as such a discovery was at the time, more common sense in Aristotle than in Plato. Against the Augustinians who, like the later Calvinists, had tended so to exalt the omnipresence and the omniscience of God that there was no place left for human freedom, he asserted the independence of the will.

> Our wills are ours—we know not how.
> Our wills are ours—to make them thine.

Aristotle in subsequent Christian thought came sometimes to be almost canonised as if he were a Christian saint. There was of course an exaggeration in this, but it was not one for which Saint Thomas was responsible. Saint Thomas inherited no tradition of Aristotle as the supreme philosopher. In so far as there was such a tradition he created it—rescued Aristotle from the underestimates of the Christian Platonists and the Moslem metaphysicians, who, as Chesterton truly says, in a highly unMoslem fashion tended to turn him almost into a pantheist. So far from being the mere worshipper of a tradition Saint Thomas got himself condemned for his novelties.

Once we advance beyond the solipsist position and admit existence outside ourselves there follows the question: 'What do we know of that existence?' Can we say more of it than simply that I know that I am not the whole of reality, that there is existence outside myself? If I distinguish between one external object and another, that is merely a distinction imposed by my own mind. There is no real meaning in saying that there are seven million people in London (or whatever may be the correct figure). It is merely my own mind by an arbitrary exercise of definition which groups together certain objects and calls them people. They have no real objective similarity to one another. So argue the nominalists. Those who argued that there was no reason to think that my body existed except as an idea in my mind thought it similarly likely that external matter only existed as an idea of a macrocosmic mind. There was, they thought, a soul of the universe. They came to be called pantheists. The trouble—or at any rate one trouble— with all such theorists was that they asked men to accept a description of reality quite different from that which every ordinary man accepted in his everyday life, when he spoke of men as each different from one another but all possessing in common qualities which differentiated them from other animals. They created a gulf between the language of ordinary men and the language of the philosophers; and, in the world of religion, Siger of Brabant even advanced the theory that there were two orders of truth, religious truth and secular truth—that one both did and ought to hold one set of propositions about reality as true when talking about religion and quite a different set when talking about the affairs of ordinary life.

Against both these extravagances Saint Thomas reacted in the name of common sense. Against Siger he indignantly protested that it was indeed true that God revealed a few truths and left us to discover the greater number of things for ourselves. That meant that we must use our reason to deal with the affairs of ordinary life and must use our reason to decide whether the Church spoke with authority, but, having decided that the Church had authority, it was but common sense to accept what it had to tell us in detail. The Bread and Wine were Bread and Wine in their accidents but the Body and Blood of Christ in their essence. That, mysterious as it was, was the revealed teaching of the Church which the Catholic must accept. But it was quite different from saying that the Bread and Wine were both Body and Blood and Bread and Wine—Body and Blood when we are talking about religion and Bread and Wine when we are talking about ordinary things. Such talk was, in Saint Thomas' opinion, both blasphemy and nonsensical blasphemy. He commented, 'it is not based on documents of faith but on the reasons and statements of the philosophers themselves'—reasons and statements in his opinion of no authority.

Similarly, the philosopher who refuses to admit any real distinction between one external object and another challenges the conclusions of common sense. Even if we approach reality from a personalist standpoint we find that one of our most certain innate ideas is that of right and wrong. To some extent experience may affect our judgement as to what in detail we think to be right and wrong. People's moral judgements on particular problems have to some extent differed in different times according to particular circumstances, but the fact that the verdicts have differed on particulars does not alter the counter-fact that there has innately been a court from which the verdict could be demanded. Therefore there are in the world forces of good and evil. One might argue whether things in themselves are evil or whether they are merely misused by men. Saint Thomas and Chesterton would both have maintained the latter and it is clearly often the explanation. There are indeed some objects of which it is difficult to see that they can under any circumstances have had a good purpose.

It may be a demand on faith to believe that there was a beneficent purpose in the creation of Professor Philimore's streptococcus. Even if we accept that there is ultimately a beneficent purpose in death, it is far from clear why God should have caused it to come about so often in such a clumsily messy fashion. Yet such incidental difficulties, real as they are, have little bearing on the central moral problem. God presumably could have made this world an ideal world. He clearly has not done so—as Christians think— because this world is not the ultimate reality. In any event he has not done so. There are plenty of evils in the world that are in no intelligible way the consequence of man's sin. But the moral problem is the important problem. We have within us two kinds of impulses, social and anti-social. The Christian explanation of this strange paradox is in original sin. Whether or not there ever was a state of innocence, a Garden of Eden, the fall of Adam, whether, if it be true that Adam ate the apple, there is in that any reason why the nature of all the rest of us should be so changed, yet, as Chesterton said in a number of places, original sin, unlike other Christian doctrines, is not a matter of opinion. It is certain and undeniable fact. There is not only evil, as well as good, within us. There is also evil, as well as good, in the universe. The disciples of progress may bluntly deny this and say 'all is for the best in the best of all possible worlds.' This is merely foolish. Extreme pessimists may say that there is nothing but evil in the world. This is equally foolish.

The wiser Persians and the disciples of Zoroaster had said that there were two forces at work in the world—a force of good and a force of evil. These Manichaean ideas of course seeped over into Christian Europe and were prevalent among the Albigensians with whom Saint Thomas and the Dominicans were so especially concerned. Of the existence of a force of evil there can be no question. It is a curiosity that, while it seems that the great temptation of the Old Testament Jews was idolatry, there is no question of idolatry as a temptation to them in New Testament times. On the other hand the world in which Our Lord lived was a world in which demons and forces of evil were prevalent. It is customary today to dismiss as naïve and anthropomorphic the belief in a personal devil or personal demons. Whether there is solid reason behind such a rejection or whether it is a mere fashion is as it may be. What is certain is that there is a force of evil in the world and it is not very easy to see how there can be a force unless there is a will. In insisting on the existence of a force of evil the Zoroastrians and the Manichees were in the right. But the difference between the Christian and the Manichaean forces of evil is that on the Manichaean view the forces of good and evil are of equal power, each independent of the other; on the Christian view, as we see so often in the New Testament, the forces of evil operate only as it were under the licence of God. When they are commanded to come out in the name of God they have no option but to obey. 'The devils see Him and tremble.' Satan is indeed at warefare with God for the mastery of the world. But it is a mastery in which his final defeat is certain.

Why in such a story Satan should have rebelled in the first place, for what purposes he wishes to fight the battle to his inevitable defeat, these are indeed mysteries to which no man can hope to know the answer. Saint Thomas does not pretend to explain why things are so. It is enough for him to say that, if they are not like this, they do not make sense. There are the facts of man's double nature with impulses that lead him to good and impulses that lead him away from good; and there is his final obstinate faith that, though he has a good nature and a bad nature, yet in some way it is his good nature which is his real self—when he betrays it, he has been unworthy of it, less than himself, a traitor to his destiny. Nor can all this be true if God and Nature are one on a merely pantheist plan. It can only be so if Nature is the creature of a God behind it.

It is curious that Saint Thomas should be saddled with the responsibility for those purely mechanical and demonstrative proofs of the existence of God in which modern metaphysicians from Kant onwards have been so ready to point out the insufficiencies. It is of course true that you cannot demonstrate the existence of God by the mere assertion that it is a condition of thought to believe that everything must have a cause. What then, ask the objectors, can be the cause of God? Such questions may be of force against many of the later, debased scholastics, concerned only to produce the mechanical demonstration and to leave the lecture before a hearer can confront them with a question. They are of no force against Saint Thomas who showed himself as fully aware of such difficulties as any modern sceptic. As Chesterton shows, far from saying that the existence of a creating God was absolutely demonstrable he confessed that, were it not for revelation, he knew of no reason to prefer the belief that the universe was created by God to the belief that it had always existed. But even supposing that it had always existed there must still, he argued, have been in it some inhabiting and creating spirit directing the developing forms which its objects took, and this, in any event true, is yet the more clearly true if, as we are now told, this universe is an expanding universe. Whence comes the expansion? Matter clearly cannot be the creator of mind. The ultimate direction must be with a *Mens Creatrix*.

Yet among the creatures of the universe Man is so obviously different in kind from any others, and has so much more obviously a moral nature that it is according to reason and not contrary to it to imagine that he has some share in the divine nature such as other creatures do not possess. Christian teaching describes this share by saying that Man was made in the image of God and that God in the person of Christ became Man. The fact that these claims, if true, explain the universe as nothing else can explain it, does not in itself prove them to be true as matters of history. The Christian before he accepts his faith is under obligation to examine the evidence of Christ's life and to decide from it whether there is any other explanation that can account for the facts. In the same way, if there is nothing beyond this life or if the future is only the future of Buddha's Sorrowful Wheel, then this life in which we have such obstinate certainties of the value of virtue and of happiness as the end of man, and in which so often virtue does not lead to happiness, does not make sense.

The nihilistic view which says that it does not make sense is tenable. The humanistic view which professes to find in this life alone a sufficiency is hardly in that form tenable. This world needs another world to make it sensible. That again does not in itself prove that the Christian promises are true. But it does prove that Christian explanations are the only explanations that give coherence to the story. The alternative is to accept that there is no explanation. It at least shows that reason is on the side of orthodoxy and that those who reject orthodoxy have to abandon themselves to a confessed relapse into unreason. This belief that the Christian doctrine, and it alone, was the doctrine of reason was of course exactly Chesterton's own belief and he was in no difficulty in showing that the subsequent revolts of Luther were revolts of unreason against reason. With Saint Francis, in his belief, the Catholic religion, having purged itself and come of age, dared to annex to itself the delights of Nature. With Saint Thomas the Catholic religion, having purged itself, dared to annex to itself the delights of reason. The lessons that Chesterton learnt from Saint Thomas were not, as we can see, for the most part new lessons. He had already in his youth and years before fought out for himself at the Slade School his battles against solipsism and nihilism and the nameless forces of perversion and had already about the time of *The Man Who Was Thursday* won for himself unaided the victory. Saint Thomas was to him not so much a new teacher as a confirmation. Just as the greatest of the pre-Christian thinkers had already for themselves come to the conclusion that the universe as we know it must of its nature be unfinished and that some further revelation was necessary if things were to make sense, so on this smaller plane Chesterton had already for himself reached the conclusion that existence had its meaning, and at the end of his life Saint Thomas came to confirm him with his assurance that he was right.

Chesterton was throughout his life in controversy with those who called themselves rationalists and his reply to them was not, of course, to take refuge in an appeal to irrational faith but rather to argue that reason was on his side and not on theirs. For this demonstration the authority of Saint Thomas was invaluable. Arrayed against religion were two formidable enemies. There was the nihilist who denied the whole existence of values, but beyond him and more common was the Manichaean, still so common in one form and another in the modern world, whose theology was no more than that of Inspiration—to him the world was in general an unimpregnated place into which from time to time God, as it were, made his raids, demonstrated his power by some sudden action and then withdrew again. Against that theory of Inspiration Chesterton invoked the authority of Saint Thomas in support of Creation. God created the world and saw that it was good. God did not create like Paley's watchmaker, simply in the sense of winding up the watch, of sending the world spinning off on its course and then leaving it to fend for itself. What was the beginning of things, who can know and how much does it matter? What indeed does beginning mean to a God who is by definition outside time? But the doctrine of Creation implies a continuing divine action. God was always and everywhere present in every action of reality.

Saint Thomas and Aristotle, in Chesterton's contention, were the great vindicators of realism which was implicit in the Incarnation. Ever since the Incarnation, he argued, 'the body was no longer what it was when Plato and Porphyry and the old mystics had left it for dead. It had hung upon a gibbet. It had risen from a tomb. It was no longer possible to despise the senses, which had been the organs of something that was more than Man. Plato might despise the flesh, but God had not despised it. The senses had become truly sanctified as they are blessed one by one at a Catholic baptism. "Seeing is believing" was no longer the platitude of a mere idiot or common individual, as in Plato's world; it was mixed up with the real conditions of real belief. Those revolving mirrors that send messages to the brain of man, that light that breaks upon the brain, these had truly revealed to God himself the path to Bethany or the light on the high rock of Jerusalem. These ears that resound with common noises had reported also to the secret knowledge of God the noise of the crowd that strewed palms and the crowd that cried for Crucifixion. After the Incarnation had become the idea that is central in our civilisation, it was inevitable that there should be a return to materialism, in the sense of the serious value of matter and the making of the body.'

Saint Francis and *Saint Thomas* were the two great religious biographies of Chesterton's post-war years. It is natural to group along with them his great work of apologetics, *The Everlasting Man*. *The Everlasting Man* must be set side by side with the *Orthodoxy* of his early years. Though there are twenty years between them and though in the interval Chesterton had taken what he without hesitation thought the most important action of his life by changing his religious allegiance, yet there is little in the one book that might not equally well have appeared in the other. For, though in arguing that Christ was unique among men, Chesterton does also in *The Everlasting Man* argue that the Church is unique among institutions, *The Everlasting Man* is concerned with the vindication of the essential Christian doctrines and nowhere in it does Chesterton turn to consider of what the Church consists. There is no argument about any such matters as the definition of papal claims and nothing in *The Everlasting Man* written about the Church which Chesterton might not as well have written twenty years before at the time of *Orthodoxy* when he still thought that the Church of England of which he was then a member was an integral part of the Catholic Church.

The Everlasting Man was largely written to correct the childishly simple story of a regular progress of history which H. G. Wells had popularised in his *Outline of History*. Its contentions were in essence two. Man was not, he argues, as so many maintained, an animal who merely differed in degree from other animals. Man was unique and differs in kind. And likewise Christ was not, as so many maintained, a man who merely differed in degree from other men. He was unique and differed in kind.

His arguments for the uniqueness of man are cogent. He goes to the evidence of the earliest man at the caves of Lascaux and finds that the first thing that we know about the most primitive man is that he drew pictures on the walls of his cave. This, he argues, is an absolute difference in kind. It is not that animals drew badly, that cave men drew slightly less badly and Michelangelo drew very well. It is that the caveman and Michelangelo both drew —the one, if you will, badly and the other well—but they both drew and the animals did not draw at all. Again man alone among animals laughs. 'Alone among the animals he is shaken with the beautiful madness called laughter.'

In the same way Christ is the great figure of history. Even if, as some theorists have argued, He never existed as a historical character, yet there was no denial of the fact that His name has dominated all subsequent history in a way that no other name can even pretend to rival. Every investigator into reality must then inevitably face the great question of the Gospels. 'What think ye of Christ?' A common answer, says Chesterton, is of course that He was a great teacher, a great social reformer, and that as a consequence His followers invented for Him the obviously spurious claims that He was the son of a virgin and the Son of God and indeed God Himself. But, argues Chesterton, the Gospels do not give us at all the picture of a great, wise, sane and balanced ethical teacher. They give us the picture of a teacher who indeed at times gave to His hearers profound and poetic maxims upon which they should base their conduct in this world and by virtue of which, had it paid them more attention, the world would today have been a greatly happier place than it is. But He also made wild claims about Himself and wild prophecies about what was to come; if they were not true, they were the claims of a madman.

As Chesterton wrote: 'Certainly it is not for us to blame anybody who should find that first wild whisper merely impious and insane. On the contrary, stumbling on that rock of scandal is the first step. Stark staring incredulity is a far more loyal tribute to that truth than a modest metaphysic that would make it out merely a matter of degree. It were better to rend our robes with a great cry of blasphemy, like Caiaphas in the Judgement, or to lay hold of the man as a maniac possessed of devils like the kinsmen and the crowd, rather than to stand stupidly debating fine shades of pantheism in the presence of so catastrophic a claim. There is more of the wisdom that is one with surprise in any simple person, full of the sensitiveness of simplicity, who should expect the grass to wither and the birds to drop out of the air, when a strolling carpenter's apprentice said calmly and almost carelessly like one looking over his shoulder "Before Abraham was, I am." '

It is of course common enough for the critic to attempt to evade this difficulty by saying that the Gospel records are inaccurate—

that Christ gave indeed perhaps His ethical teaching but that His apocalyptic pronouncements or His own claims about Himself were invented or a misunderstanding. But such an evasion is not tenable. We need not at this stage of the argument beg any question about the inspiration of the Gospels. They may or may not have been written by four gentlemen called Matthew, Mark, Luke and John. They may or may not have been written at the dates commonly ascribed to them. All that is certain about them are two things. First, they were documents selected by the early Church out of a considerable corpus to represent what the early Christians believed about Christ—they are the Christian evidence in the case. Secondly, however composed, they are very remarkable documents. True or false, they tell a remarkable story. We need not haggle over details whether the words of every anecdote are exactly accurate, whether the great sayings recorded in Saint John's Gospel were delivered in one single discourse, as we are told, or at separate times, whether or not there has been in places some confusion and transference of minor miracles. The certain fact is that these stories and sayings have dominated the mind of man ever since they were recorded as have no other stories or sayings. There they are, written down in the Gospels. The Gospels, if they are substantially the record of fact, are very remarkable documents. If they are not the record of fact somebody must have invented them, and to believe that these stories were invented is almost more difficult than to believe that they were true. Who invented them? Who was this extraordinary crook-novelist—perhaps these yet more extraordinary four crook-novelists—who imposed this story upon mankind? And for what purpose? Was it the invention of Saint Paul? There are those who have argued that Saint Paul imposed a new theology of his own, different from the theology of Christ. The evidence is not convincing. But in any event we know a good deal about the literary style of Saint Paul. What is quite certain about him is that he did not possess the poetry of Christ.

So, argued Chesterton, Christ, whatever He was, was certainly unique—entirely different from other men. He compared Christ with the other great founders of religions and exposed the difference.

Moses and Confucius and Buddha and Mahomet taught doc-trines about the nature of things. They said that things were of such and such a sort and that people should behave in such and such a way. But Christ did not primarily teach doctrines. He primarily claimed to be someone. 'I am the way and the truth and the life.' He made the astounding claim, 'Heaven and earth shall pass away but my words shall not pass away.' Such a claim, argues Chesterton, is not the claim of a great ethical teacher, of a Socrates or a Confucius, a university lecturer or even a founder of a religion, as that phrase has been elsewhere used. It is the claim of a blaspheming lunatic—except on the one extraordinary hypothe-sis that it is the claim of Truth. If there are parallels to be found to Christ, they are to be found not among the great religious and social teachers of mankind but among its deluded lunatics in its padded cells.

So, argues Chesterton, our choice is not whether Christ was the Son of God or whether He was merely a good man and a great teacher. Our choice is whether He was the Son of God or a de-luded freak—*aut Deus aut malus homo*. If all that we knew of Him was that He claimed to be the Son of God, obviously the reason-able conclusion would be to accept the latter. History is full of persons—conscious impostors or deluded fanatics as the case may be—who have made claims of such a nature. Some of them have attracted a band of followers for a time. None of them has founded a cult which has survived over the generations in any way at all comparable to the cult of Christ. Here His story is clearly that of a man who is unique. That is a simple fact of history, however we may explain it.

Yet of course the Christian case is not merely based on the survival of the Church. Were that all, the sceptic might fairly ask, how long has it survived, anyhow? Perhaps longer than any other existing institution—perhaps long enough to merit consideration as a remarkable institution, as Macaulay admitted. But long enough to sustain its extraordinary claims? After all the Incarnation was only yesterday—two thousand years in a world that has been going on for some millions. None of us can indeed foresee the future, but, as we look at the world today, it may indeed be that the Church is still in her infancy and has a long future before her. It seems on the whole more probable that the first disciples who believed that they were living at the end of time were right. The Church will doubtless survive until the end of the world. But it does not seem improbable that the end of the world is fairly close at hand.

In any event the longevity of the Church is hardly among the most important of the arguments for Christ's divinity. Christ was not merely a teacher. Yet it is His teaching which makes it impossible to believe in a deluded lunatic. Can anyone believe that the Sermon on the Mount was the discourse of a madman? We accept the divinity of Christ, as indeed we accept any great but controverted truth not for one single reason but, as Bishop Butler and Newman were so constantly arguing, for a cumulation of reasons, each one taken by itself establishing no more than a probability but taken together establishing a proof—the actual detective evidence for the Resurrection, the witness of the early Christians and their willingness to die for their faith, their conquest of the Roman world, the survival of the Church through the ages, Christ's ethical and spiritual teaching, the pre-Christian world's consciousness of insufficiency, the feeling that all had not yet happened that something more must be going to happen if things were to make sense.

It was therefore natural enough that Chesterton, having in the earlier part of his book established that Man was unique among animals, should go on to ask why he was unique and what it was that he did with these unique faculties. It was a fact that he painted when the animals did not paint, that he laughed when the animals did not laugh, that men communicated with one another by writing—an achievement of which animals knew nothing. But it was not only interesting to discover that man did express himself in art. It was equally interesting to ask why he should want to do so. It was indeed interesting to notice certain physical similarities between man and the ape. Both had fingers and toes and feet and nose and eyes and the like. But, if a scientist went on from that to say without qualification that this proved that men were very like apes, it was pertinent to note that, while they might be like one another in many respects, they were at the least unlike in that Man noticed his similarity to the apes but there was no reason at all to think that the ape noticed his similarity to Man.

Concerned with religion and with Christ's divinity, Chesterton was most naturally interested in what pre-Christian men thought about religion. For it is one of the deepest mysteries of any orthodox faith that, if the Incarnation was to come to rescue Man from the effects of the Fall, there should have been this large gap of time between Fall and Incarnation. Why did God delay so long to come? Man, says Chesterton, has from the beginning of time always believed that there were forces from beyond this world acting upon this world. From the beginning of time Man has had this inevitable sense that 'all goes out into mystery.' That he has given many mistaken explanations of this mystery is true enough. But he would not have given a wrong explanation unless there was something to explain. 'Man found it natural to worship,' wrote Chesterton in *The Everlasting Man*. And indeed he still finds it so. There may be some men who do not at all feel this need and, if so, that does not indeed rob them of the title of Man, but, just as the tone-deaf man is so much less a man in that he has no music, so the man who does not worship is so much less a man for having no religion.

The religion of the pre-Christian world was mythological. They believed, indeed they knew, that Man was not his own master, that he was the victim of forces from beyond this world, and, since they had no clear voice from beyond the world, since they saw those forces only as they acted through Nature, they very sensibly saw God in Nature. That was reasonable. It may be that Nature is obedient to its own laws, they said. But whence come the laws of nature? The apple falls on the head of Sir Isaac Newton through the law of gravity. But 'the law of gravity' is an invented phrase to record what is observed to happen. It explains nothing. Who understands why gravity has these laws? The child is born as a result of certain physical processes. That is how it happens, but who knows why it happens? Who knows why the child grows up year by year some twenty years and then ceases to grow? So the pre-Christians very sensibly saw that there was some mysterious force behind nature, 'a strength and stay upholding all creation'. But what exactly that force was and how it operated, they had no means of knowing. So they made up their mythological tales, explaining the sort of way in which it operated. They did not pretend that there was evidence of the historical reality of these events of myth, that they actually happened on such and such a date. They were myths—tales—that they half believed and half did not believe, not knowing themselves exactly what they believed. At the same time, the philosophers sought by pure reason to establish what was the nature of things. Their search was unaffected by the myths. Philosophy and religion went forward on their separate roads, unconnected with one another. They only came into any sort of contact when the deepest of pagan minds, ready as a rule to talk the conventional language of polytheism, yet recognised at moments of highest tension the unity of things and of a God behind the gods. Thus Virgil, having filled his story of Aeneas with details of the activities of the gods and goddesses, spoke at the last

O passi graviora, dabit Deus his quoque finem,

(Ye whose sufferings are yet more grievous, to these, too, God will give an end.)

or as Socrates said to his condemning judges, 'I go my way and you go yours and which is the better God alone knows.'

It is of course the fashion in certain quarters to contrast this allegedly happy, or carefree pagan life with the twisted tortures of the soul which Christian asceticism was later to introduce. Chesterton naturally rejected such a view, as anyone who had studied pre-Christian literature must necessarily reject it. The Christian way was a middle way, as he had shown in his *Saint Francis*, between excessive indulgence and excessive restraint, each when unrestrained so closely linked to the other. It was not Christianity which invented the notion that the world was full of demons. The pre-Christian world had already come to believe that. What Christ taught was that the power of God could control the demons, who previously had so often appeared to be invincible. 'Hold thy peace and come out of him.'

The trouble obviously with worshipping Nature is that there are so many forces in Nature, some of them good and fruitful and some of them bad and destructive. He who gives himself to the satisfaction of impulses will soon grow weary of the normal and healthy impulses and, in a mad search for novelty, turn to the abnormal and the unhealthy. The trouble with the worship of Nature is that it leads to the unnatural. The things of this world may, if you will, in themselves be good, but they are only good if they are properly used, and man has within him a propensity to misuse them—the flaw which the theologians have named original sin. Nor could this be unless God, who is indeed immanent in Nature is also at the same time trancendent to and beyond Nature—unless God was *Deus absconditus* whose existence indeed we certainly know but who has in some mysterious way hidden His face from us.

Now to the pre-Christian all these were speculations in which the wisest might indulge. 'And that is all we can know,' wrote Plato, 'unless indeed a voice from some God should tell us something more.' There must be further revelation coming, said Virgil.

Iam nova progenies caelo demittitur alto.

(Even now a new being comes down to us from high heaven.)

He could write thus. But could he really believe it? Could it really be true that such a thing was going to happen? The Incarnation, if it could be accepted, was the assurance that God cared for Man and that there was a purpose in his life—that men were not merely, as it might be most natural to believe, like a hive of ants whom God crushed carelessly with his boot, indifferent as to any individual whether he crushed him or missed him.

> Has some vast imbecillity,
> Mighty to build and blend

> But impotent to tend,
> Framed us in jest
> And left us now to hazardry?

asked Thomas Hardy.

The Trinity, if it could be accepted, was the assurance that God did love because He was Love—that God Who was one God was also Three Persons, bound to one another in a bond of love.' This is my Beloved Son.'

> So the All-Great were the All-Loving, too . . .
> The madman saith he said so. It is strange.

Of course all this does not in itself prove the divinity of Christ and Chesterton nowhere in this book analyses as a detective the evidence for the Resurrection as he could very well have done and as was done in such a book as Mr Morrison's *Who Moved The Stone?* All that he was concerned to do was to show that the Incarnation was the logical conclusion of rationalism, in that with Christ the universe made sense and without Him it did not make sense. It might be no more than a foreshadowing of a fuller truth beyond itself, and indeed every Christian must believe that in a certain sense it is so. There is no claim that the Christian is the possessor of the totality of truth or that more than a small corner of it has been revealed to him. But the battles that the Church has fought against heresy have always from Arius' time onwards been battles against those who would detract from the full belief in the nature of Christ, and, detracting from it, would make it less rational. For, if the Father existed before Christ, then there must have been a time when God was no more than a single Person and He cannot therefore be fully perfect love. To the Victorians the problem of the Fall had been an argument whether the account of *Genesis* was literal historical truth. Chesterton was not much interested in that argument. His interest was in the assertion that Man had a double nature—that he was a man subject to sin yet one who had within him this obstinate feeling that his true nature was something different from the defective nature of his actual being in this world. What was this but a story of the Fall—a story that Man was made for beatitude but had fallen from it?

It is for the reader to judge how far he accepts Chesterton's reasoning, more fully developed in this than in any other of his books. He who reads him casually may be inclined to criticise his arguments as too disjointed; he who reads him carefully, as too syllogistic and impersonally rational. Obviously we cannot prove the truth of Christianity or even the existence of God in the sense in which we can prove that the three angles of a triangle are equal to two right angles. The fact that there are many reasonable, honourable and well read persons who, having investigated them, rejected the propositions, proves that they cannot be of the class of propositions which necessarily command assent. All that Chesterton professes to show is that faith is the logical conclusion of reason, that a measure of faith is necessary if we are not to resign ourselves to 'the puerilities and the despairs', and that, as Bishop Blougram put it, faith 'has our vote to be so if it can.'

The general level of Chesterton's argument is extraordinarily high and cogent. He does incidentally betray some of his characteristic weaknesses. In a purple passage for instance he compares Hector with Achilles and makes the point that the vanquished Hector has survived in legend almost as a Christian hero and that the name of the victorious Achilles has wholly perished, and is never found today as a Christian name. At the time he wrote his book the Pope was Pius XI, whose name was Achille Ratti. Chesterton speaks characteristically of the contrast between Europe the Christian, and Asia the unchristian continent. 'If the Church had not entered the world then,' he writes, 'it seems probable that Europe would be now very much what Asia is now.' He does not seem at the moment to have recollected that it was in Asia that the Church entered the world, or to have remembered Christopher Dawson's judgement that 'Africa was actually the creator of the Western tradition.' All but two of the great Western theologians of the early Church were Africans.

15

Chesterton and His Survival

Fashions change, and with few exceptions the sales of writers decline after their death. This has doubtless always been so, and it is more true than ever today in this plethora of mass communications. A few authors have come back into popularity because their works have been adopted by the television. Shaw has had a curious and spurious survival because of the derivation of *My Fair Lady* from *Pygmalion*. How many of those who go to see *My Fair Lady* return to read *Pygmalion* I do not know, but at least they are reminded that there was such a work. One or two of the Father Brown stories have appeared on television, but Chesterton's novels in general are clearly not suited for such a presentation—indeed would hardly be intelligible there. So the television has not been of much use to him, master as he was of the radio talk during his last years.

Those of us who were young Catholics in the years between the wars remember the time when he was held up before us almost to weariness as the inevitable Catholic champion, and the very old whose memories go back to the first decade of the century can perhaps recall the time when the young Chesterton was accepted and quoted by all the reading world as the most brilliant *enfant terrible* of the age. His readers today—for the moment at any rate —are not very many. It is said that the young—even the Catholic young—know little of him. In Mr Wicker's *Culture and Liturgy* there is only one reference to him, and that derogatory. If it be so we can be sure that, had it been foretold to him, he would not have been surprised and would have cared very little. For he always thought of himself as primarily a journalist, concerned with what were the inevitably passing problems of the day, and he used frequently and gaily to prophesy that his works had no prospect of survival.

He was the humblest of men and it would never have occurred to him to claim any of the gifts that deserved immortality. The last time that I saw him, I took, with some apology, a couple of visiting Spanish schoolboys to have tea with him at Beaconsfield, for they had asked to meet him. When the time came to go, they very properly thanked him for his hospitality, and with touching sincerity he replied: 'Oh, no, but it's so good of you to come. Do come again next time you are in England.' It clearly never occurred to him for an instant that he was the more important person who had been conferring the favour. He was indeed surprised and a little shocked at the reputation that he was given by his contemporaries and if, after his reception into the Church, he was told that that step had lost him some popularity and publicity, he would welcome that loss as both proper and desirable. Of petty vanity in others he was not excessively censorious. As vices go it was among the lesser of the vices, but he certainly had no touch of it himself. He considered it merely comic that a man should take himself very seriously. His 'democracy', his belief in the utter equality of men, his belief that he could not conceivably be of more importance than his undistinguished neighbour, was of a mystical kind rather than of the political kind that is so greatly bothered about purely political arrangements. His complaint against the Germans was a complaint against their pride. Other nations, he alleged, in easy vanity thought that causes which they were championing were, as it happened, the causes of God. The Germans thought that the causes that they were championing were the causes of God merely because they were championing them. They thought of truth as a German quality which Germans had the right to invent, and of God as a German. Whether this accusation against the Germans was justified, whether, if the Germans had been guilty of it, they alone had been guilty of it, we need not at the moment discuss.

The important point is that to Chesterton pride—the sin of Lucifer—was the arch-sin, and humility—the virtue of Christ—

was the arch-virtue. The other virtues which the Christian code praises—truth, courage, love, honour—had already, he argued, been found and praised by the greatest of the pre-Christians. The one original virtue which Christianity brought into the world— the virtue that had never previously been suspected as a virtue— was humility. So Chesterton in all simplicity and without quali- fication would have thought that it was the duty of a Christian to bear witness to the Christian truth. But each age had its own habits of language and it was only to be expected that methods of ex- pression that captured one generation would be out of fashion in the next. These matters of fashion were of no importance. If to- morrow's young men should change their tastes and wish to turn to new writers for their stimulation to truth it bothered him not at all. What can be less important than to be remembered after you are dead?

But it would of course have bothered him greatly if he had been told that a generation that was to come would say that he had misunderstood the Christian truth, and were to preach as Chris- tianity contentions that were in some way in contradiction with his contentions.

In ecclesiastical circles ecumenism is today the fashion. Reli- gious leaders talk about how much they have in common with the leaders of other denominations and dream of a recreation of Christian unity. Certainly Chesterton, though, unlike Belloc, he felt no sundering enmity for those from whom he differed, yet did not dream that any reunion was possible save through the acceptance by others of the papal claims. 'The kiss of Kikuyu' seemed to him an absurdity deserving only of mockery. Far from seeking out how much he had in common with those from whom he differed, he rather entered with gusto and without apology into the battles of debates and delighted in exposing their con- tradictions. Perhaps he enjoyed debate too much. Like MacIan in *The Ball and the Cross* he loved an antagonist simply because he was an antagonist, and had too *simpliste* a belief in the supreme validity of mere logical processes; he did not allow enough for the psychological suasions which led different men to argue from dif- ferent premises. He fought a battle that was perhaps valuable in his time when there was a bubble of arrogance in the enemies of the faith which needed to be pricked and when the Catholics lacked self-confidence, but it is out of date in the world of Pope John and Cardinal Bea. There has been a change there.

As has been said, Chesterton's detailed plans of distributism and the return to the land are not today much advocated either in secular or in Catholic circles and indeed have almost explicitly been rejected by Pope John. It is hard to see how his particular remedies could indeed be practicable save perhaps in a world whose population had been drastically reduced by some terrible calamity and whose communications had already broken down. Yet criticism of Chesterton's distributist policies are not really very relevant to a full estimate of his opinions. The accident that he felt an obligation of honour to continue his brother's work had the effect that his name was much more commonly associated with distributism than it should have been. His opinions on that field were never very deeply informed nor at all original to himself, and he would have been the last to expect that his essays in it would still have been read when the world had passed into a new age. It is likely enough too that the horrors of the new weapons which have now totally destroyed any last possibility of seeing conflict as an exercise in high-spirited chivalry would have prevented him from the praise of mere battle for battle's sake. In his closing years, as he foresaw so rightly the inevitable approach of a Second World War, it was in no sort of spirit of excitement that he welcomed it.

Our danger today is that in concentrating so much on irrelevant and secondary points we overlook the great truths which he saw at a time when they were not generally apparent. The battle of his day was essentially a battle between two rival materialisms— the materialism of the capitalist, which taught that the desire for a higher standard of living was the one motive of man's action, and the franker materialism of the Marxist, who accepted from the capitalist philosophers the principle that a higher standard of living was the end of man but professed to have found a better plan by which that higher standard could be given to the poor as well as to the capitalists. Today there is growing up a younger

generation to whom the battle between capitalists and Communists
is as irrelevant a sham battle as was the battle between Conservatives and Liberals to Chesterton in his day. His attacks and
Belloc's attacks on the party system, in their day a paradox, are
today accepted as a platitude. The revolt is against the impersonality of the gigantic units—it matters little whether the unit is
called General Motors or called the State, Berkeley University or
the party machine. They are in revolt against the gigantic units
whether in industry, in politics or in education. They do not know
any more than Chesterton knew how to introduce personal relations into these gross impersonal organisations of society, and new
Catholic thinkers like Mr Wicker, who believe that a solution is
likely to be found by transferring Catholic support of the Right to
a Catholic support of the Left, are—with all respect—likely to
find themselves out of date a great deal more rapidly than ever
Chesterton did. The practical demand of the students in their
days of riot are today singularly incoherent. The people of England
most certainly have not spoken yet—at any rate in any intelligible
form. Yet the proclamations of 'their riot and their rest' and of
'God's scorn for all men governing' are, little though they know it,
in many ways singularly like the proclamations of Chesterton's
Secret People—and perhaps as irresponsible in their blindness to
the ultimate dangers into which an appeal to violence can so easily
escalate.

The young have indeed provided a more complete refutation of
the materialist ethics, so popular but a few years ago, than have
any of the philosophers or the theologians. For science has provided them with the material standards for which they were supposed to be asking on a scale which would have seemed to any
previous generation to exceed the bounds of avarice. They are
offered educational facilities of which their parents never dreamed.
Though the world's productivity is now so great that it could
satisfy its demands under almost any economic system, and therefore it is exceptional madness to quarrel bitterly about whether we
should have one economic system or another, yet the nations insist
on denying themselves abundance by piling up against one another
gigantic and useless armaments; and such money as they are not

able to waste on these absurdities they contrive to dissipate by financing expeditions to the moon. And yet even in spite of all this madness people have a greater abundance of goods than they have ever had, and yet in spite of it are desperately unhappy, and indeed, it sometimes seems, most unhappy and most discontented in the developed countries which offer the greatest abundance of goods. Could there be a more eloquent demonstration that materialism is not enough—that Man cannot live by bread alone? Chesterton would very certainly have reminded them with humour and pity that their discontent was inevitable because men without a final philosophy are inevitably discontented.

> The world is wild as an old wives' tale,
>   And strange the plain things are,
> The earth is enough and the air is enough
>   For our wonder and our war.
>   But our rest is as far as the fire-drake swings
>   And our peace is put in impossible things
>   Where clashed and thundered unthinkable wings
>   Round an incredible star.
>
> To an open house in the evening
>   Home shall men come,
> To an older place than Eden
>   And a taller tower than Rome,
>   To the end of the way of the wandering star,
>   To the things that cannot be and that are,
>   To the place where God was homeless
>   And all men are at home.

Yet, even if it be argued that Christianity should be the logical resting point of the modern revolt, it cannot be pretended that it is in fact recognised by the young as such—apart from those who look to the Church for a social programme.

There are today devoted disciples who proclaim as the special champion of Christian truth to the modern world Teilhard de Chardin. Teilhard de Chardin in his lifetime had his difficulties with religious authority. With such stories we need not here be concerned. Whatever one may think of Teilhard's opinions no one can wish to defend the methods by which in Cardinal Merry del Val's day authority attempted to discourage their propagation—the theft of documents from his drawer and the like—and we can be certain that Chesterton, if he had ever heard of Teilhard and heard of such stories, would have been indignant in his denunciation of them. However that is not here the issue. The issue is that of the contrast between Teilhard's interpretation of the Christian religion and that of Chesterton. The contrast at any rate at first sight appears striking and almost total. To Teilhard evolution and progress were not only true, but he commonly spoke of them as the main evidence of God's working in the world. Chesterton was not especially concerned to deny that evolution had happened as a biological fact. He did not know whether it had or not. But, whatever the story of the origins of Man, what was important to him was that he was a product of a special creation in so far as he was radically different from all other creatures. He was a fallen being, if not in the sense that the Garden of Eden was historical truth, at least in the sense that he had a double nature. There was Man, as he was in his fallen nature, the creature of original sin, and Man as he ought to be, the Man which God has designed him to be. Common phrases about the true Man, Man being worthy of himself, the man deranged as being a man 'beside himself', bore witness to Man's double nature.

In the same way Chesterton was not concerned to deny the possibility of progress. New inventions were made. Some of them —though by no means all—proved to be for the benefit of Man. Man's life in this world was in its nature a battle, and those battles sometimes ended in victory. In that sense it is possible to say of some episodes in human history that they are episodes of progress. But at other times the battle ends in defeat. There are episodes of regress. There is no inevitability of victory or progress. It was not necessarily true that

> When science has discovered something more
> We shall be happier than we were before.

And Chesterton, when he used such words as evolution and progress, usually used them in mockery and as terms of some derision.

This is no place to attempt a general exposition of Teilhard's opinions, but he has so much set a stamp on modern Catholic intellectual thinking that it is important to set them against those of Chesterton for contrast. Teilhard's opinions are by no means altogether easy to discover, because owing to the difficulties put in the way of publication by authority he was not able to set them before the world in publicised and coherent form so that they might be submitted to criticism. We have to piece them together from scattered and private notes. Nor with his many gifts had Teilhard in any way the gifts of an artist, and his work was of course peppered with strange neologisms like 'noosphere' which may have been convenient for his own private mind but for which he would probably have found more normal synonyms had he been writing for a public. Thus something like the following would, I think, be a fair summary of what he had to tell the world. As a scientist and a palaeontologist, in which of course his qualifications were abundant, in contrast to Chesterton, who had none, Teilhard was of the opinion that the evidence in favour of evolution was overwhelming. There had been a period of inorganic matter, then a period of organic matter. Then out of unconscious life came the 'noosphere', the life of Man who alone among creatures was aware of his own existence. Now Teilhard's beliefs about the past were derived entirely from scientific study. On that plane he asked no more of the theologians than that they should not make fools of themselves by denying in the name of mistaken authority propositions that could be demonstrated to be true. Some believers in God thought of the material world as an obstacle between themselves and God. The religious man, they thought, had no duty towards the material world except to despise it and turn from it lest it distract him from God. The materialist on the other hand thought that the material world was all that there was and disliked talk about God as impossible chatter which distracted him from reality. Teilhard of course repudiated both these positions. Man was the creature of God and his first business was therefore to establish a true relationship with God. But the world was God's creation. It was through the world that God acted and a man must not turn his back on the world in indifference. He must act in the world in co-operation with God. Whatever the Buddhist might say or do, the Christian could not be indifferent to the world into which God Himself had deigned to become incarnate.

In all such assertions there was of course no conflict between Chesterton and Teilhard. Chesterton would have agreed wholeheartedly. 'These are they for whom their omnipotent Creator did not disdain to die.' He repudiated as heartily as Teilhard would have repudiated the doctrines of Swift which taught so bitter a contempt for the human race. The conflict of the Victorian Protestants against Darwin arose because they had been brought up to accept the stories of the Old Testament as literal history and repudiated an account of the Origin of Species that was in conflict with *Genesis*. Chesterton, brought up in his father's liberal, freethinking household, was never in youth under any temptation to be bothered by such literalisms. Still less was he under such a temptation in later life as a Catholic. To him, as we see from *The Everlasting Man*, his quarrel with evolutionists was with those among them who derived from the assertion of Man's common physical ancestry with the apes the conclusion that the difference between man and other animals was only a difference in degree. But, whoever among them might be guilty of this error, Teilhard was certainly not guilty of it. Whatever Man's ancestry, Teilhard was as explicit as Chesterton in his assertion of his uniqueness. 'Because we are reflective we (men) are not only different,' wrote Teilhard in *Le Milieu Divin*, 'but quite other. It is not a matter of change of degree but a change of nature, resulting from a change of state.'

Biology showed that Man was unique among creatures, and theology and the Incarnation confirmed it. God became Man—not merely an animal. There was an old controversy between the Thomists and the Scotists. The Thomists asserted that the Incarnation was necessary because of the Fall—to redeem Man from his sin. Had there been no Fall there would have been no Incarnation. The Scotists asserted that God was Man and would have shown himself as such in any event. Redemption was to them an accidental task. The universe was of its nature Christo-centric. On this issue Teilhard was Scotist, and, though I do not know that he ever discussed the problem exactly in those terms, there is no reason to think that Chesterton would not also have been Scotist.

So the difference between Teilhard and Chesterton about past history was not so much on what was true as on what was important. Chesterton was not particularly concerned to deny that evolution had happened. He did not think that it was very important whether it had happened. There was Man. Why did it so greatly matter how he had come to be? What was important was Man's moral struggle to triumph over the weakness of his original sin and to make himself what God had created him to be. That battle had to be fought out by every man. The physical conditions under which he fought it were of very secondary importance. To Teilhard evolution was the law of God. It had been through evolution that God had worked in the past and it would certainly be through evolution that he would work in the future. The assertion that the future would be like the past seemed at first sight sensible, but in fact the more that one examines Teilhard's speculations the more does it appear that the similarities of future to past are merely verbal and the dissimilarities real. Man has been the product of an evolutionary ancestry. Are we then to expect that in the future Man will evolve into something beyond himself—into a physical Superman of some sort? That is what might have been expected from the argument. But it does not appear to be what Teilhard expected. He does not expect the individual Man of the future to beget a being who is something other than Man. What he expects is rather with Sir Julian Huxley a moral progress of the human race at large—not the appearance of a Superman so much as of a Supermankind. Whereas up till now the story of progress has been a story of increasing diversity, in the future Man, having established his diversity, will rediscover unity in his diversity and men will come together again in the unity of Omega Point—where all men will be one and ready to receive the Parousia of the Second Coming of Christ.

281

There are a number of difficulties about such a theory. In the first place it is not very clear why Teilhard calls this picture of the future evolution at all. Evolution, as it happened in the past and in the most natural sense of the term, describes the physical process by which one form of life is produced from another form of life, but it does not seem that Teilhard foresees a transformation of man's physical nature in the future. What he foresees is a moral progress as a result of which man in the future will come more fully to recognise the unity with his fellow men. This, one would have thought, might fairly be called Progress. It is not very clear why it should be called Evolution.

Secondly there is a radical difference between Teilhard's theories about the future and his theories about the past. His theories about the past are the theories of a scientist, derived from careful observation of facts. But his theory about the future, whether it be just or not, is in no way a scientific theory. He tells us that the modern intercommunication of the different parts of the world must inevitably compel mankind to learn the lesson of his essential unity. It could be most plausibly argued that our intercommunication makes it both sensible and desirable that we should learn the lesson of the world's unity, that it makes it sensible to work for that unity, that, if unity be not achieved, Man with his present weapons will inevitably destroy himself. But to say, as Teilhard does say, that the world is in fact moving towards unity is hardly scientific. It is possible indeed, as one looks over the world today, to find certain examples where mankind has to some extent learnt its lessons and is now willing to co-operate more fully than it has in the past. But it is, alas, also possible to find at least as many examples where dissensions are now more bitter than they have ever been. Great Empires have broken up. Small independent nations, often bitterly hostile to their neighbour, have taken their place. Ideological conflicts divide the world. International institutions such as the United Nations have indeed been established but national rivalries play a bedevilling part in their policies. Looking at the world today the dispassionate judge could surely find rather more evidence that the world was moving towards division and final destruction than he could that it was moving towards unity. That would be the more reasonable prophecy of a pure scientist who considered the world solely through the eyes of the scientist. The world does indeed change. The scientist records the facts of change but science gives him no law to justify an assumption that changes are for the better. The fitter, it may be, survive but only those who are fit for their own survival. There is no reason to think that the fittest will be those who most effectively contribute to the survival of the total scheme. Man-eating tigers survive, but they survive by eating men, not by protecting them. Their survival does not help the survival of man.

There is indeed a reason for prophesying the survival of the world, but it is not a reason that is at all to be discovered from the collation of data from the researches of the laboratory. Pope John, in his most famous allocution inaugurating the Second Vatican Council, rejected the prognostications of 'the prophets of doom'. Had he been asked why he did so, doubtless he would not have answered by painting some picture of Panglossian folly which averted attention from all the suffering and wickedness that was abroad in the world. John was too wise a man and a man of too deep experience of life to be unaware of the world's suffering and its wickedness. His opinion was religious rather than scientific. If one believes in God and believes, as one must then believe, that the world is the expression of the purpose of God, then indeed it is a mystery that there should be evil in the world and sin in Man; but it is a mystery which the evident facts make it folly to deny. Yet, even if we accept the fact of evil, we cannot believe in evil's ultimate triumph. Simpler logic-mad Calvinists might be prepared to believe in the final damnation of millions through no fault of their own and find such a belief in no way in contradiction to a belief in the greater glory of God. Most of us are not so much concerned to discover any logical flaw of detail in such a demonstration but to reject it as evidently mad and obscene. The belief in purgatory—the belief that man requires some cleansing of himself before he is fit to enjoy the company of God—involves no violence to reason. But to the normal man the belief in hell is indeed a difficulty. It is difficult to understand how an omnipotent and loving God can have created souls to be utterly and finally damned. If we agree with the theologians that Man cannot be saved unless he commits some action that has some trace of goodness in it, then on that formula we cannot think that the ordinary run of men with their mixture of goodness and badness, selfishness and unselfishness, is utterly irredeemable; but we admit, though most of us have only read of and have never seen such a person, the possibility of some strange souls—the master, for instance, of a gas chamber or some wholly evil blackmailer—who have utterly surrendered themselves to evil and hatred and callousness and cruelty and in whom no chink of love is found. But, if such there be, they must, we say, be utterly exceptional. How far they are sane, how can we know?

In any event the notion that a loving God could make the generality of his creatures simply to damn them is utterly unacceptable. Therefore, while accepting, whether in the physical or in the moral order in Man's soul, the existence, or at least apparent existence, of evil, we accept it as a mystery and cannot but believe by faith in the ultimate triumph of good; and indeed it can well be argued that such a faith is inevitably inherent in Man's nature, and that a man cannot help himself but hold such a faith, and that nihilists who profess to see no more in life than utter futility or the victory of evil are merely indulging in an intellectual exercise, playing a game extracting for themselves a kind of twisted pleasure from an insincere pretence that all is for the worst. If there is no purpose in anything, what purpose is there in bothering to proclaim this purposelessness? So no doubt when John rebutted 'the prophets of doom', he had in mind an expression of faith, a rebuke to those who proclaim purposelessness and ultimate failure; and doubtless it was a similar faith in God's purpose which enabled Teilhard so confidently to look forward to the ultimate triumph of unity, to Omega Point and to the Second Parousia. But, if so, this was the vision of a man of faith and not the discovery of a scientist.

Chesterton would certainly have had no difficulty in associating himself with Teilhard in his belief in an ultimate triumph of good, nor would he have denied that the ultimate triumph must in some way be associated with a recognition of the unity of mankind; but

he would as certainly have said in criticism that Teilhard was too
naïvely ready to take for granted that unity would be expressed in
the obvious mechanical form in which it was first offered. Chesterton had seen the League of Nations and listened to the rhetoric
with which its birth was proclaimed; he had seen the purpose for
which its machinery had been used. We can hardly doubt that,
had he survived to see it, he would have had similar suspicions
about the United Nations. He would have replied to some of
Teilhard's too confident prophecies—

> And when the pedants bade us mark
> What cold, mechanic happenings
> Must come, our souls said in the dark
> 'Belike, but there are likelier things.'

It is arguable that Chesterton appreciated insufficiently the
achievements of science. He did not allow for the fact that the
increased population of which he approved could never have been
supported had not new inventions made possible increased production of goods, nor did he appreciate that curiosity about the
nature of the world was one of the divine gifts to Man and that he
who gave his life to the investigation of nature's secrets was en-
larging Man's understanding of the ways of God. On the other
hand Teilhard, so fully appreciating all this, was as certainly
naïvely indiscriminating in his praise of progress. Any discovery
which makes it easier for Man to survive and to survive in health
is certainly a good. But how many of the products of modern
industrialism are merely futile, adding nothing to Man's true
well-being or only increasing the turmoil and confusion of his life?
How many are sellable on the markets only because they are ram-
med down the consumers' throats by the press of advertisements,
compelling them to think that they want what they do not really
want? The finger of God is not very notably to be discovered in
some newly invented detergent, and there is at least as much to be
said for Chesterton's belief that industrialism is making the world
more beastly and noisy and discontented as there is for Teilhard's
contention that it is making it better. Both are the product of

highly selective evidence. How many of the most recent discoveries of science have been directly destructive? The truth was that Teilhard, living the strict life of a religious, only saw science as an intellectual achievement. Living away from the world himself, he did not allow for the world's worldliness—for the senseless modern pursuit of the so-called higher standard of living, pointless in itself and when seen side by side with the absolute poverty of a large proportion of the human race, positively obscene.

There is one self-evident difficulty for a Christian who sees the evolutionary process as the supreme revelation of God. That is that if Man is destined to move forward to yet higher forms of life, then it would seem that Christ was not incarnate in the highest form of being. If Teilhard's evolutionary belief had been a belief that Man was destined to evolve into a Superman—something other than, and superior to, Man—it is hard to see how this difficulty could have been avoided. Indeed in one place Teilhard does speak of the Christ of the Second Coming as a 'super-Christ' —a singularly unhappy phrase—but Teilhard elsewhere adequately shows that he did not mean what his phrase might appear to mean. We must always remember that he was not a man of much sensitivity to language, and that the fact that his thoughts had of necessity to be entrusted to private notes and not submitted to the discipline of publication was the cause of many verbal confusions.

If we do not therefore take him up on this verbal point and allow it to pass as a slip, no one can possibly question the total sincerity of his devotion to Christ—the historical Christ. Christ was to him a unique figure as certainly as He was to Chesterton. Nor can we quarrel when Teilhard complains of his fellow Christians that, though it is as certain an article of Christian faith that Christ must come again as it is that He has come already, yet the certainty of this Second Coming has been strangely little emphasised by modern Christians. They have written as if this world was going on for ever and this, if true of other Christians, is perhaps also to some extent true of Chesterton. So far then as Teilhard emphasises the Parousia, the Second Coming of Christ, he can justly claim that, far from being unorthodox, he is more orthodox —or at least more insistent on orthodoxy—than others. But the question that one cannot refrain from asking is rather this. Certainly a Christian is under obligation to believe in the Second Coming of Christ; and, if he believes that men in their progress towards unity must take into themselves the spirit of Christ if they are to succeed, he has the powerful support of Saint Paul and Saint John and many other Christian saints for such a belief. But one is tempted to say that the Christ to whom Teilhard looked was the metaphysical Christ—the Christ 'within you' of Saint Paul—more than the Jesus of history, the master of the parables and of the Gospel stories. He argues, it is true—and argues with palpable sincerity—that the universe was a Christo-centric universe and that if Christ was the world's centre it was essential not only that He come again at the Last Day but that He should have been born into the world as a historical fact. But again we cannot but feel that it was the metaphysical necessity of the Incarnation rather than the story of the child of Bethlehem who was born in a manger that appealed to Teilhard. Teilhard was no poet and insensitive to the magic of stories. There need indeed be neither insincerity nor heresy in the faith of such a man, but there must be a certain deficiency in it as of a man who is tone-deaf or colour-blind. To Chesterton on the other hand it was in the story—the Gospel story, the story of Christ as He walked the streets of Jerusalem or the hills of Galilee—that the great appeal lay. Christ was to him not merely the teacher of love. He was the Great Lover.

Similarly let us suppose that Teilhard is right—that it is the divine purpose to lead mankind to the final unity of Omega Point. That is then very important and it is doubtless the duty of each of us in our humble way to help mankind to that consummation. The moral decisions that we have to take in our life of every day—to be kind and honest and charitable—doubtless if taken rightly, help mankind one tiny step forward to its consummation. But who thinks of that consummation when he takes these decisions? And what purpose would be served by thinking of them? God doubtless has his cosmic purposes but Christian language commonly speaks not of the attainment of these purposes but of God's love for me here and now, living, as I do, in a world where Omega Point is still far distant. Of that love of God for a person, of the pursuit of the Hound of Heaven, Chesterton has more to tell us than Teilhard. The great reality is Death and each man dies. To all prophecies of a cosmic future it is only possible to say 'Who knows if they are true?' and 'I shall not be there.' Though we be travelling towards Omega Point, yet Christ died among others for those who had died when the journey was not yet completed. What is to happen to them?

Behind all these differences there is perhaps one curious similarity between Teilhard and Chesterton. Christianity in its essential nature is not only a creed of life but also a creed of death. Many who do not find it reasonable or easy wholly to live with it yet find in it a creed in which it is most comfortable to die. For in Christian belief death is not the end of all but the gateway to the true reality beyond itself, and throughout the ages insistence on this has always been the main burden of Christian advocacy. Whatever your achievements in this life, the Christian has argued to the unbeliever, its ultimate end is death and none of your inventions, whatever the additions that they may make to the comfort of life, have any effect in abolishing death. Today we are told—I do not know if it is wholly true—that people are reluctant to think or talk about their deaths. If it be so, one might have expected that the Christian at any rate would have refused thus to attempt to evade the inevitable—would have insisted, in age at any rate, that speculations about the nature of death were the only speculations of any real importance and that it was religion alone which had any light to throw on them. But it does not seem to be altogether so. Christians, rightly rejecting the naïve confidence of earlier ages when men professed absurdly to know exactly and to describe in detail just how the future life works, tend now hardly to talk about it at all and to concentrate on the effects of religion in this world. Now Teilhard doubtless held orthodox beliefs about the survival of the individual soul, but the survival in which his mind principally dwelt was that of the distant future of the human race—Omega Point—the 'one far-off divine event', more reminiscent of Tennyson or of Bernard Shaw than of Christian tradition, and in itself offering little in the way of comfort to the individual who dies before the consummation is achieved.

It might be thought that here at any rate Chesterton would have had a more definite comfort to offer than Teilhard, but it is not altogether so. The Christian, unable to see or say exactly in what form survival takes place or what the future life is like, should nevertheless in logic look forward to his death with a certain inevitable apprehension which the very dignity of so unique an event indeed deserves, but nevertheless with excitement and welcome as to the door to the new and truer life. Tennyson's faith is too much a mere matter of hope, and there is perhaps a certain false bravado in Browning's boast to 'greet the unseen with a cheer' as if it were a racehorse winning a race. Nevertheless the Christian should certainly await it with eagerness, if with resignation. Many do so. I fancy that this welcome to its approach is not as rare as it is nowadays the fashion to pretend, and one might have expected to find it as a logical and inherent consequence of Chesterton's firm faith and high spirits. But there is little trace of it. Monsignor Knox once told me that Chesterton had in him something of Dr Johnson's morbid obsession with the terrors of death. It is difficult to believe that a man like Chesterton, any more than a man like Johnson, had much need to expect a fearful fate from the verdict of a loving God. Yet it seems that his mind was strangely not at ease. I do not think that Chesterton ever confided such fears to print. His innate reticence would have prevented such a public display. It was a display, if for anyone, for the private company of his wife. He would have said with Browning in *One Word More*—

> God be thanked, the meanest of his creatures
> Boasts two soul-sides, one to face the world with,
> One to show a woman when he loves her.

But I have no doubt that Monsignor Knox who knew him so intimately had good reason for saying what he said. In his *Saint Thomas Aquinas* Chesterton protested against Dante's readiness to condemn his enemies to hell; and it may very well be that Chesterton spoke but little of death as an exciting adventure because he could not find easily comfortable the traditionally orthodox teaching about final punishment, and at the same time was not willing to take upon himself the responsibility of openly challenging it. He thought it best to leave such matters as an unknowable mystery.

For whatever reason, the result was that Chesterton's references to death in his published writings are very few—a salute to 'the decent inn of death' as a finale to a drinking song in *Wine, Water and Song*—a refusal to discuss it in his *Ecclesiastes* on the ground that

> There is one blasphemy—for death to pray,
> For God alone knoweth the praise of death.

There are no Browningesque words of welcome and defiance for it and Keats' half-love would have seemed to him morbid. His defence of religion is almost invariably a defence of religion's action in this world. Of that there can be no complaint. The writer is under no obligation to reveal the whole of himself to his readers. He has a right to his reticences. Yet, critic of the world as he was, it was a world whose values came to it from beyond itself—a world interpenetrated by forces of another world. As Ronald Knox wrote of him in a sonnet after his death, after he had enumerated the men of this world to whom he owed and had paid his debt

> So much while Peter fumbled with his keys
>   And justice for a little strove with truth
>   Clouding the difficult passage of Heaven's door;
> Till other wiser counsellors came than these.
>   Take him, said Thomas, for he served the truth.
>   Take him, said Francis, for he loved the poor.

G. K. CHESTERTON
1874 – 1936
SELECT BIBLIOGRAPHY

Verse

The Wild Knight and Other Poems (1900)
Greybeards at Play (1900)
The Ballad of the White Horse (1911)
Poems (1915)
The Ballad of St. Barbara and Other Verses (1922)
The Queen of Seven Swords (1926)
Collected Poems (1926, 1933)

Essays, History, Criticism

The Defendant (1901)
Twelve Types (1902)
Robert Browning (1903)
Heretics (1905)
Five Types (1905)
Charles Dickens (1906)
Orthodoxy (1908)
All Things Considered (1908)
George Bernard Shaw (1909, 1935)
Tremendous Trifles (1909)
William Blake (1910)
Alarms and Discursions (1910)
The Victorian Age in Literature (1913)
A Short History of England (1917)
Irish Impressions (1919)
The Uses of Diversity (1920)
The New Jerusalem (1920)
St Francis of Assisi (1923)

The Everlasting Man (1925)
The Outline of Sanity (1926)
Robert Louis Stevenson (1927)
Chaucer—A Study (1932)
St. Thomas Aquinas (1933)
The Well and the Shallows (1935)
Autobiography (1936)
The Common Man (1950)
Lunacy and Letters (1958)
The Spice of Life and Other Essays (1964)

Fiction

The Napoleon of Notting Hill (1904)
The Club of Queer Trades (1905)
The Man Who Was Thursday (1908)
The Ball and the Cross (1909)
The Innocence of Father Brown (1911)
Manalive (1912)
The Wisdom of Father Brown (1914)
The Flying Inn (1914)
The Man Who Knew Too Much (1922)
The Incredulity of Father Brown (1926)
The Secret of Father Brown (1927)
The Scandal of Father Brown (1935)

BIBLIOGRAPHICAL NOTE

This book, as can be seen, is mainly dependent upon Chesterton's own works which are here criticised. By far the two best biographical sources for Chesterton's life are his own *Autobiography* (1936, reissued 1969), and Maisie Ward's biography of him (1944).

In addition may be mentioned

Father Brown on Chesterton by Monsignor J. O'Connor (1937)

The Laughing Prophet, the Seven Virtues and G. K. Chesterton by E. Cammaerts (1937)

G. K. Chesterton As Seen By His Contemporaries by C. Clements (1939)

On the Place of Gilbert Chesterton in English Letters by Hilaire Belloc (1940)

Paradox in Chesterton by Hugh Kenner (1948)

Return to Chesterton by Maisie Ward (1952)

Christ and Apollo by Rev. William F. Lynch

Chesterton, Man and Mask by Garry Wills

Chesterton the Classicist, an essay by Margaret Clarke in *The Dublin Review* (1955)

G. K. Chesterton: the Giant Upside Down, an essay by Elizabeth Sewell in *Thought* (Winter, 1955–56)

G. K. Chesterton: A bibliography by John Sullivan (1958)

The Centre of Hilarity by Michael Mason (1959)

CHRISTOPHER HOLLIS

Index

on God - Tempting - God etc - p.7?

5 Preposterous about God - 68-76